IMAGES
of America

WASHINGTON COUNTY

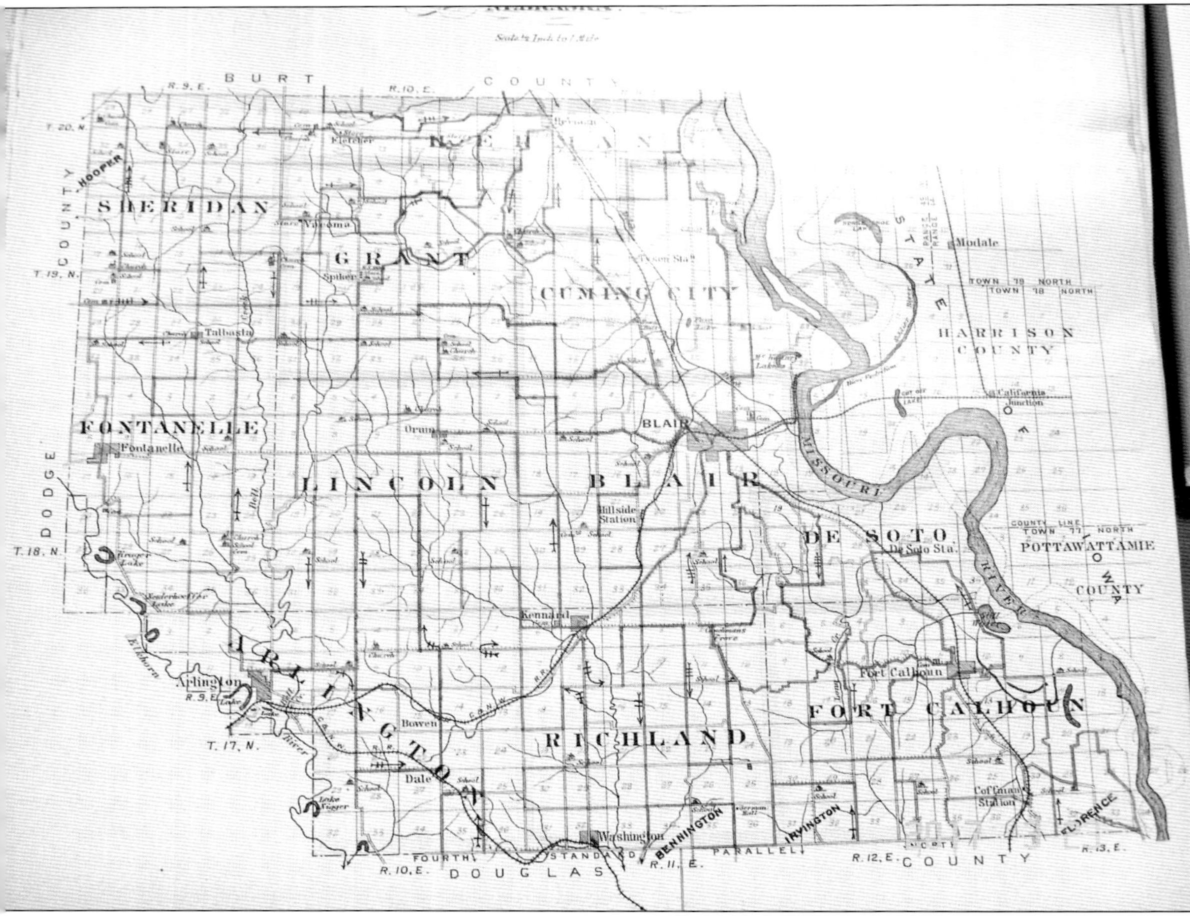

Nebraska was organized into territories by acting governor Thomas B. Cuming. A year later, Washington County was reorganized by the territorial legislature on February 22, 1855, the anniversary of Pres. George Washington's birth. On March 1, 1867, Nebraska achieved statehood. As of the 2010 census, the population of Washington County was 20,234. Washington County took its name from Pres. George Washington. By 1908, the towns and villages of Washington County were established. This 1908 Washington County plat map details the towns and villages, some dating back to the territorial settlement and a few that would disappear. (Courtesy the Washington County Historical Association.)

ON THE COVER: In this 1930s photograph, a crowd of young boys eagerly take part in the moving of the city jail as it is pulled on a Minnesota Moline tractor to its new home. (Courtesy the Washington County Historical Association.)

IMAGES
of America

WASHINGTON COUNTY

Kathy Haley Buhrman

ARCADIA
PUBLISHING

ISBN 978-1-4671-2628-1

Published by Arcadia Publishing
Charleston, South Carolina

Printed in the United States of America

Library of Congress Control Number: 2017953086

For all general information, please contact Arcadia Publishing:
Telephone 843-853-2070
Fax 843-853-0044
E-mail sales@arcadiapublishing.com
For customer service and orders:
Toll-Free 1-888-313-2665

Visit us on the Internet at www.arcadiapublishing.com

To the good people of Washington County—our ancestors that walked this land before us and the generations that will follow

Contents

Acknowledgments

I have always enjoyed writing the story of my ancestors. When Arcadia Publishing editors approached me to write the story of Washington County, I welcomed the opportunity to share the story of our pioneer citizens, offering the reader a snapshot of the communities and world in which they lived. It is almost an impossible task to tell the entire story in depth in a pictorial book, but I never lost sight of my goal to represent every community and enclave in our county, and I hope I gave them justice. The story of Washington County could not have been told without the contribution of her sons and daughters who walked this land long before me. They penned their memories and preserved the history of our land and her people, and as I turned the pages, their words took me back into time, offering me a treasured glimpse of what can only be told and not witnessed. I am indebted to them. This project could not have been possible without the assistance of the Washington County Historical Association and Faith Norwood. She dug into her files, opened her books and folders, and let me browse. Unless otherwise noted, all photographs are from the Washington County Historical Association. A huge thank-you goes to Dixie Lambert, Jonnie Andrew, and LeMara Eicke, who enthusiastically shard their images of their beloved hometowns. Special thanks go to Salem Lutheran Church; Janine Carlson; Bobbi Anderson; Ryan Thompson of the Blair Preservation Alliance; the Danish American Archive and Library in Blair; and the DeSoto National Wildlife Refuge for use of the Bertrand Steamboat. Individual credit is given throughout. Much thanks and appreciation goes to the good citizens of Washington County who contributed their stories and to the committee who compiled the 1980 *Washington County History* book, which holds our past. Finally, to my family, always my cheerleaders.

Introduction

Before the steamboats and trains that would open up the vast unexplored frontier west of the Missouri River, the famed expedition led by Meriwether Lewis and William Clark to explore and map the newly acquired US territory reached the bluffs separating the lower bottoms and the higher prairie overlooking the Missouri River.

The first council ever held with Indians and whites west of the Missouri River took place between Lewis and Clark and six Indian chiefs on the western banks of the Missouri River in July 1804. The Lewis and Clark expedition discovered abundant fur-trapping resources in the region and believed the bluffs along this portion of the Missouri were a good location for a fur-trading establishment and military fortification. In 1812, the fur trader Manuel Lisa established Fort Lisa, about six miles south of the original council, influencing other trading centers to be established.

Fifteen years later, in 1819, by order of Secretary of State Calhoun, a military expedition, known as the Yellowstone Expedition and led by Col. Henry Atkinson, established the first military post west of the Missouri River, below the same bluffs where Lewis and Clark held council with the Indians. For the next eight years, the fort was home to the Rifle Regiment and the 6th Infantry, which included the soldiers, traders, trappers, and a few frontier people.

Atkinson's military expedition was joined by a scientific one. Named Engineer Cantonment, it was located on the Missouri shores of Washington County, about six miles south of Fort Atkinson, near the future site of Rockport and along present-day Douglas County. The scientific studies conducted at Engineer Cantonment are believed to be the first biodiversity research undertaken in the United States.

Steamboats carried the occasional explorers and the fur traders into the region along the course of the Missouri River, but for 25 years after the abandonment of Fort Atkinson the territory had no permanent settlements. In the spring of 1847, the Mormons, wintering in the city of Florence, north of Omaha, sent farmers north into what would soon be Washington County, to grow food for their westbound caravans traveling to Utah. Nebraska was still a territory in 1854, when the frontier line reached the Missouri River.

One

River Towns

Taking a Gamble on Pushing the Frontier

The early towns in Washington County were river towns along the Missouri River, established during the steamboat era before the railroad was built west of the Missouri. Fort Calhoun, DeSoto, and Cuming City were established along the river. Fontanelle (a misspelling that was never corrected) was a territorial town overlooking the Elkhorn River on the western edge of the county but had no river traffic. People, livestock, and necessary provisions arrived by steamboat, flatboat ferry, the occasional canoe, on horse-and-wagon teams, and sometimes by foot. In the summer of 1854, after the Nebraska Territory was opened for settlement, the first permanent settlement in Washington County was established two miles west of the original fort, and the name Fort Calhoun was adopted. On December 25, 1854, acting territorial governor Thomas B. Cuming appointed Thomas J. Allen, one of the first pioneers to settle in Washington County, as the first territorial sheriff of the county.

Fort Calhoun was the county seat and held that position until 1858, when a crowd of armed DeSoto citizens took the county seat by force. In 1866, by popular vote it was again moved to Fort Calhoun. In 1869, the county seat was moved to the newly formed railroad town of Blair, where it has remained.

Fontanelle, a village of some 200 settlers, was incorporated and became the county seat of Dodge County, in which Fontanelle was then located, in March 1855. Fontanelle remained the county seat of Dodge County until January 12, 1860, when the western boundary of Washington County was redefined and extended to the west side of the Elkhorn River.

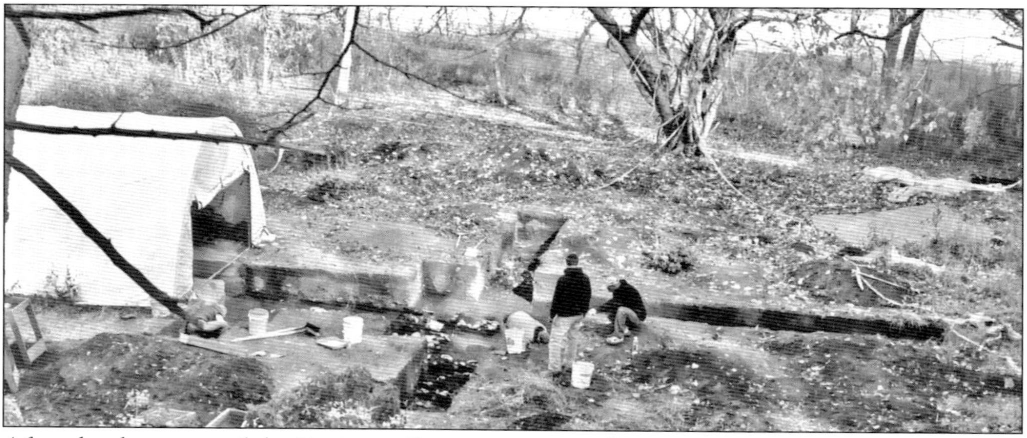

After the departure of the Engineer Cantonment expedition in 1820, the site was abandoned and the exact location lost. In 2002, archeologists discovered the location and excavation began. Building ruins, lead balls, a smoking pipe, ceramic pieces, and other artifacts of early 19th-century living began to emerge. In 2015, it was listed in the National Register of Historic Places. (Courtesy the Nebraska Historical Society.)

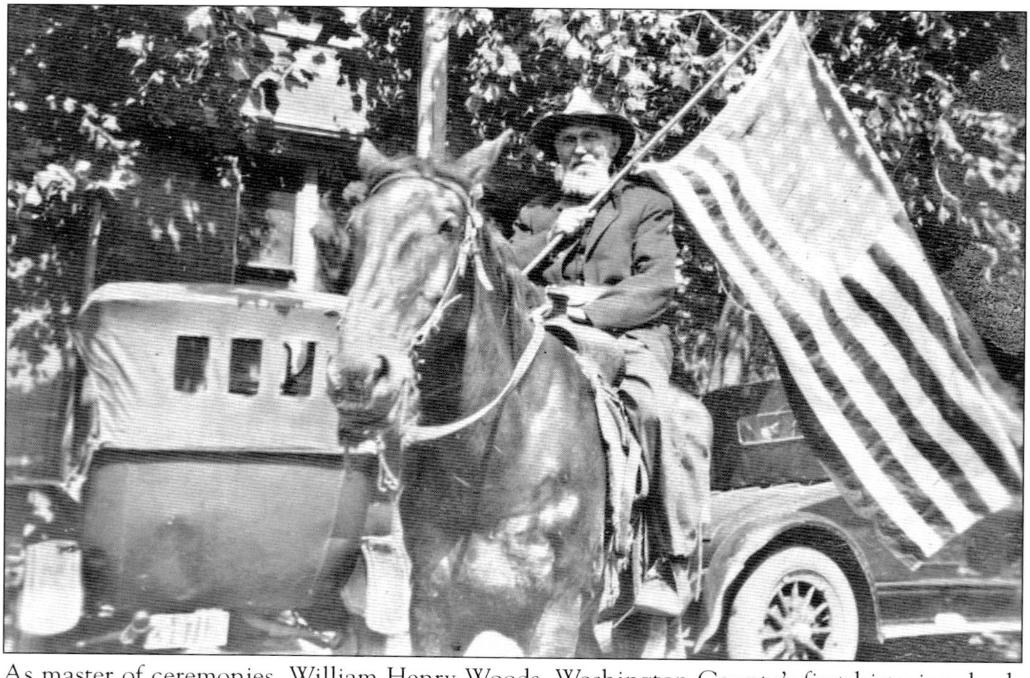

As master of ceremonies, William Henry Woods, Washington County's first historian, leads the 1919 centennial parade of Fort Atkinson. Born in England in 1839, Woods emigrated to America as a boy. A recognized archeologist, he studied and excavated the grounds of the fort, discovering valuable bones of prehistoric animals, Indian relics, and the remains of soldiers in the cornfields (once the site of Fort Atkinson). Through Woods's tireless efforts over the next 55 years, the history of the fort and the site of the Lewis and Clark expedition were preserved for future generations. Well known in and instrumental in preserving the history of his adopted community, Woods had a wish that Fort Atkinson be recognized as a national cemetery for the soldiers buried there. He died in 1927 and is buried in the Fort Calhoun Cemetery.

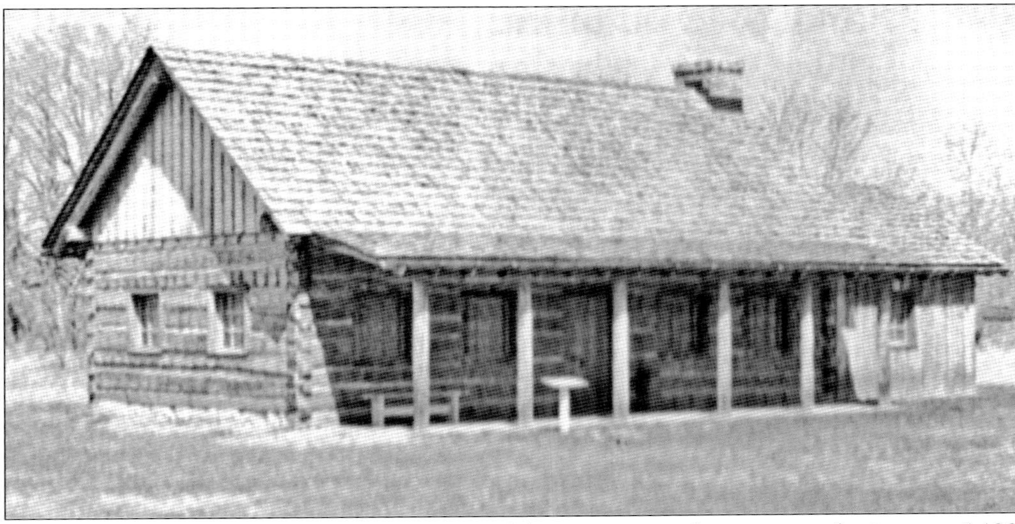

Fort Atkinson was the first military post west of the Missouri, with troops numbering over 1,100. The soldiers protected the fur traders but spent most of their time hunting, fishing, and farming. In 1827, the garrison transferred to a new camp at Jefferson Barracks in Missouri and the fort was abandoned.

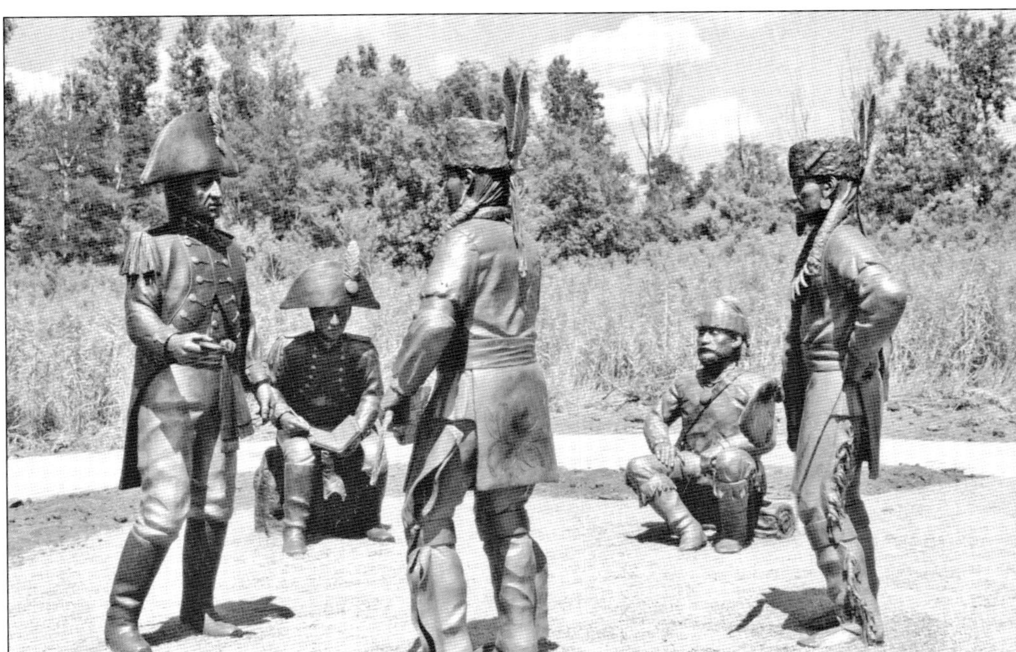

In 1971, the Nebraska Game and Parks Commission began reconstructing the fort. Today, Fort Atkinson is a Nebraska State Historical Park and a National Historic Landmark. In 2003, a life-size bronze depiction of the Lewis and Clark historic meeting was installed on the grounds of Fort Atkinson. The bronze men were sculptured by artist Oreland C. Joe.

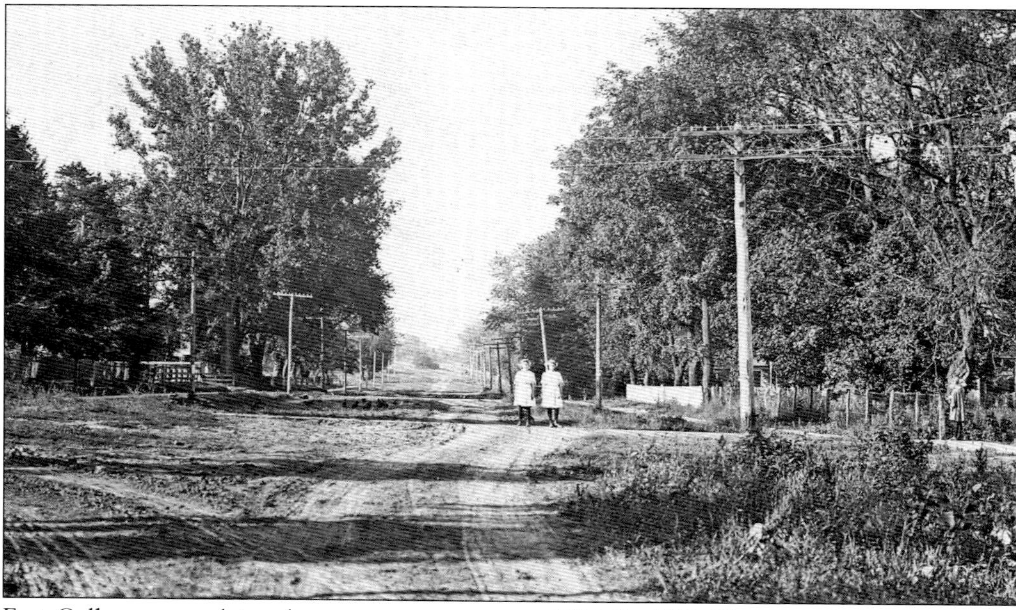

Fort Calhoun was claimed as a company town in 1854. In 1855, Elam H. Clark surveyed and platted the town into lots, and 100 lithographs were printed to advertise the rising settlement. In 1856, Fort Calhoun was incorporated and Elam Clark was mayor. Some of the early settlers in Fort Calhoun and the county were the Allen brothers and the Craig, Beale, Rohwer, and Arnold families.

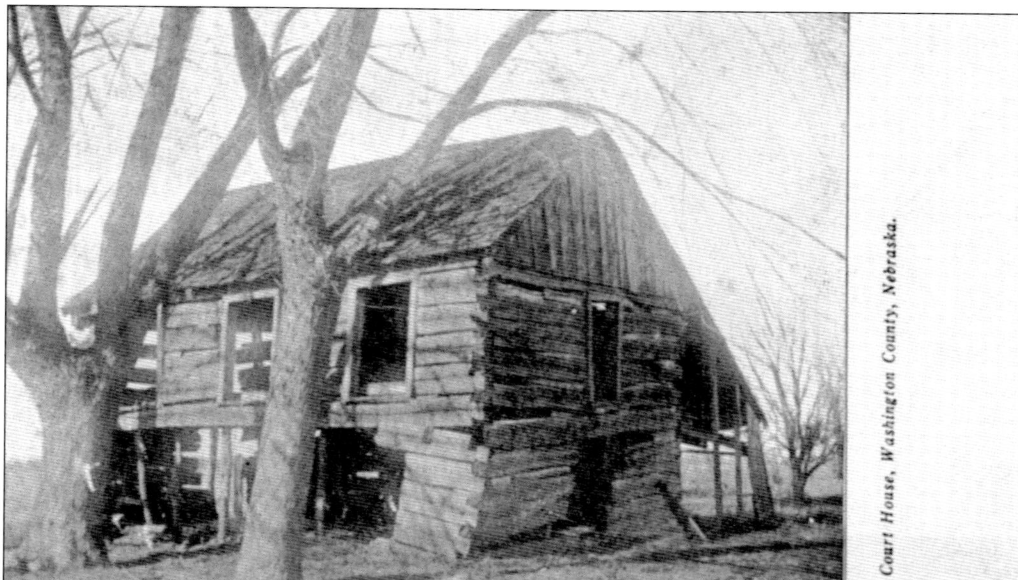

A company cabin was built on the site of the old fort, in which to administer laws in the fledgling settlement. The first district court proceeding in the county was in June 1855, involving a case of claim jumping, common throughout the West in the early settlements. A courthouse constructed of logs and cottonwood boards was built in 1856 (pictured). It also served as the first church and school.

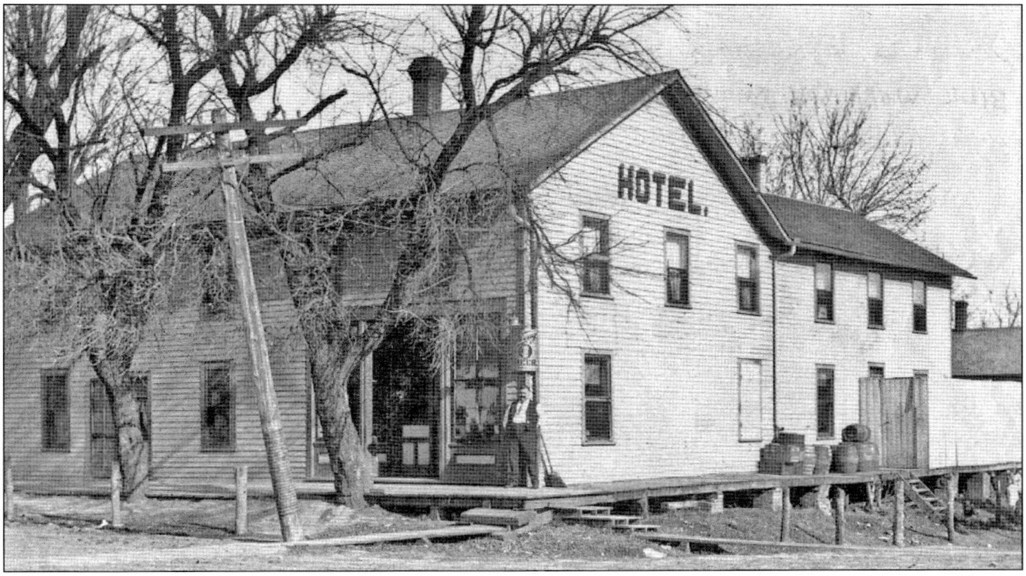

In 1854, a post road was constructed using old Indian trails. As communities settled, Fort Calhoun became a stopping point along the road. The Tew hotel, later known as the Worline Hotel, was originally a four-room log house of cottonwood built in 1856, for travelers to rest and dine. The hotel was one of the best-known hotels in the early West for many years. It was torn down in 1937.

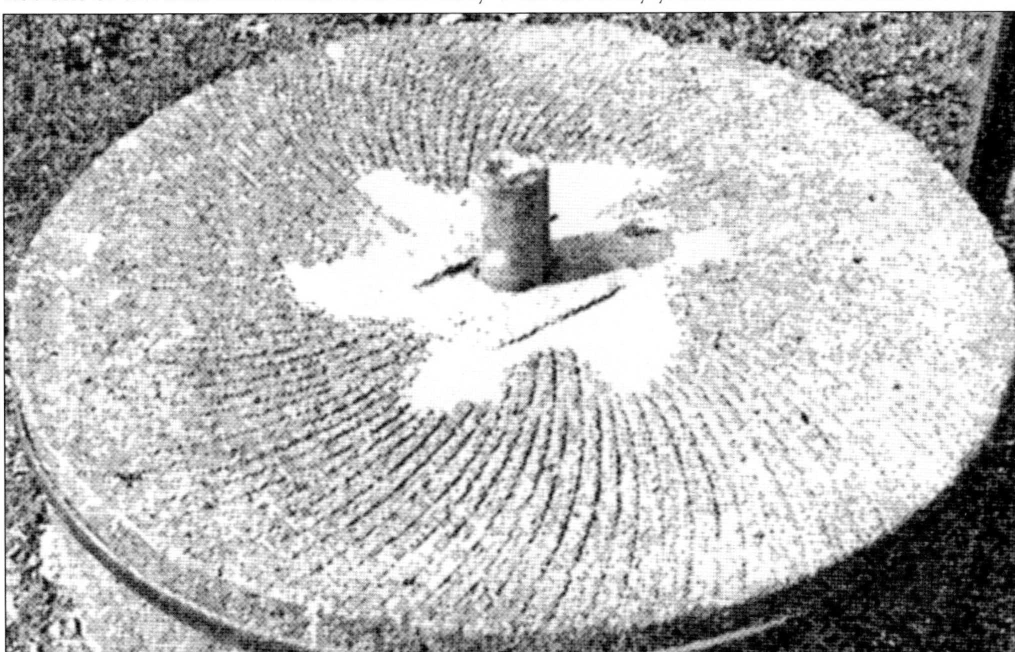

In 1858, the Fort Calhoun flouring mills were put in operation by Z. Vanier & Brothers. Three years later, they became the property of Hon. Elam Clark. Clark built a law practice, was a member of the Nebraska Legislature, and was prominent in business, civic affairs, and public life for 40 years. Grindstones from the Elam Clark Mills and the Rohwer Farm were moved to the city park in 1925.

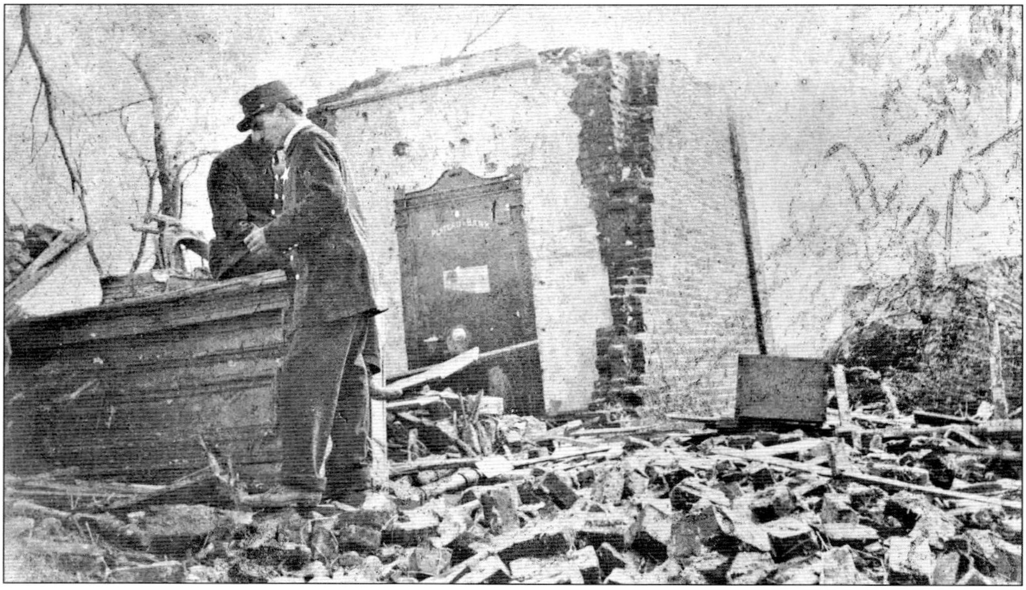

The town grew, and by 1856 the community was a booming frontier town. Brickyards were a necessity in the early towns. Willard Franklin "Sourgham" Miller is pictured standing at the Fort Calhoun brickyard, started by his brother Bethuel on the old Fort Atkinson site.

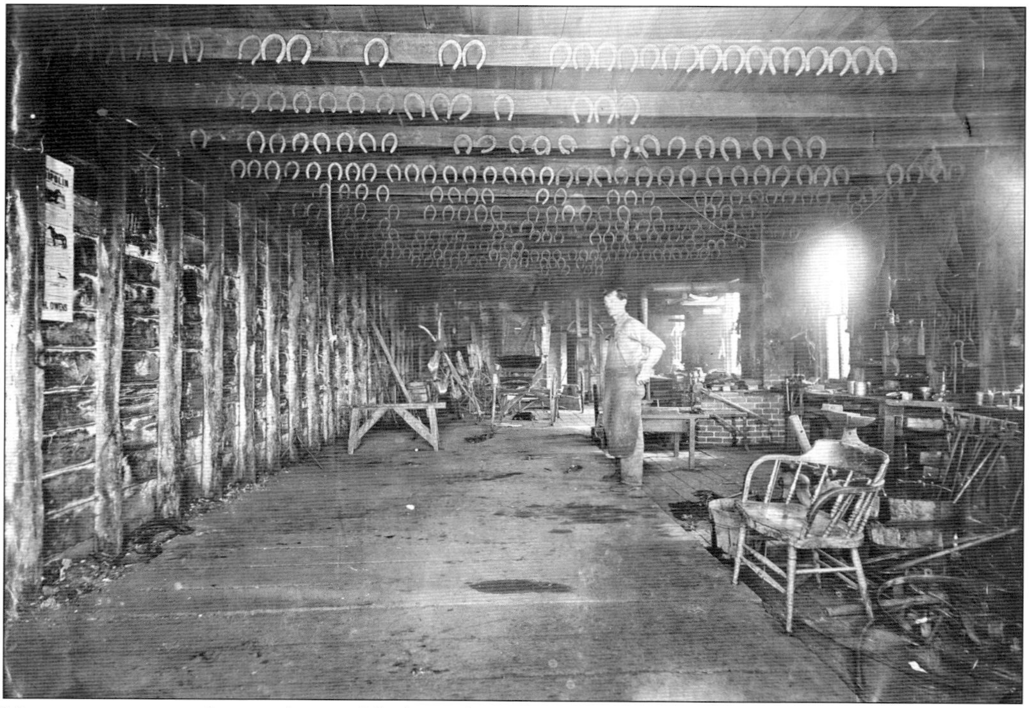

No town was complete without a blacksmith. Horseshoes hang on hooks next to the brick oven in Henry Schmidt's blacksmith shop. Born in Germany, Schmidt was a wagonmaker and, for a time, a Fort Calhoun marshal. His shop put new iron tires on wagon wheels, sharpened plows, made tools, and repaired farm equipment.

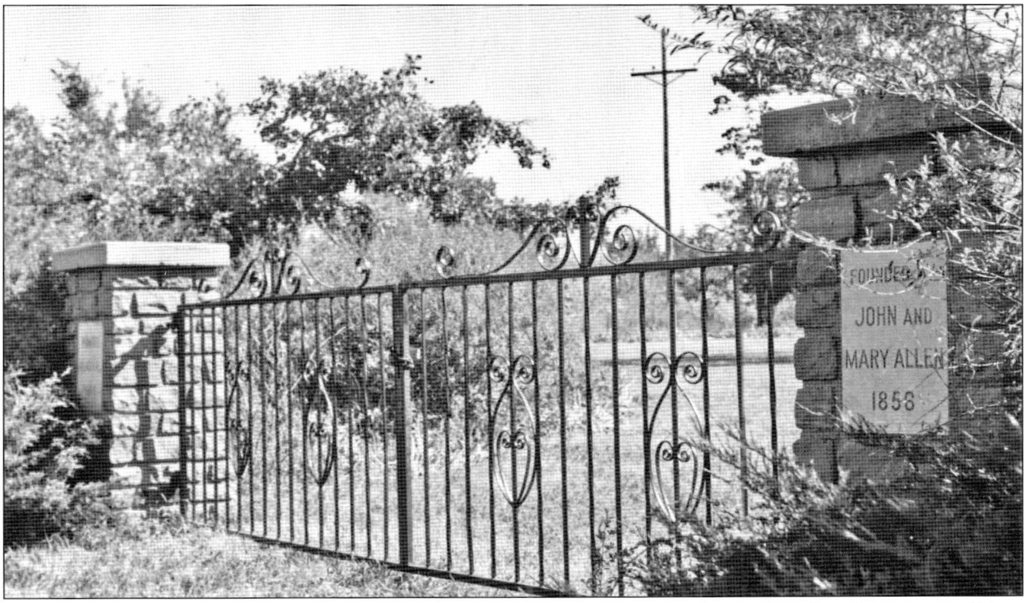

The Allen brothers were very early settlers, playing an active role in the development of Fort Calhoun. Thomas J. Allen became territorial sheriff. John Allen was appointed Washington County commissioner and was involved in the education of the pioneer children. John and his wife established one of the earliest cemeteries, the Allen Cemetery, also called the Pioneer Memorial Cemetery, after the accidental death of their daughter, Martha Catherine.

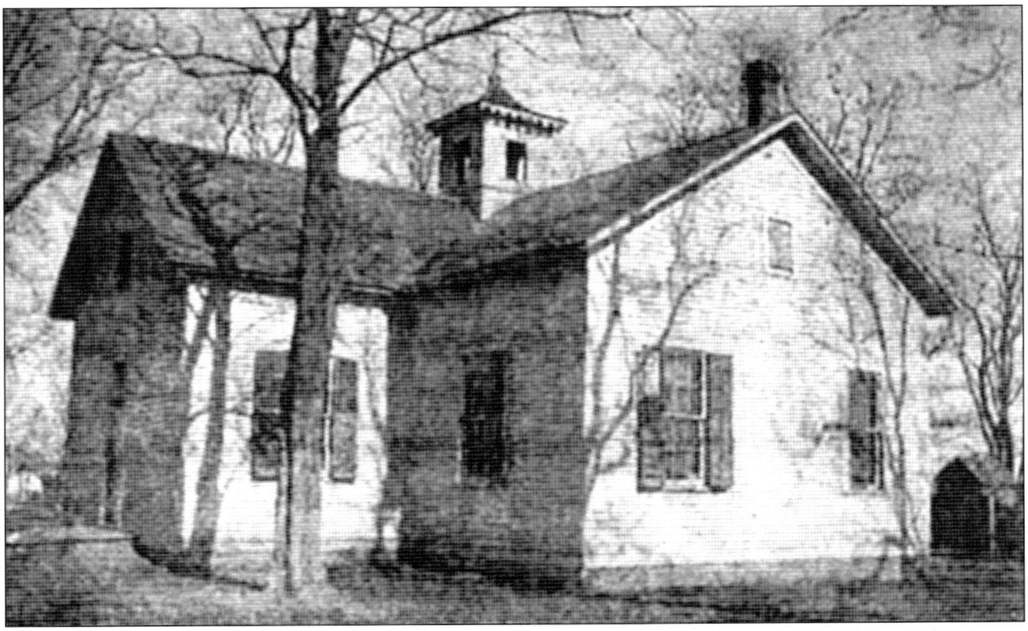

Education was of utmost importance. The first schoolhouse, constructed through a tax levy, was approved in May 1865. It cost less than a $1,000, which included the costs of a belfry and black locust trees planted on the grounds. The school served the community for 30 years until a larger school was approved. The original building was torn down to make way for the new school.

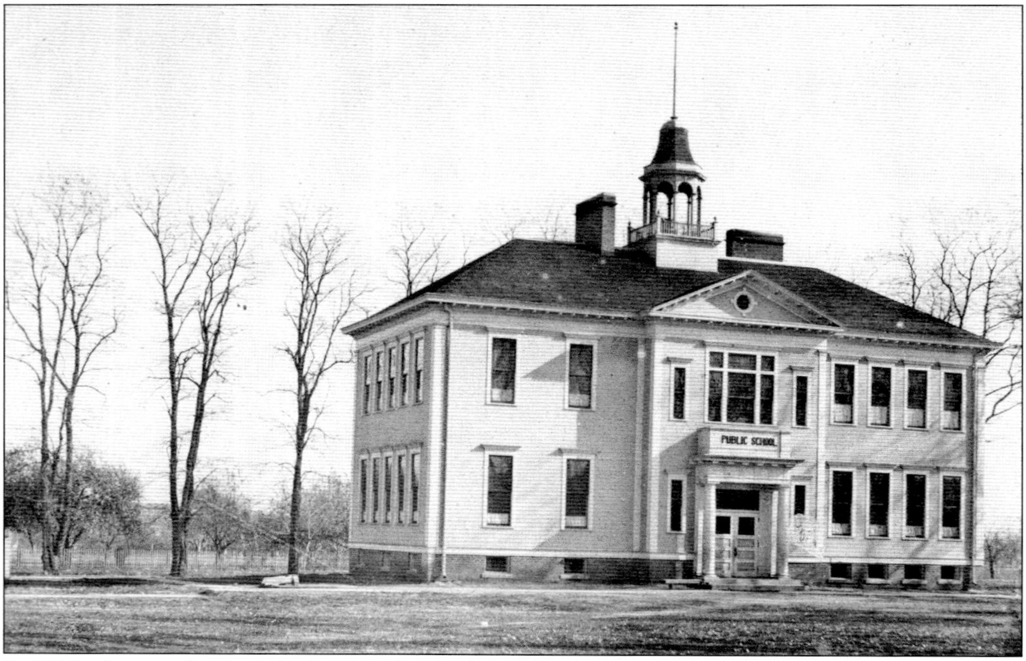

In 1899, a larger school was built, complete with the modern conveniences of the time, demonstrating the pride of a growing and prospering community. The first graduates were Catherine Beales, Otto G. Frahm, and Ella Blodgett. The school was torn down in 1972.

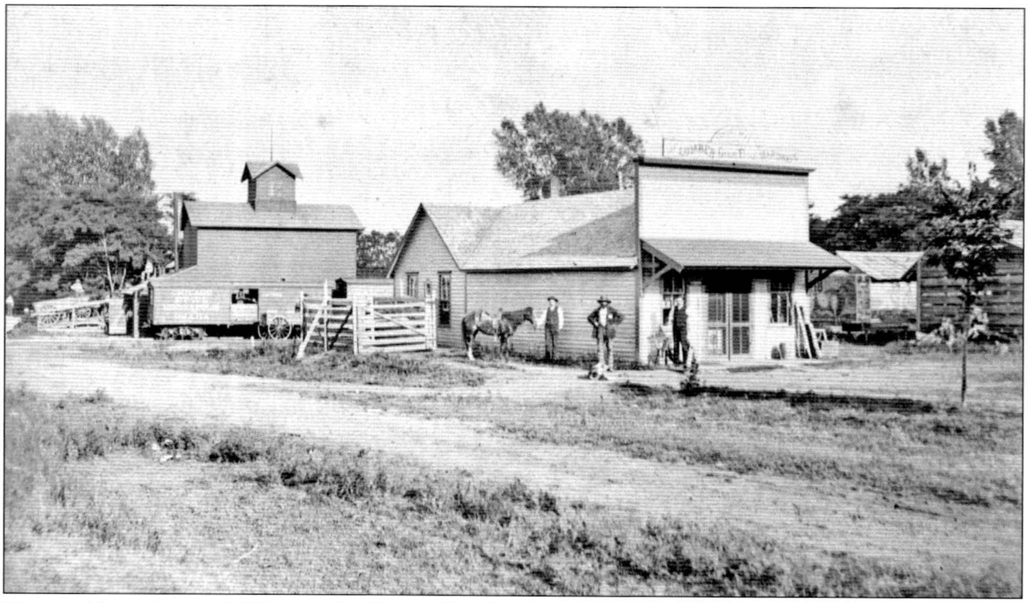

Pictured here in the 1880s are the Henry Rix lumberyard, feed and hardware store, and elevator. Rix expanded his business operations and eventually branched out into the banking business. He formed the Washington County State Bank of Fort Calhoun, which soon became his principal occupation. He sold his interests in the store to his brother-in-law Fred Frahm, who was employed in the general store retail business at the time.

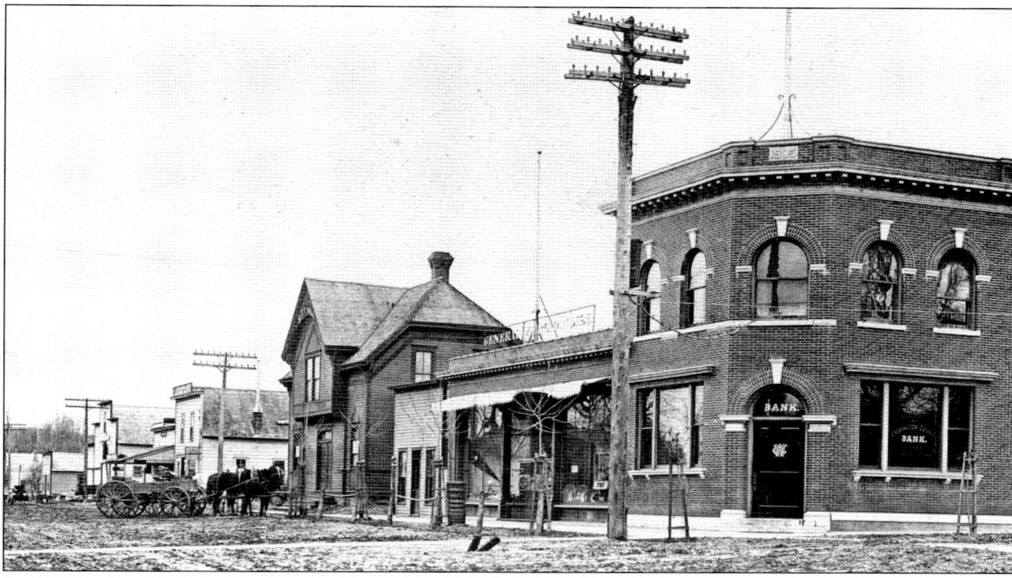

In 1905, the Frahm General Merchandise store and the Washington County Bank, pictured here in 1905, moved into a new brick Masonic building on Main Street. The Washington County State Bank of Fort Calhoun served the community for over 30 years but did not survive the Depression.

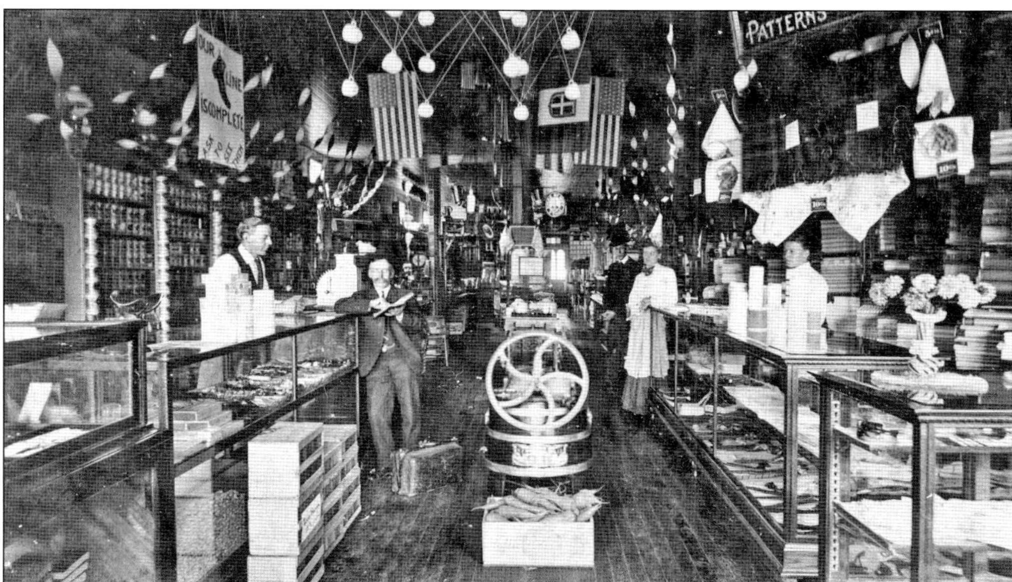

The general store of a frontier town sold everything a settler needed but as the population and competition in businesses grew, general merchandize stores were finding their own niche to draw in patrons. The Rix General Store was carrying a large inventory of household consumer goods for the comforts of home.

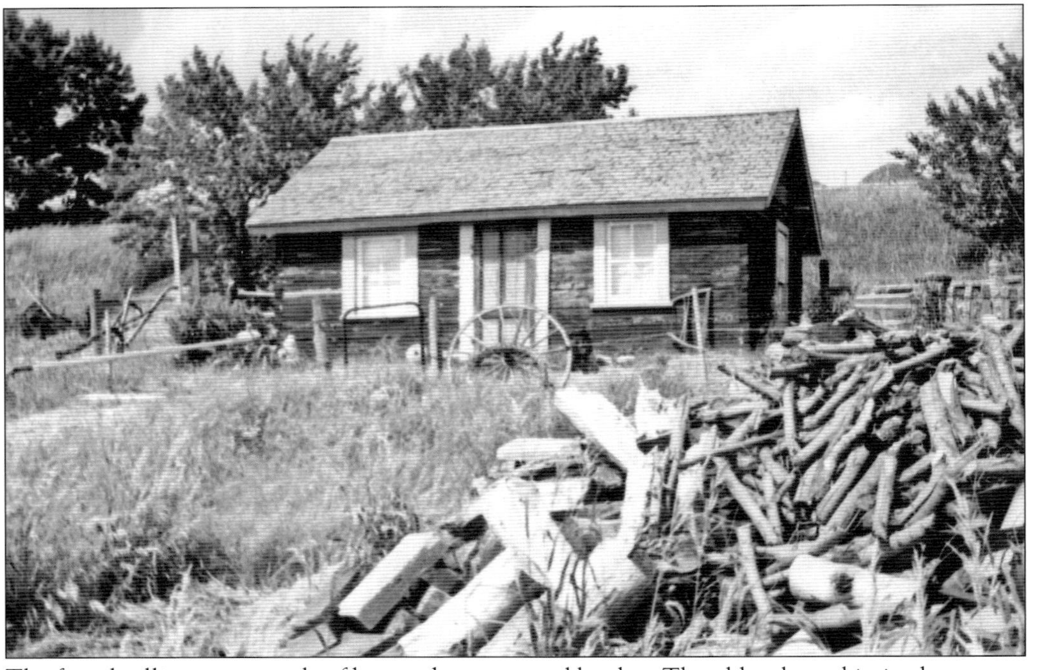

The first dwellings were made of logs and cottonwood lumber. The oldest log cabin in the county was the Thone cabin, built in 1857. The cabin was eventually owned by Niels Miller, who rebuilt it log by log. Bill Kistler purchased the Miller property, acquiring the log cabin in the 1990s.

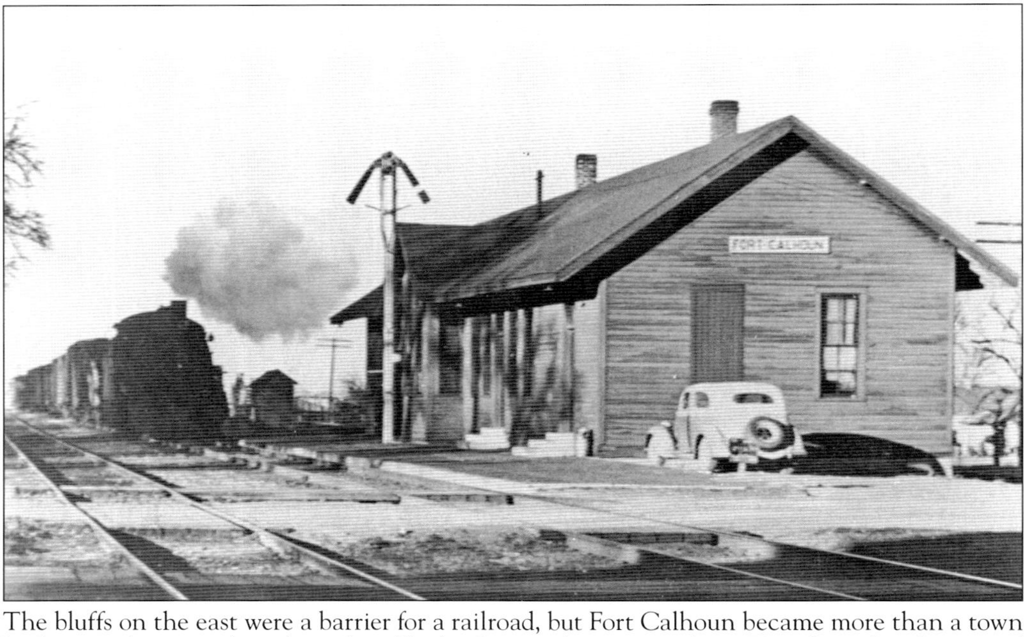

The bluffs on the east were a barrier for a railroad, but Fort Calhoun became more than a town built upon the river when the railroad built a line to the town in the 1870s. The railroad operated as a commuter line to Omaha and other towns in the Missouri Valley. The Chicago & North Western eventually owned the line. The original Fort Calhoun depot burned in 1920, and a new one opened in the fall.

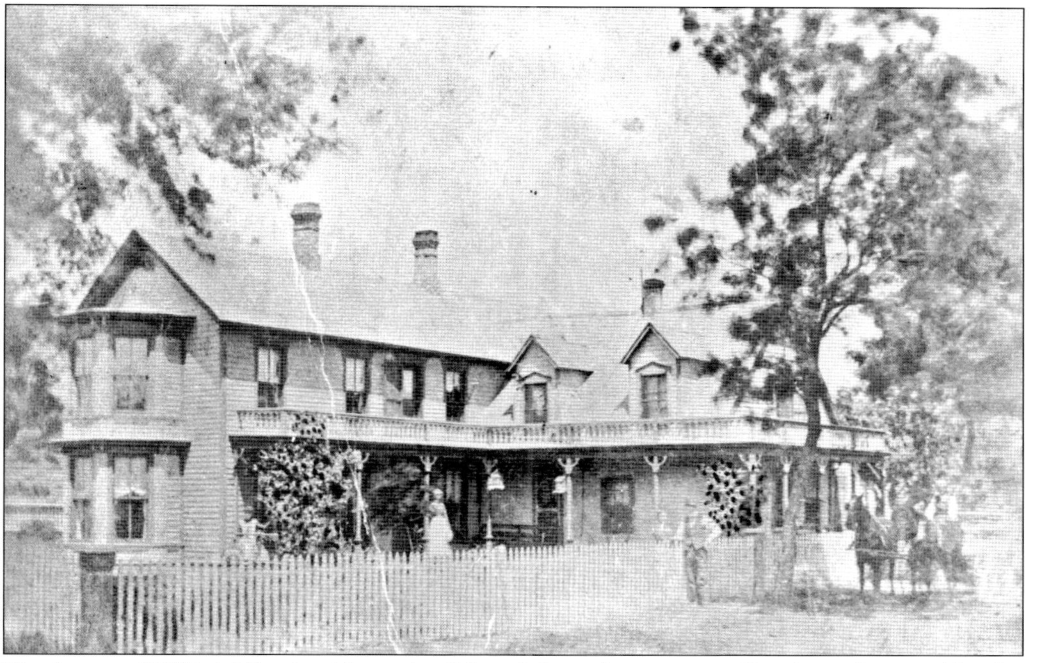

The home of W.H. Miller (and later the Schmidt home) was originally a log cabin used by the railroad laborers in building the railroad in 1871. In the 1880s, a new addition was built butting up to the original log house and the log structure was removed.

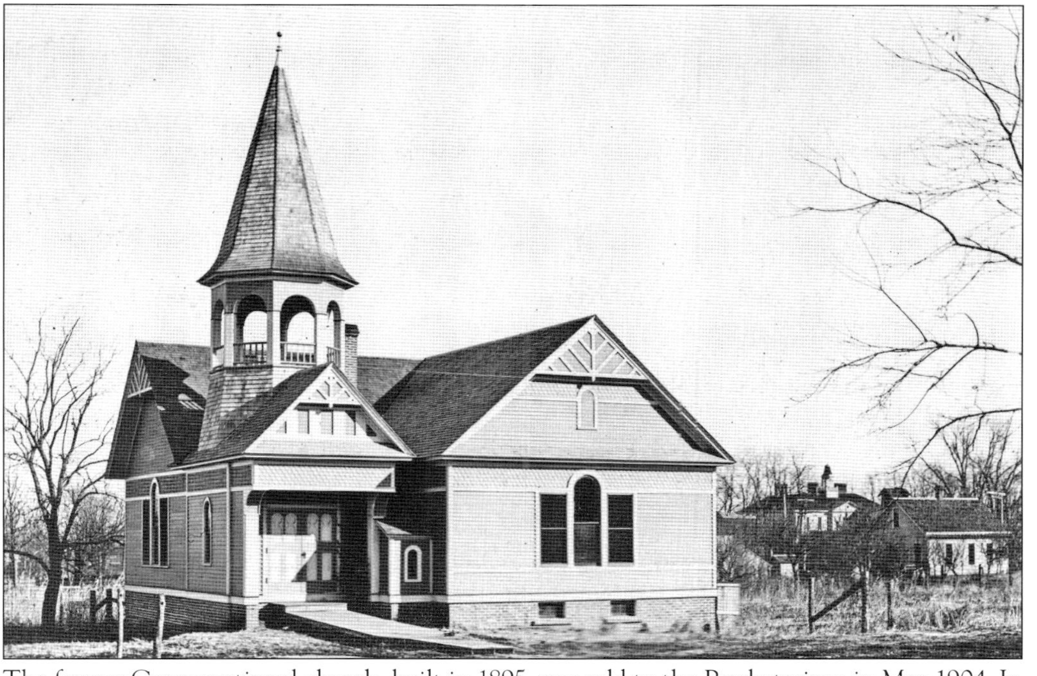

The former Congregational church, built in 1895, was sold to the Presbyterians in May 1904. In 1921, a new bell rang for the first time. The church celebrated its 50th anniversary on May 16, 1954, its 75th in 1979, and continues today as an active Presbyterian congregation, 112 years later.

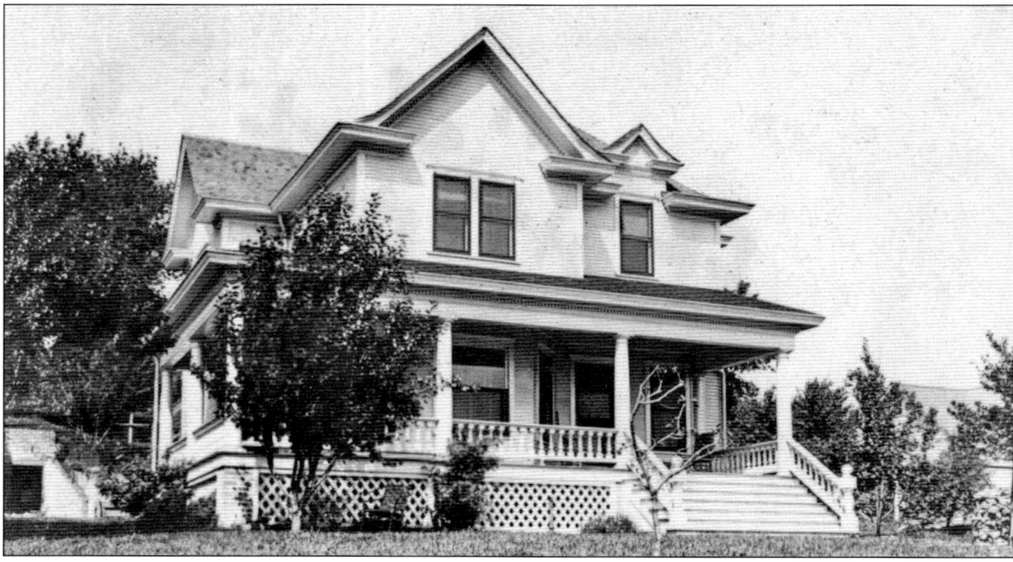

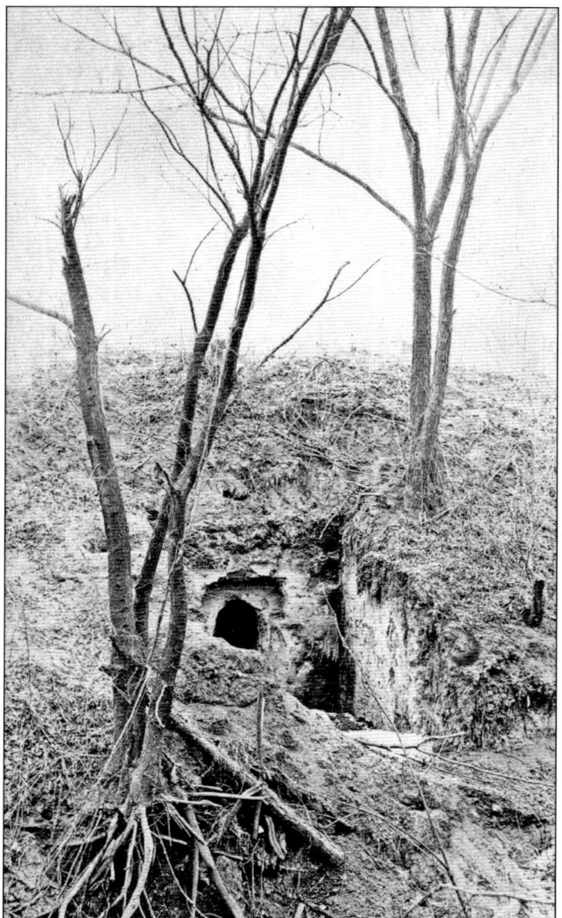

Fred Frahm was born in Fort Calhoun in 1872, of German immigrant parents. He bought and operated the general merchandise store and was active in the Fort Calhoun community, having served three terms as mayor. His house, built in 1906, was a Colonial Revival structure built on a hillside overlooking the community he called home. The Frahm House is part of the Washington County Museum collection.

Every community has some folklore or a mystery or two. Pictured here around the early 1900s, this cave under the bluffs in Fort Calhoun had long been reputed to be the soldiers' tunnel to the river from the old fort. This theory seems unlikely, but the truth of the tunnel may never be known.

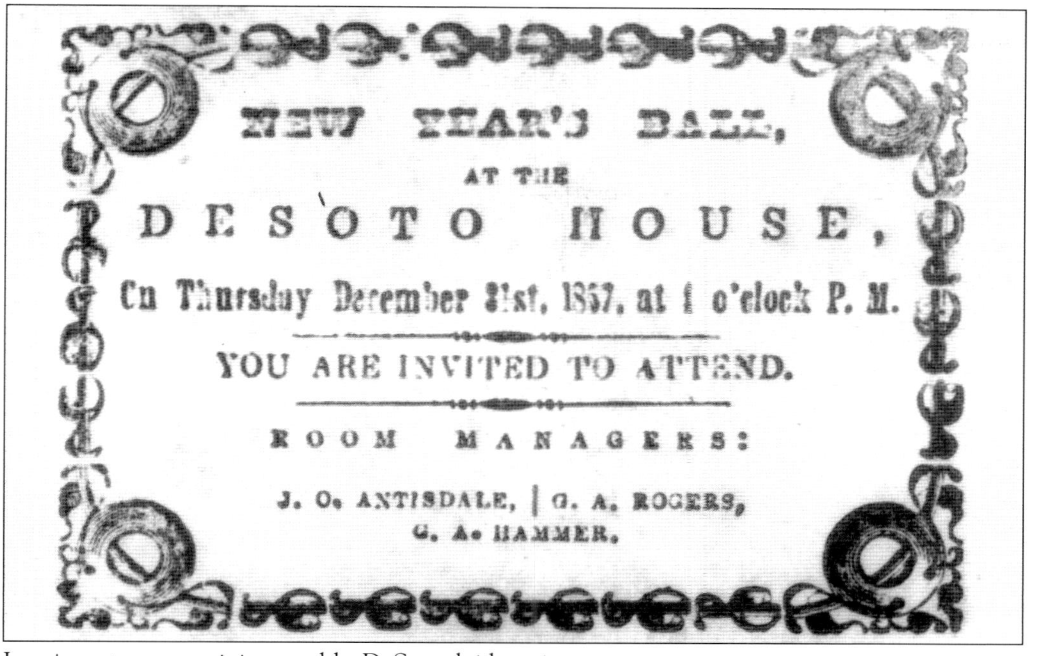
NEW YEAR'S BALL,

AT THE

DESOTO HOUSE,

On Thursday December 31st, 1857, at [illegible] o'clock P. M.

YOU ARE INVITED TO ATTEND.

ROOM MANAGERS:

J. O. ANTISDALE, | G. A. ROGERS,
G. A. HAMMER.

Immigrants were arriving weekly. DeSoto, laid out in the fall of 1854, was located about six miles north of Fort Calhoun along the Missouri River and was a popular river steamer port when water was the chief means of transportation. One of the first buildings to go up was the DeSoto House hotel.

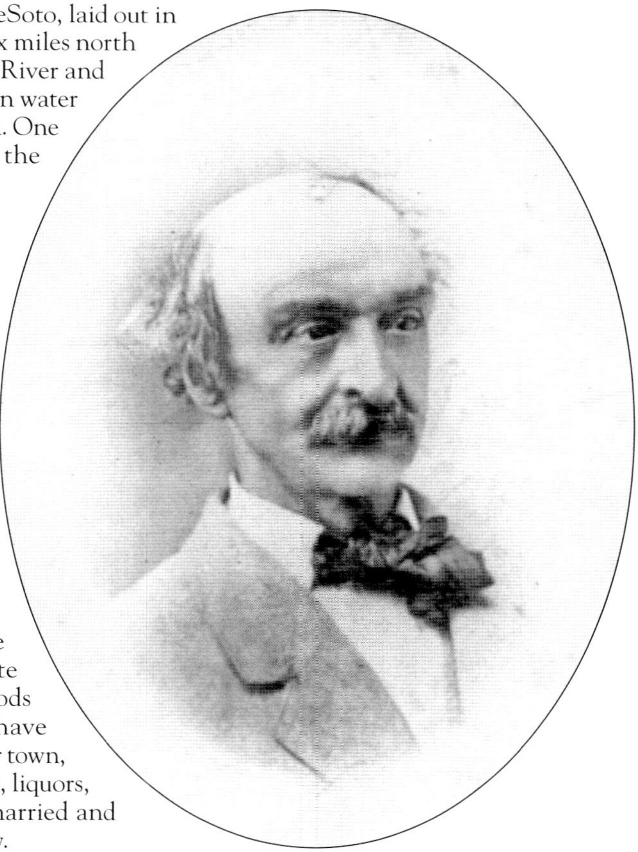

Charles Seltz was a fur trader along the Missouri River when he stopped at DeSoto in the fall of 1855. He was the second merchant to locate in the town and received all his goods by steamboat. Seltz's store would have carried provisions needed in a frontier town, including molasses, chocolate, spices, liquors, cigars, and bottles of bitters. Seltz married and remained in the DeSoto community.

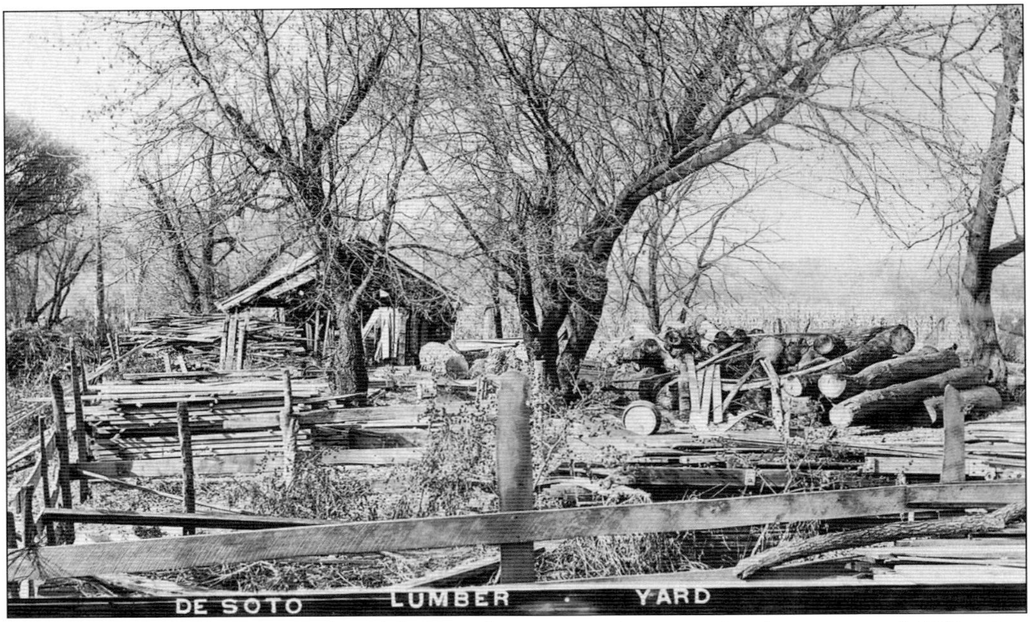

Timber for construction was plentiful along the rivers and streams. In the summer of 1855, using the cottonwood found along the riverbanks, 30 hewn log houses (usually with wooden floors) were built, keeping the lumberyard busy. Wages for cutting a cord of wood were 75¢ in the 1880s and 1890s, but a cord of hardwood could sell in Omaha for $5.

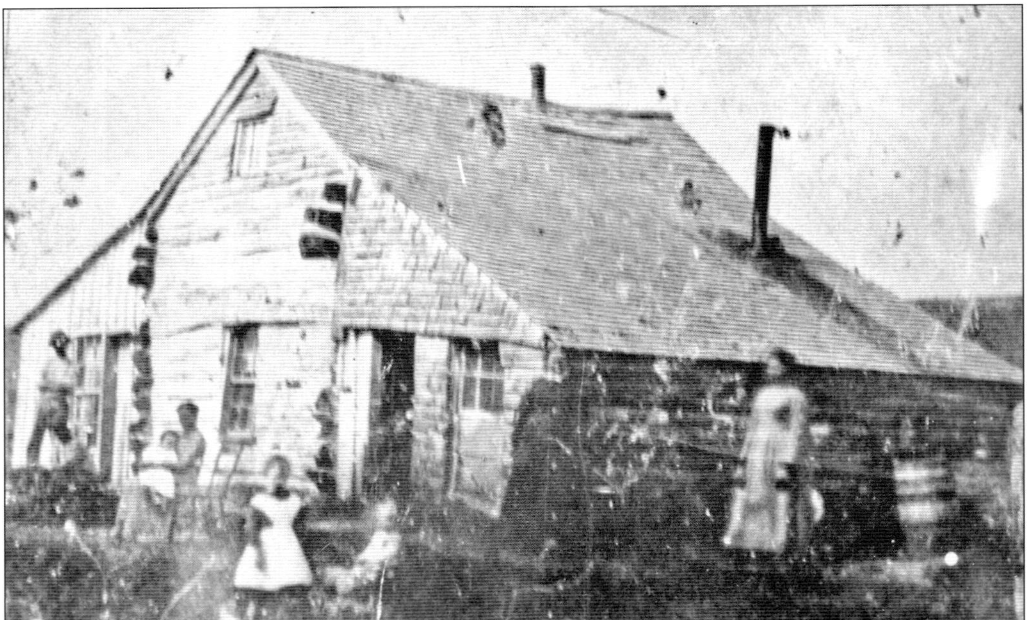

The Louis Bouvier log home was built in 1856. This c. 1878 photograph shows the central main dwelling with the lean-tos later added, a common practice as the family grew or income allowed for expansion. By the 1870s, most houses were wood-frame or brick.

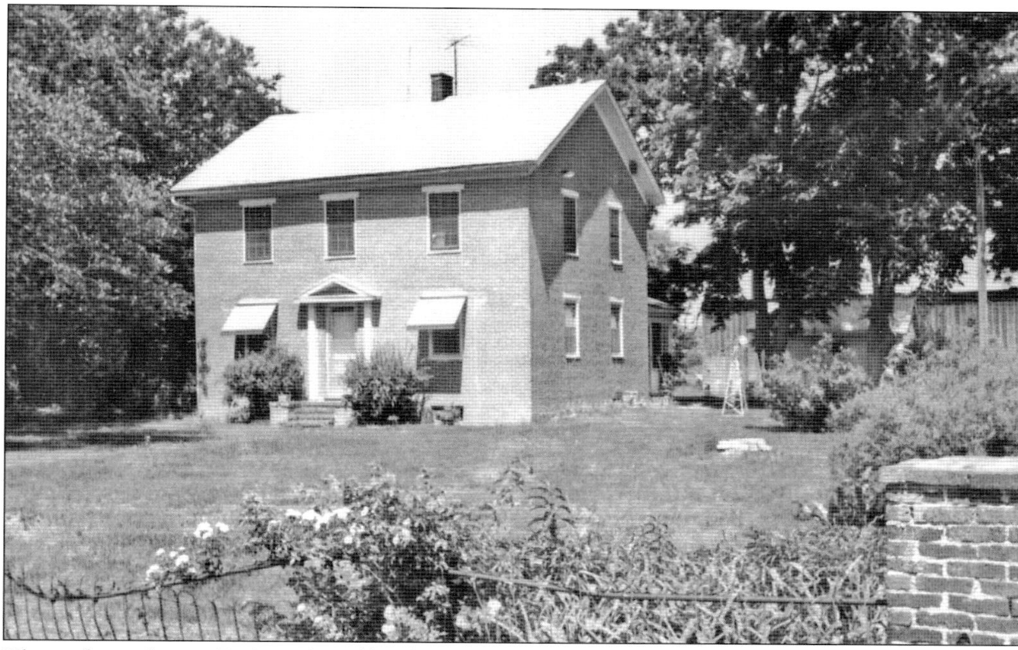

The early settlers in DeSoto found brick in considerable quantities (a result of the Mormons' brief settlement in the area) and used them in walling up wells and fireplaces. Brickyards later allowed the use of brick in homes. The Roland Smith home in DeSoto, built in 1867 in the popular Greek Revival style, was made of brick from the area.

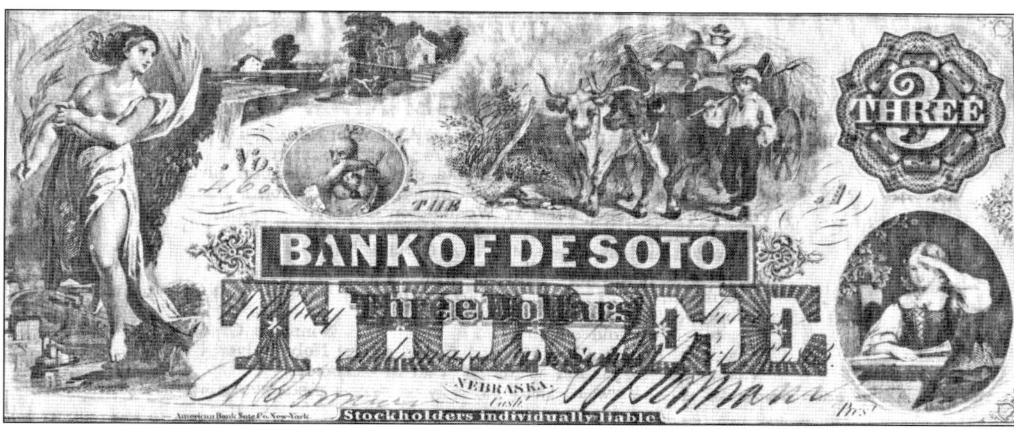

DeSoto had three banking houses and four newspapers. The Bank of DeSoto, the Waubeek Bank, and the Corn Exchange Bank were wildcat banks. Operating, as most banks were in the new territory of the West, as private institutions and without sufficient capital to back their free issuing of bonds, they folded in the panic of 1857. Banking houses, if they survived, were later incorporated.

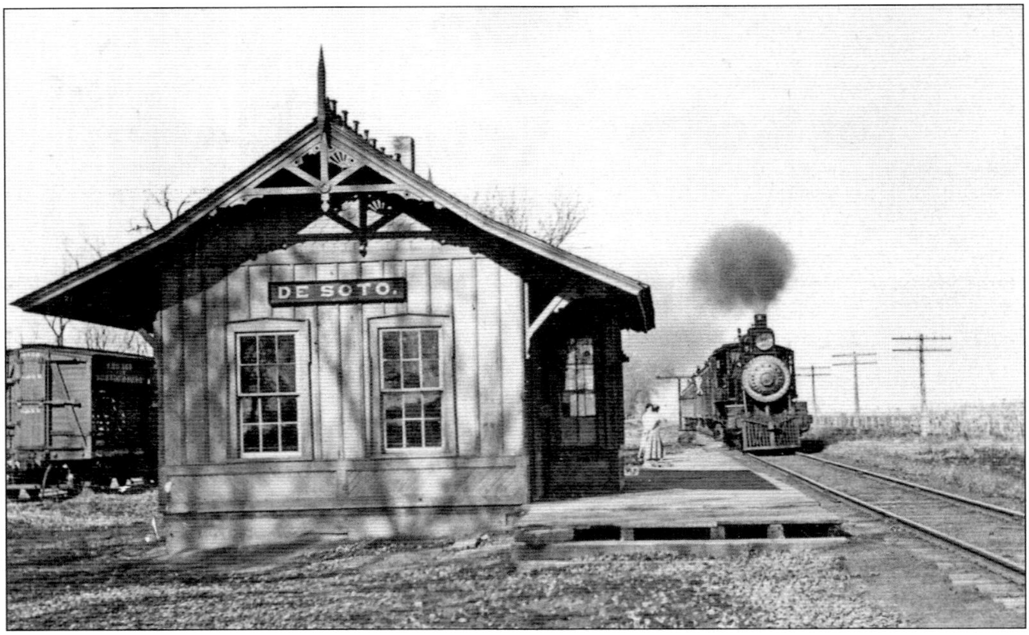

DeSoto was a booming city with a population of 600. In 1867, plans were to build a railroad west from DeSoto to Fremont, in the adjoining county of Dodge. A railroad camp was established and a depot built. A decision to locate the bridge two miles north denied DeSoto's hopes of a railroad changing the history of the town forever.

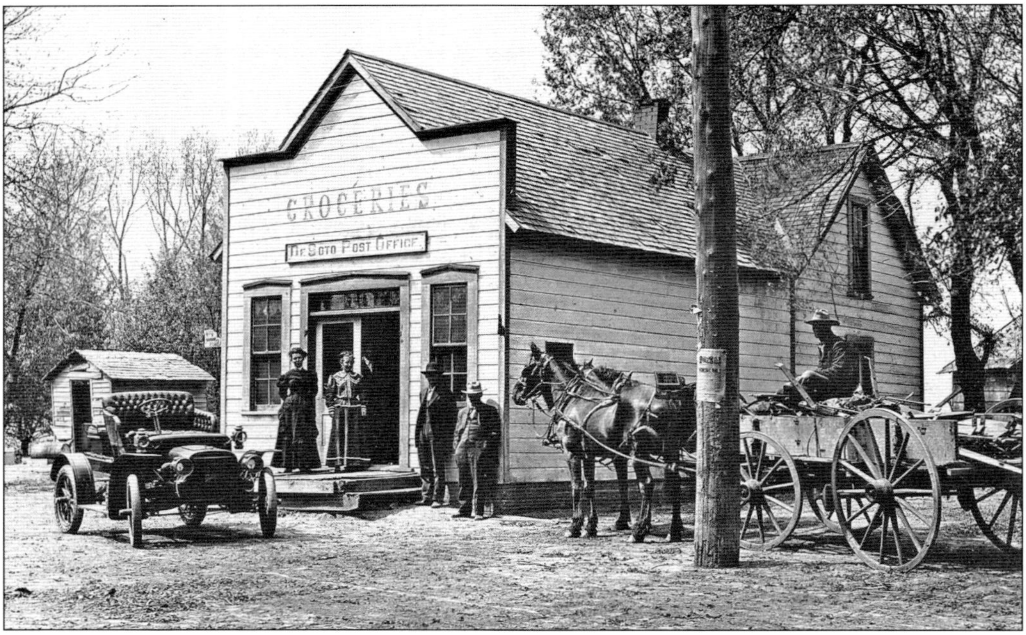

The DeSoto general store and post office served the farming community until the 1920s. After the US Army Corps of Engineers straightened the river with dams, many of DeSoto's farms became part of the DeSoto National Wildlife Refuge. Today, the community of DeSoto is the site of the nuclear plant just outside Blair's city limits.

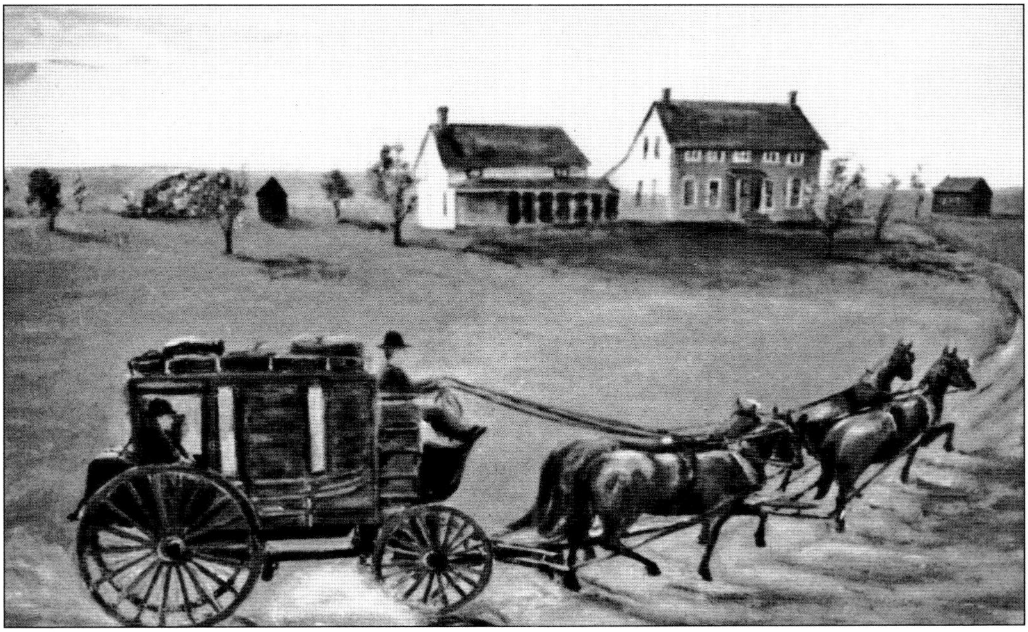

Another early town, now a ghost town, was Cuming City. Claimed in 1854, it stretched along the Missouri River six miles north of the present site of Blair. The hotel in Cuming City became known as the Halfway House, for it was a day's journey in either direction from the ends of the post line. Extra horses were kept for the stage line and food and lodging provided for travelers.

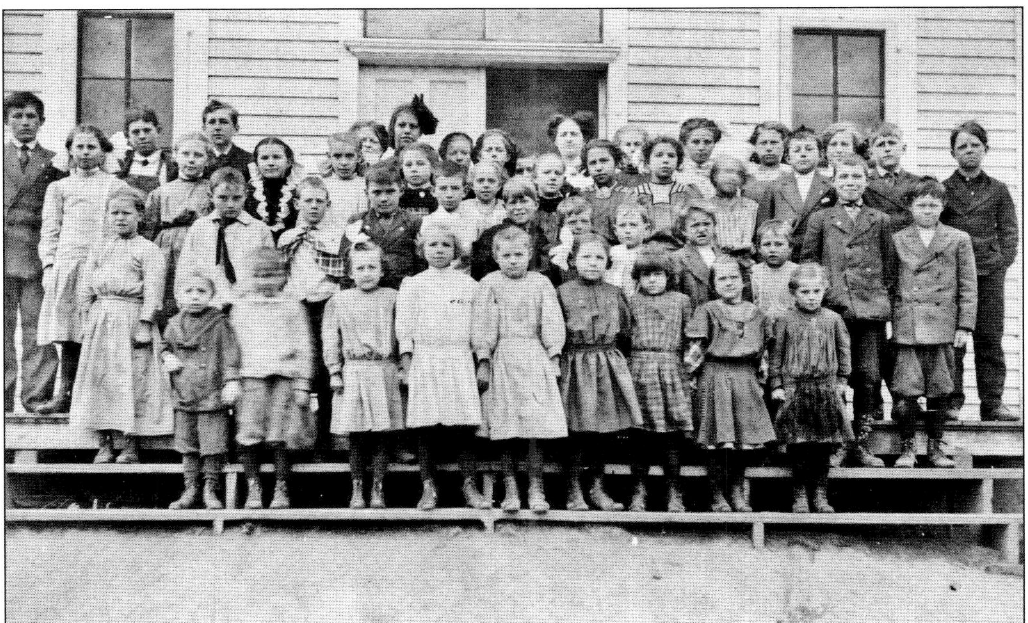

Unidentified students pose in front of the school in Garryowen, a hamlet located in Nashville, near the old Fort Lisa trading post and Rockport. Rockport was located near the old Engineer Cantonment and was an important steamboat landing at the height of the fur-trading era. Nashville is an unincorporated established community situated in the southeast corner of the county.

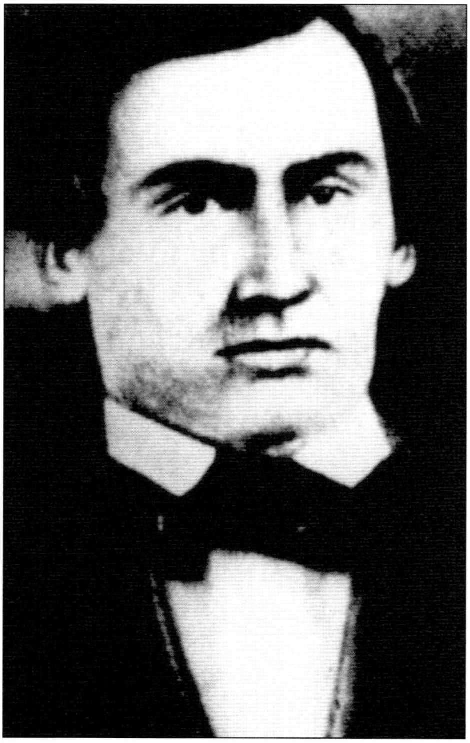

Fontanelle, overlooking the Elkhorn River, was founded in 1854 by the Nebraska Colonization Company from Quincy, Illinois. These pioneers met Logan Fontenelle, the son of a French trader and Omaha chief Big Elk's daughter, while crossing the Missouri River at Omaha. He led the party along the Elkhorn to the present site of the town, 40 miles north of the city of Omaha, and they named their new home in honor of Fontenelle.

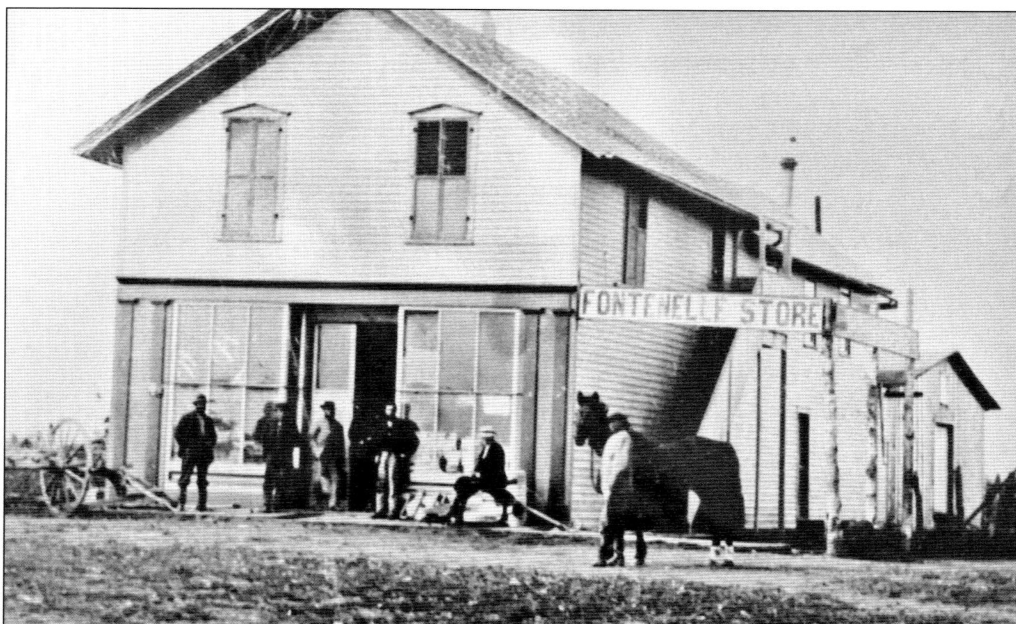

William Davis kept the first hotel, the Fontanelle House. The Fontenelle Store would have many owners throughout its history and operated for a 105 years. The first sawmill was put into operation in the summer of 1856. A creamery turned out 5,000 pounds of butter a day. Built by Ira Cahoon in 1895, it is believed to be the first incorporated creamery in the state of Nebraska.

In 1855, the original founding fathers, many of whom were represented in the first territorial legislature, secured a charter for the first Nebraska University. It was the first college in Nebraska. The first college building was completed in 1858 operating under the Congregational Church.

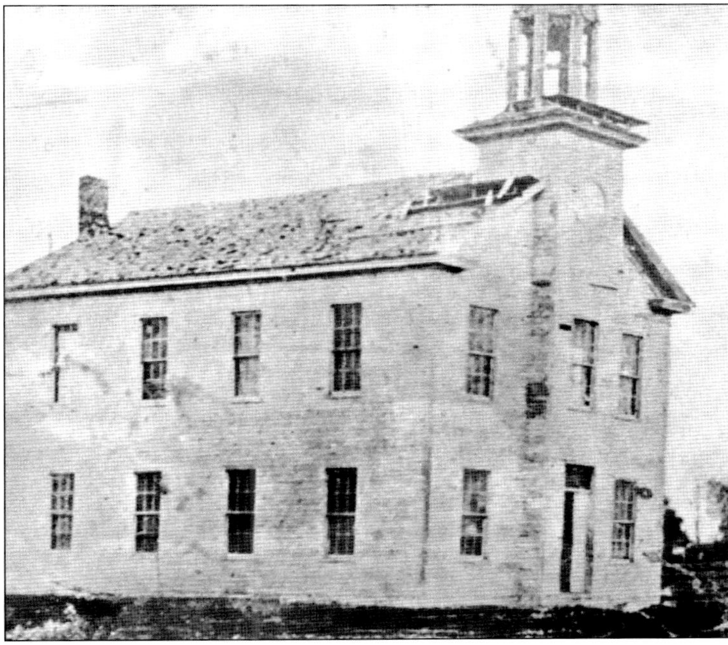

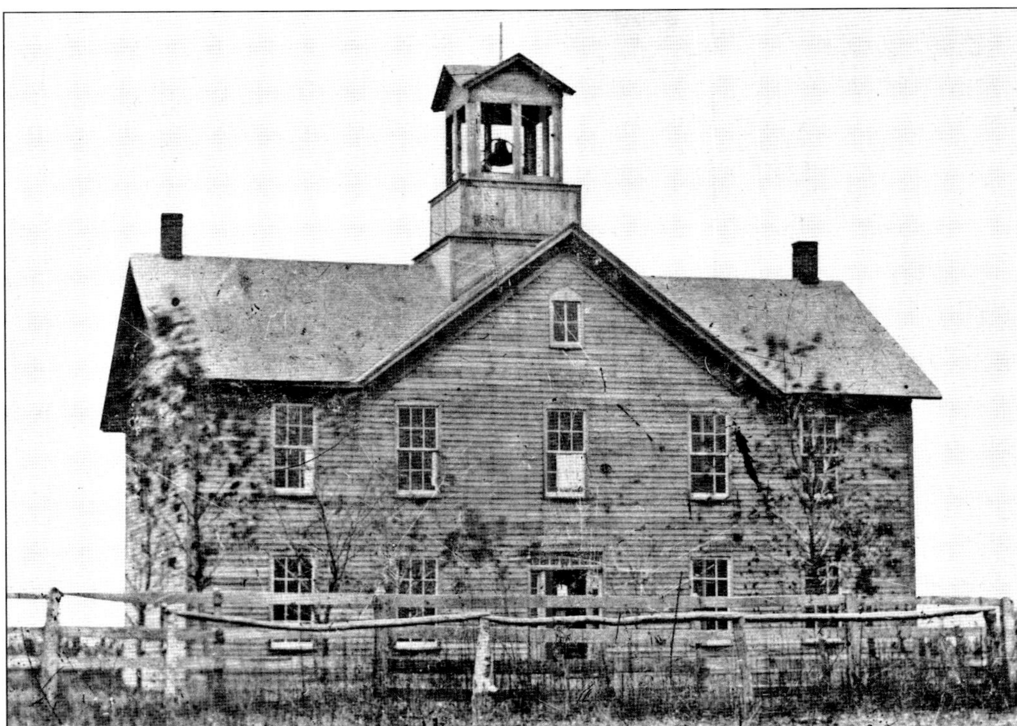

In 1865, the college burned to the ground. It was rebuilt, but when it burned again a decision was made to not rebuild the university. The school was disbanded in 1870 and began a new life as Doane College in Crete, Nebraska, which exists today. The city of Lincoln became home to the state university.

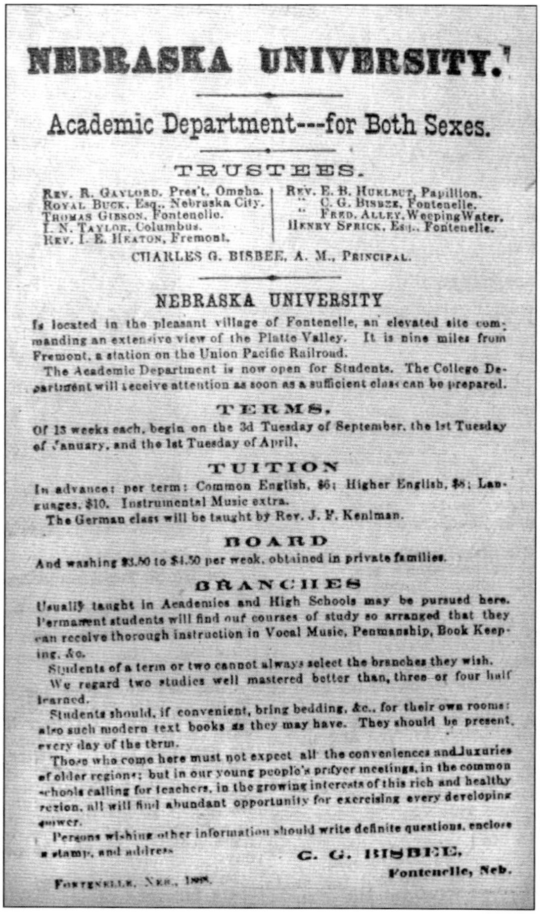

NEBRASKA UNIVERSITY.

Academic Department---for Both Sexes.

TRUSTEES.

Rev. R. Gaylord, Pres't, Omaha.
Royal Buck, Esq., Nebraska City.
Thomas Gibson, Fontenelle.
I. N. Taylor, Columbus.
Rev. I. E. Heaton, Fremont.
Rev. E. B. Hurlbut, Papillion.
" C. G. Bisbee, Fontenelle.
" Fred. Alley, Weeping Water.
Henry Sprick, Esq., Fontenelle.

CHARLES G. BISBEE, A. M., Principal.

NEBRASKA UNIVERSITY

Is located in the pleasant village of Fontenelle, an elevated site commanding an extensive view of the Platte Valley. It is nine miles from Fremont, a station on the Union Pacific Railroad.

The Academic Department is now open for Students. The College Department will receive attention as soon as a sufficient class can be prepared.

TERMS,

Of 13 weeks each, begin on the 3d Tuesday of September, the 1st Tuesday of January, and the 1st Tuesday of April.

TUITION

In advance: per term: Common English, $6; Higher English, $8; Languages, $10. Instrumental Music extra.

The German class will be taught by Rev. J. F. Kenlman.

BOARD

And washing $3.50 to $4.50 per week, obtained in private families.

BRANCHES

Usually taught in Academies and High Schools may be pursued here. Permanent students will find our courses of study so arranged that they can receive thorough instruction in Vocal Music, Penmanship, Book Keeping, &c.

Students of a term or two cannot always select the branches they wish.

We regard two studies well mastered better than three or four half learned.

Students should, if convenient, bring bedding, &c., for their own rooms: also such modern text books as they may have. They should be present every day of the term.

Those who come here must not expect all the conveniences and luxuries of older regions; but in our young people's prayer meetings, in the common schools calling for teachers, in the growing interests of this rich and healthy region, all will find abundant opportunity for exercising every developing power.

Persons wishing other information should write definite questions, enclose a stamp, and address

C. G. BISBEE,
Fontenelle, Neb.

Fontenelle, Neb., 18[illegible].

Advertisements for the college were printed to help promote the town that had established a school of higher learning in hopes of attracting settlers. Many of the town pioneers were immigrants from Westphalia, Germany, who first settled in Quincy, Illinois.

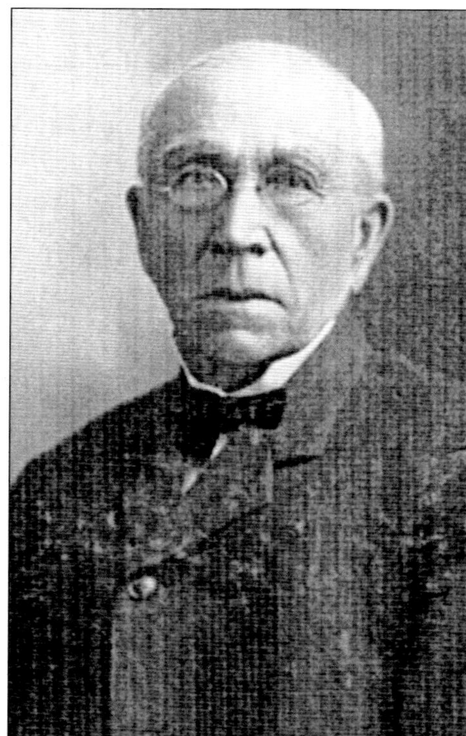

Henry Sprick was instrumental in the settlement of Fontanelle and establishing Salem Lutheran Church. He was one of the largest landowners in the county, owning over 3,000 acres. Sprick served three consecutive terms as a member of the senate. In 1878, Sprick was the US presidential elector for James Blaine on the Republican Party ticket. (Courtesy Salem Lutheran Church and Washington County Historical Association.)

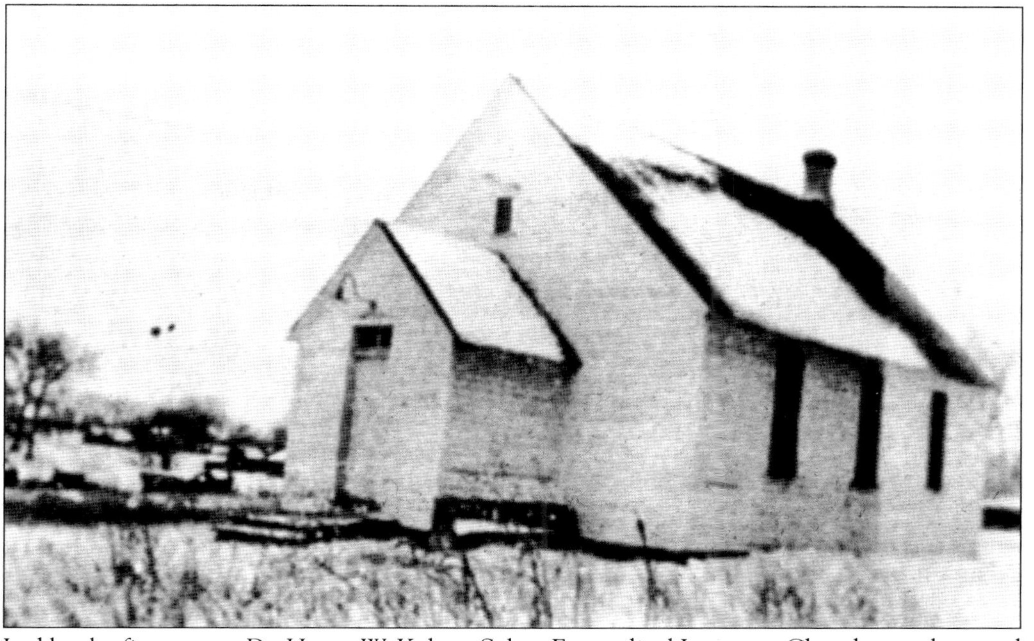

Led by the first pastor, Dr. Henry W. Kuhns, Salem Evangelical Lutheran Church was chartered with 33 members in June 1860. Built in 1865 from lumber hauled out of Omaha in wagons driven by the congregation, the church was dedicated in June 1866 with a German-speaking pastorate.

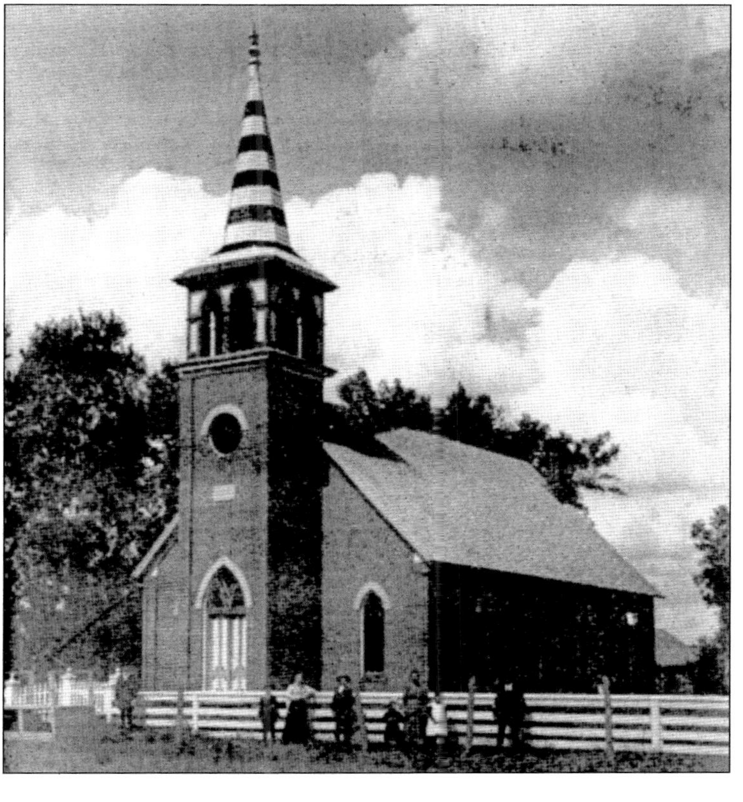

A fire in the original church led to the building of a new church in 1888. The Salem congregation purchased four acres of land across the road from the old church remains and a brick church building was erected at a cost of $3,500. The bricks were from the brickyard of Waterman and Edelmeyer of Fontanelle. The new church was dedicated on October 12, 1888. (Courtesy Salem Lutheran Church.)

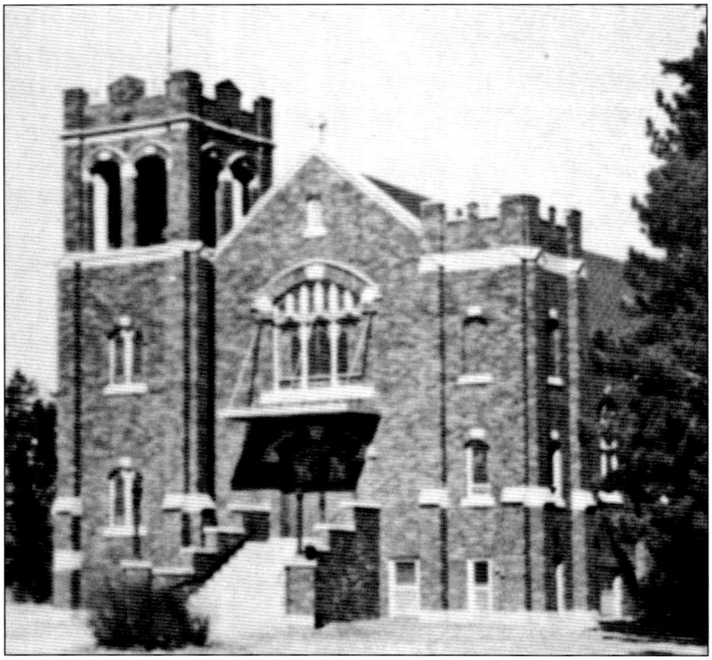

The present church, built in 1929, seats 300. The congregation, many of whose members are descendants of the original pioneers, celebrated its centennial in 1960. Salem Evangelical Lutheran Church is the oldest continuous Lutheran congregation in Nebraska and remains an active church serving the community.

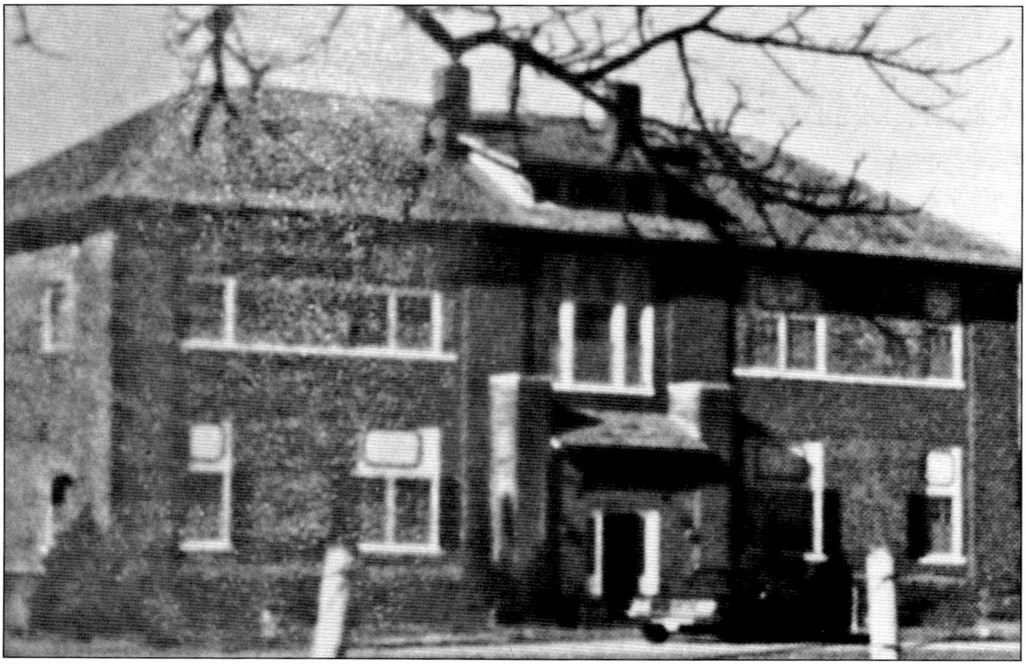

The first schoolhouse—a 28-by-40 building with 100 feet of blackboard, a cupola, and bell—was built in 1876. In 1912, a new schoolhouse was built with pine and birch interiors and a ventilation system. The school closed in 1963 and was later remodeled into a home.

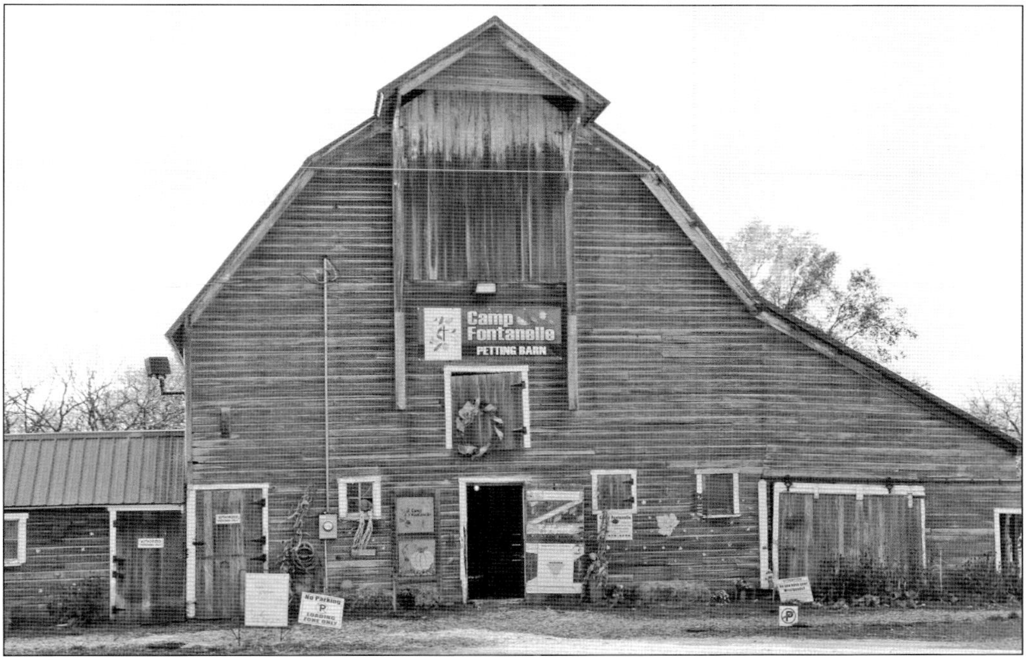

This barn located in Camp Fontanelle and owned by the United Methodist Church is believed to be the oldest barn in the county. In 1957, a parcel of 185 acres of land was donated to the Methodist Church and a campground was established in Fontanelle. The barn is used for the camp's annual Halloween festival, which includes a corn maze and is open to the public during the fall season.

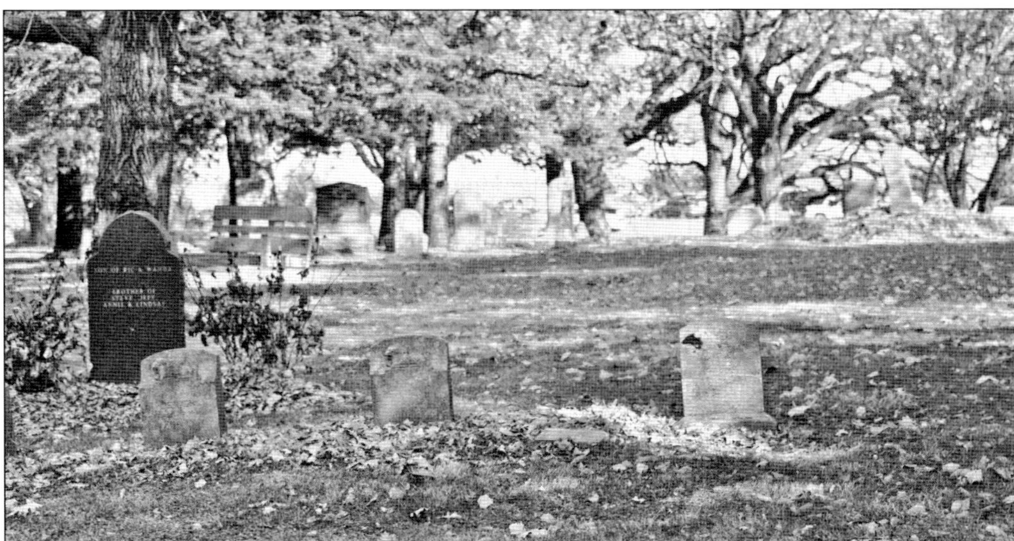

The Hartung Cemetery, otherwise known as the Fontanelle Pioneer Cemetery, is reputed to be one of three known cemeteries to have been established upon sacred Indian burial grounds. It is located south of the city near the Elkhorn, and many of the earliest pioneers were buried here. The cemetery was signed over to the Methodist Church by the Hartung family in 1957 for perpetual care. It is a private cemetery today.

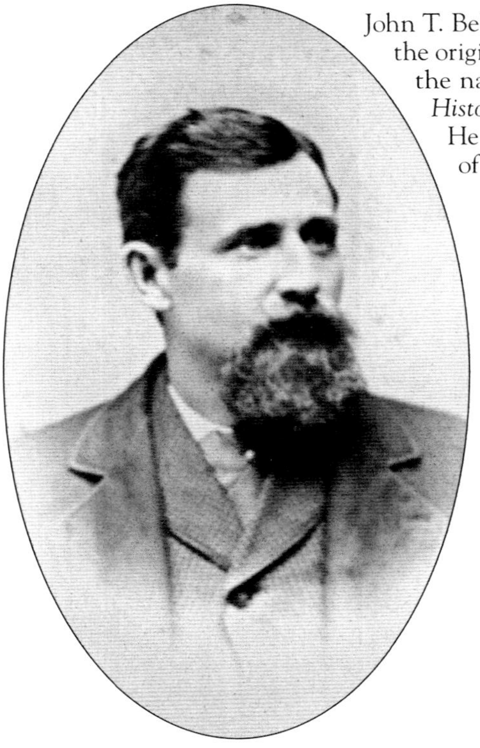

John T. Bell, born in 1842, was the son of James Bell. One of the original members of the Quincy colony, James was also the namesake of Bell Creek. John wrote two books: *A History of Washington County* and *A History of Omaha.* He was instrumental in recording and preserving much of the early history of Washington County.

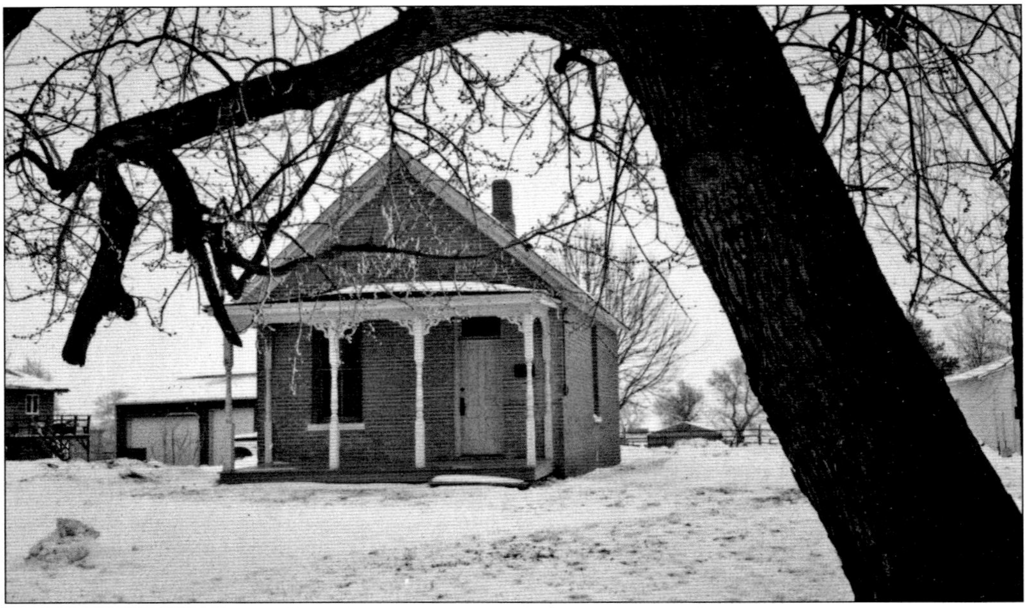

The town hall (pictured), built in 1896 as a community meeting hall and voting place, has been maintained by the Washington County Historical Association and is listed in the National Register of Historic Places. The lack of a railroad caused the people to move, and the population dropped from 500 to a few dozen families by the turn of the century. Many of the descendants of the original pioneers live in the community today.

Two

Railroad Towns

We Heard the Whistle

The building of railroads revolutionized transportation, and there is no doubt as to the role that the railroad industry has played in the state of Nebraska. There are examples everywhere. The iron rail spurred the quick growth of the American West. It was paramount to local settlement to replace wagon trains and canals with a more economical and faster means of transportation into the territories of the new frontier.

In 1862, President Lincoln authorized the construction of the first transcontinental railroad, with construction to begin across the river from Council Bluffs terminal, at Omaha, Nebraska, when he signed the Pacific Railroad Act into law. The same year, Lincoln signed the Homestead Act, legislation that allowed the purchase of government land in the unsettled West by any citizens at a reduced price in exchange for improvements to their land, usually 160 acres. The Union Pacific and the Sioux City and Pacific Railroads owned 20,000 acres of land, which they offered as homestead grants.

Railroads offered easy and affordable fares, and the government enticed with cheap land. Railroads were connecting folks from town to town by 1872, and growth spiraled. Civil War veterans and European immigrants came by the thousands to claim their stakes. Four towns owe their existence to the railroad: Blair, Arlington, Herman, and Kennard. People came, they settled, they stayed, and they traveled by rail. The Danish, German, Irish, and English settled in Washington County with dreams and ambitions. And Washington County grew.

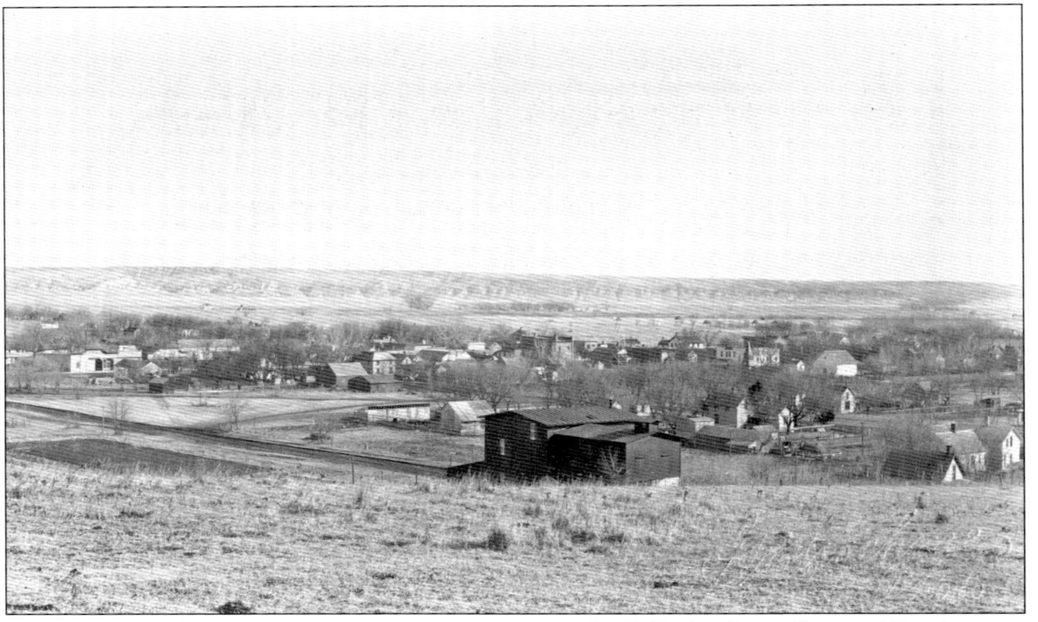

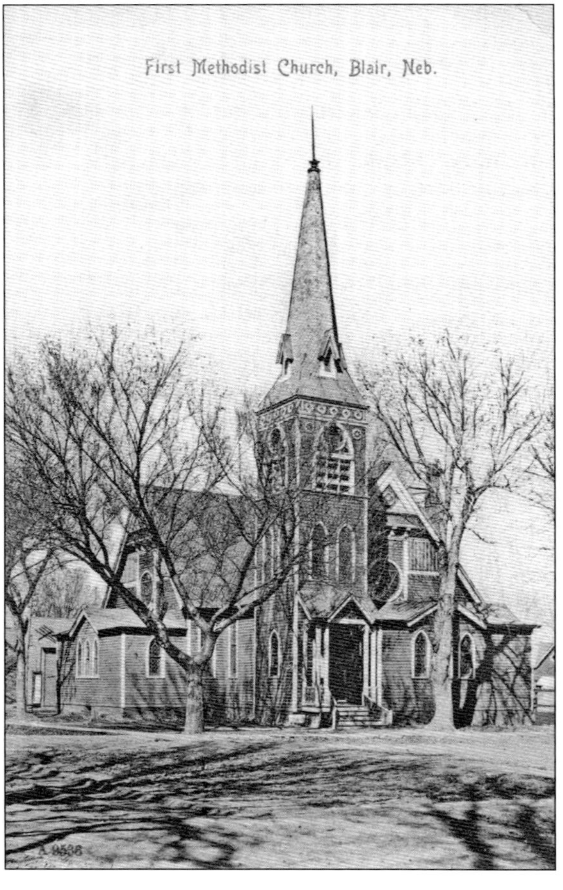

In 1868, the Sioux City and Pacific Railroad was sold to John I. Blair and his associates. A decision was made to build the railroad two miles north of DeSoto, where the crossing of the Missouri was aided by a natural valley on the banks of the river. As a result, a railroad town named Blair was created. A three-story hotel and depot was built alongside the tracks in 1869.

The Methodist church (with additions) moved from Cuming City in 1869, becoming Blair's first church. The first sermon preached to the Baptists was in April 1869, on the platform of the railroad station. Their church building was moved from Cuming City in the fall of 1872.

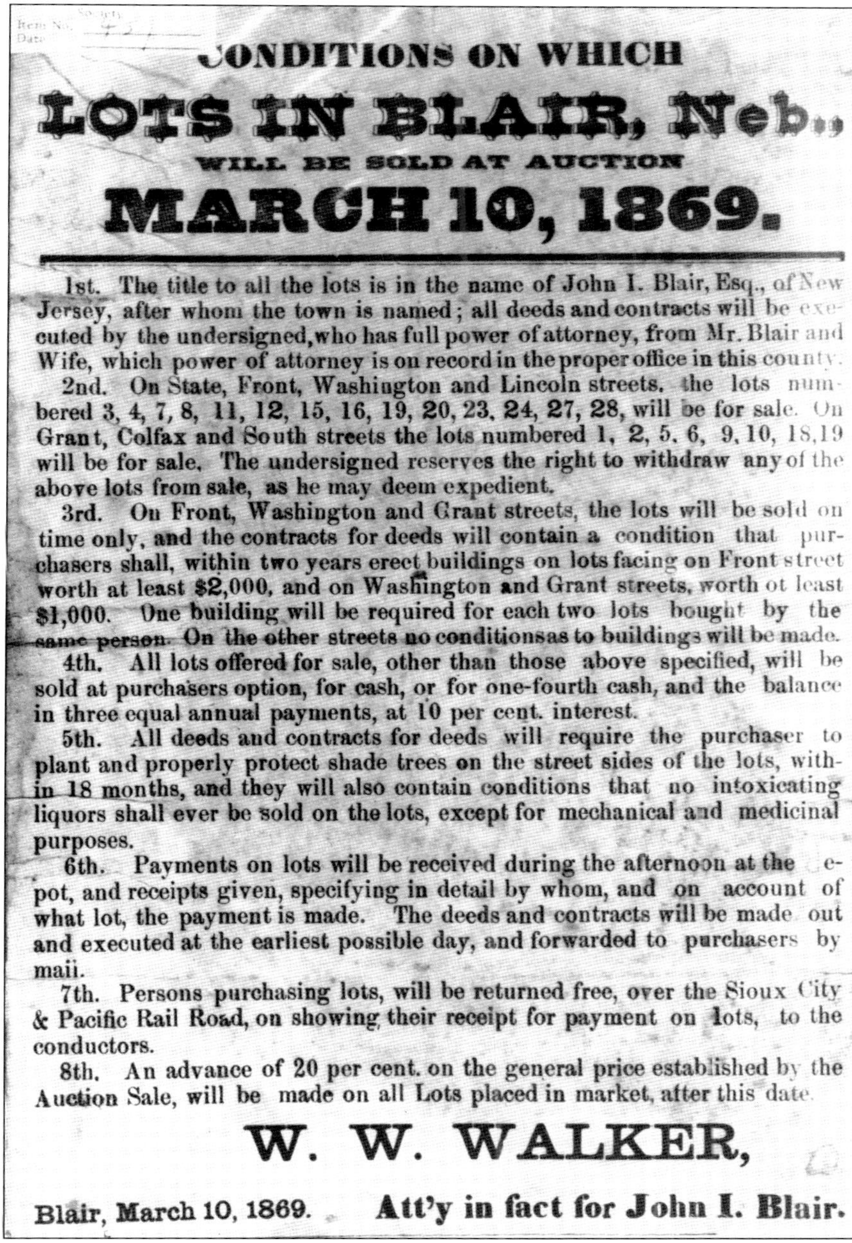

CONDITIONS ON WHICH

LOTS IN BLAIR, Neb.,

WILL BE SOLD AT AUCTION

MARCH 10, 1869.

1st. The title to all the lots is in the name of John I. Blair, Esq., of New Jersey, after whom the town is named; all deeds and contracts will be executed by the undersigned, who has full power of attorney, from Mr. Blair and Wife, which power of attorney is on record in the proper office in this county.

2nd. On State, Front, Washington and Lincoln streets, the lots numbered 3, 4, 7, 8, 11, 12, 15, 16, 19, 20, 23, 24, 27, 28, will be for sale. On Grant, Colfax and South streets the lots numbered 1, 2, 5, 6, 9, 10, 18, 19 will be for sale. The undersigned reserves the right to withdraw any of the above lots from sale, as he may deem expedient.

3rd. On Front, Washington and Grant streets, the lots will be sold on time only, and the contracts for deeds will contain a condition that purchasers shall, within two years erect buildings on lots facing on Front street worth at least $2,000, and on Washington and Grant streets, worth ot least $1,000. One building will be required for each two lots bought by the same person. On the other streets no conditionsas to buildings will be made.

4th. All lots offered for sale, other than those above specified, will be sold at purchasers option, for cash, or for one-fourth cash, and the balance in three equal annual payments, at 10 per cent. interest.

5th. All deeds and contracts for deeds will require the purchaser to plant and properly protect shade trees on the street sides of the lots, within 18 months, and they will also contain conditions that no intoxicating liquors shall ever be sold on the lots, except for mechanical and medicinal purposes.

6th. Payments on lots will be received during the afternoon at the depot, and receipts given, specifying in detail by whom, and on account of what lot, the payment is made. The deeds and contracts will be made out and executed at the earliest possible day, and forwarded to purchasers by maii.

7th. Persons purchasing lots, will be returned free, over the Sioux City & Pacific Rail Road, on showing their receipt for payment on lots, to the conductors.

8th. An advance of 20 per cent. on the general price established by the Auction Sale, will be made on all Lots placed in market, after this date.

W. W. WALKER,

Blair, March 10, 1869. **Att'y in fact for John I. Blair.**

Blair was platted on land purchased by the railroad builder from three Carter brothers who lived in the valley. From the date of sale, the town grew rapidly. Lots were sold by John Blair's company, the Nebraska Town Company, on two conditions: that the owner plant a tree and sign an agreement (with the company) not to sell any liquors. The streets were built in a grid running east-west and north-south, from 80 to 120 feet wide, and were shaded with trees that were planted with the sale of the lots. Stores and homes were moved from Cuming City and DeSoto into the new town, and newcomers arrived weekly. H.C. Riordan moved his hardware store from DeSoto. Judge Jesse T. Davis and Dr. F.H. Longley moved in from DeSoto in April 1869. Everyone was anxious to move to the railroad city. By 1870, Blair boasted 470 people.

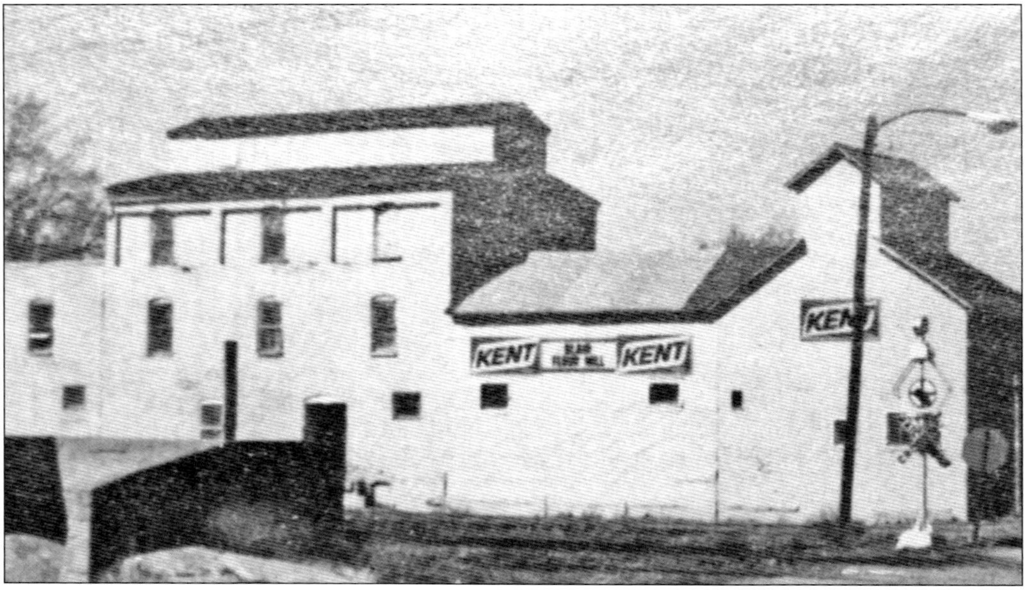

Originally built on the ground occupied as winter quarters by the Mormon pioneers, the DeSoto flouring mill, operated by Christopher Crowell, moved operations to Blair. Renamed the Blair Milling Company, it produced Maintop flour and livestock feed. The Blair flour mills would change hands over the years until mills in town were no longer needed.

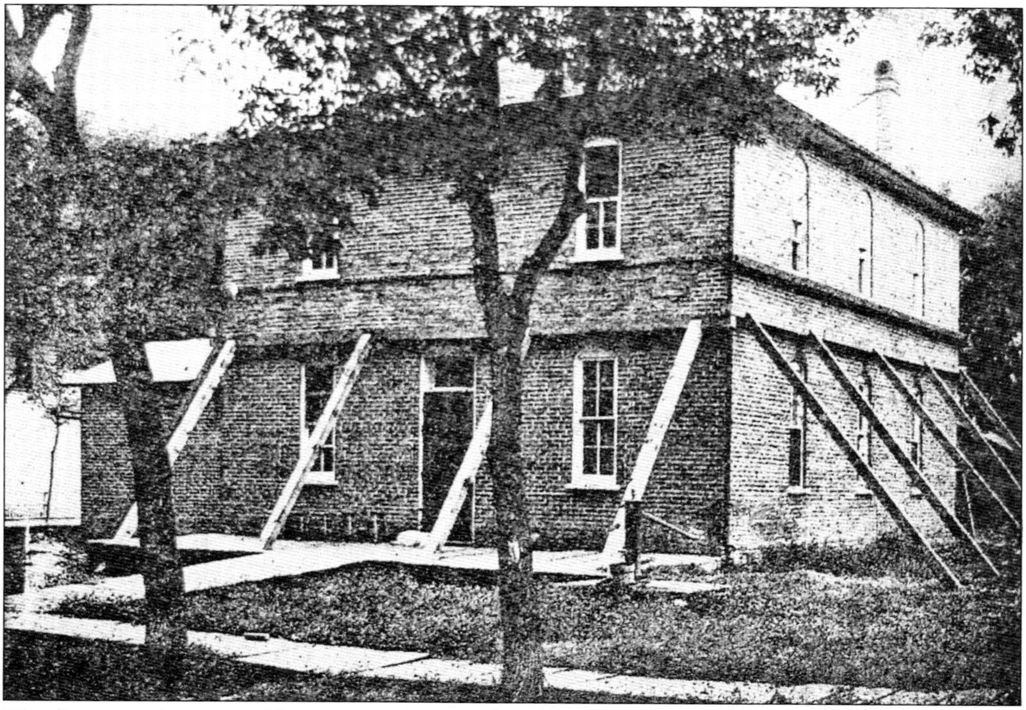

The first courthouse in Blair was a 40-by-40-foot brick building originally built as a school but sold to the county to be used as a courthouse about 1870. The county commissioners declared the building unsafe and boarded it up. A bond was passed and a new courthouse built in 1899.

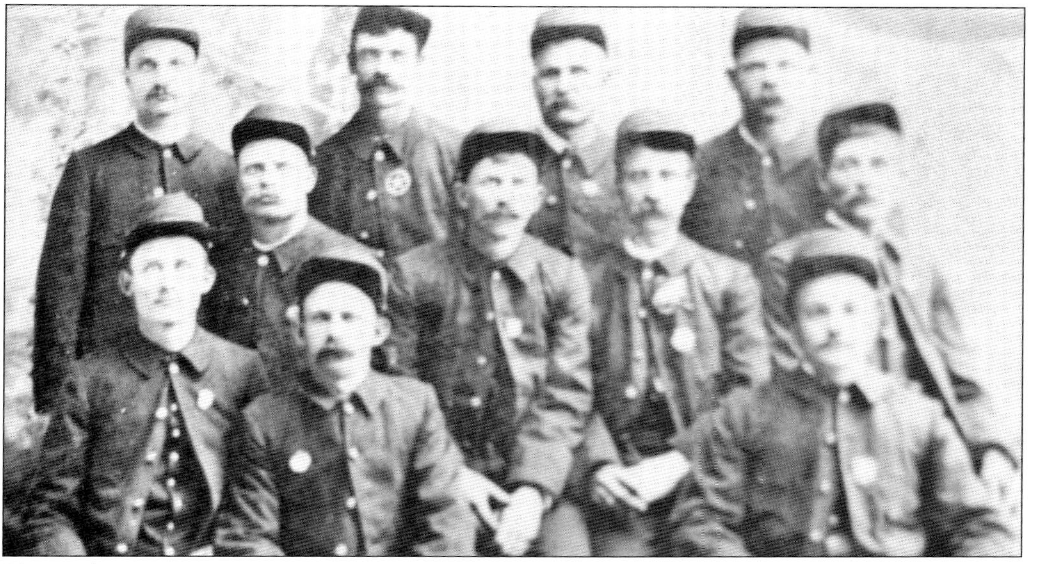

Blair Volunteer Fire Department, founded in 1870, was made up of a traditional bucket brigade with 13 members and 13 buckets. The hose carts replaced the buckets in 1886 after the town of Blair installed an updated water system. Hose carts were used until 1927, when a hose truck and pumper were purchased. Pictured here are some of the earliest members.

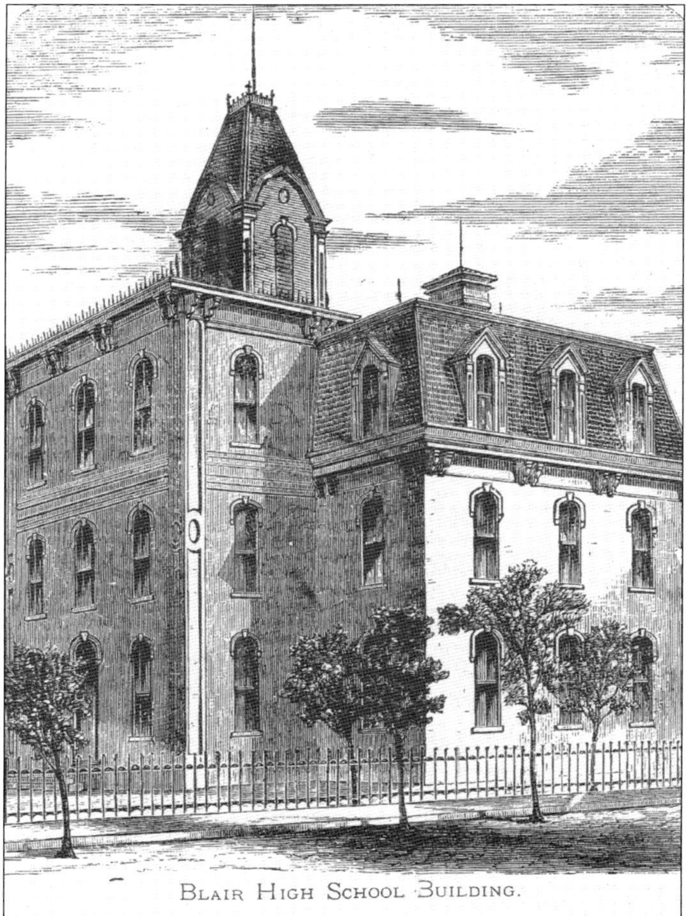

A three-story high school building was built in 1872 at a cost of $15,000, replacing the school the town had outgrown. The first two graduates, both of whom became teachers, were Vesta Noyes and Mary Fawcett.

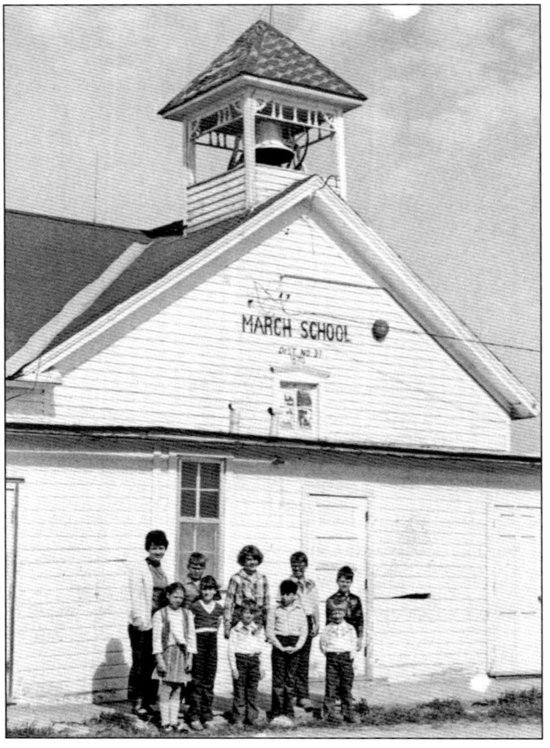

County schools were established about every two or three miles in either direction. The March School, eight miles west and three miles south of Blair, began serving the community in 1870, with 20 pupils. It celebrated its centennial in 1970, and in 1980 it held the distinction of being the oldest country school still serving area students.

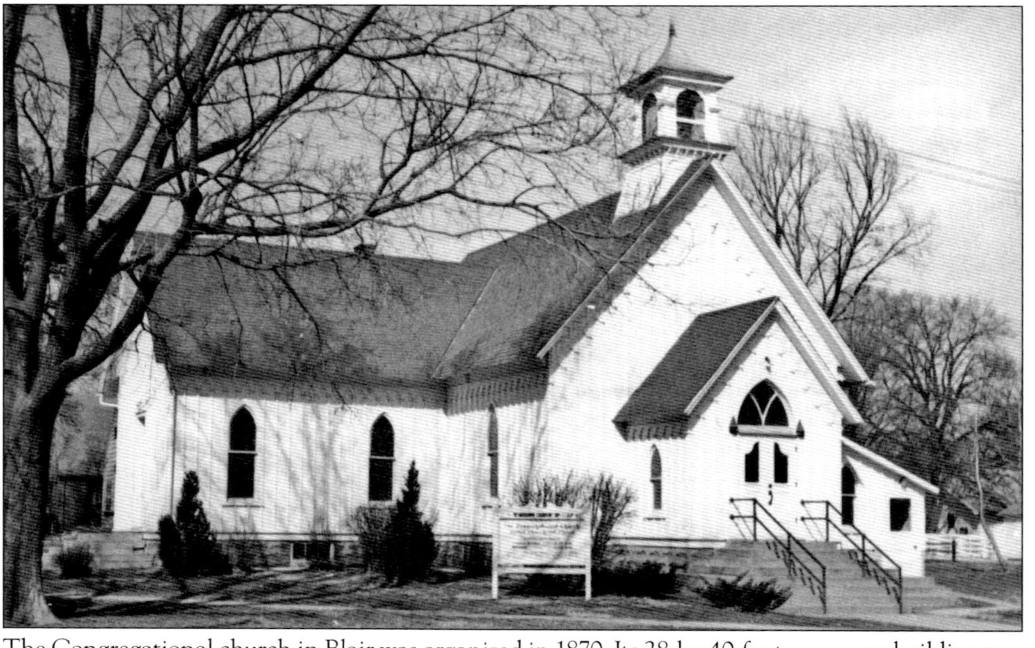

The Congregational church in Blair was organized in 1870. Its 28-by-40-foot one-room building was built in 1874 in a combination of Colonial and semi-Gothic styles. In 1969, the church combined with Grace Methodist of Kennard. In 1974, it celebrated its centennial. It is the oldest church building in Washington County still in use and is a National Historic Landmark.

In 1871, the first Catholic church, named St. Joseph, was built on the corner of Colfax Street. In 1889, a new church was built in the same location and named St. Francis Borgia. In 1958, the St. Francis Borgia parish built a new church, which today serves over 450 families. St. John the Baptist Catholic Church in Fort Calhoun is the only other Catholic church in the county.

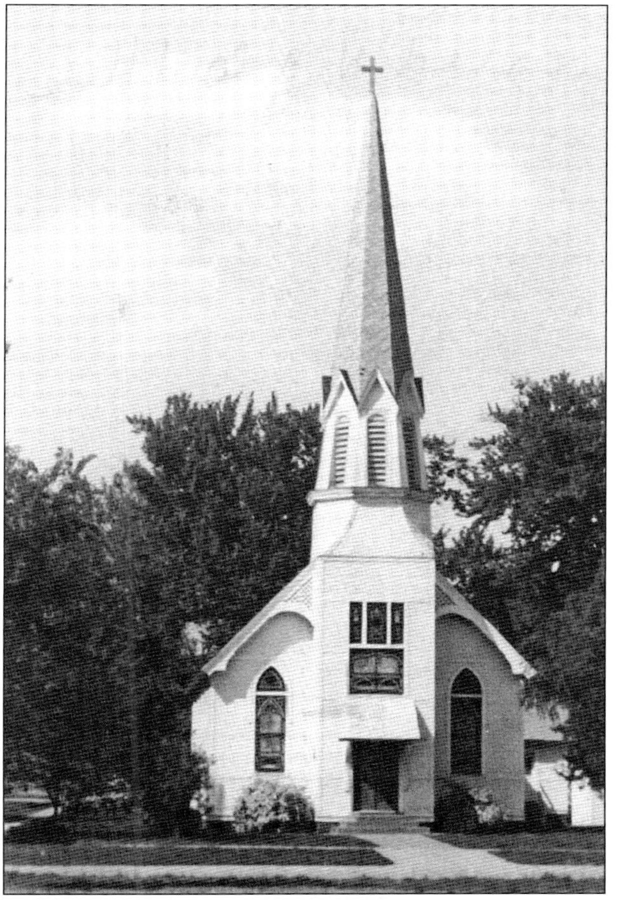

As early as 1880, Blair operated a hospital—then a room in the back of the Maher Hotel. The hospital was moved to the back of city hall with four beds. In 1904, with more room needed, the old East School on Thirteenth and Grant Streets (pictured) was purchased and converted into a hospital, used until a new modern hospital was built in 1956. A medical society was formed in 1903.

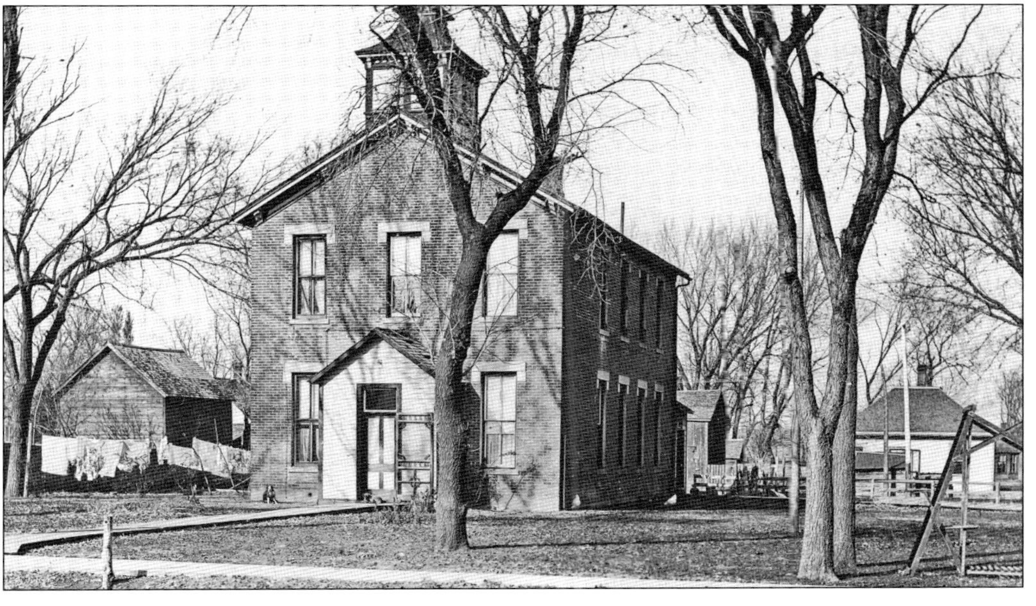

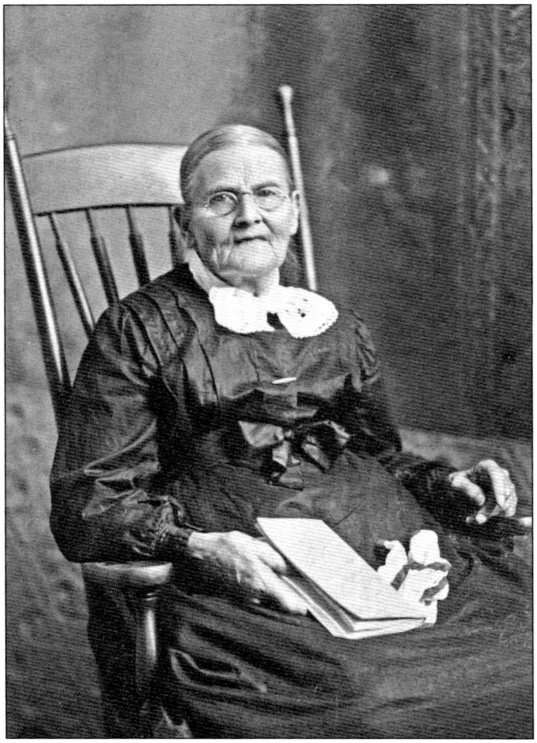

Arriving with the founding of the town, Indiana Fox was the first female to practice medicine in the territory of Washington County. The allopathic school of medicine was almost universally used, with a doctor occasionally practicing herb medicine. Dr. J.P. Andrews was the first physician to settle in the county.

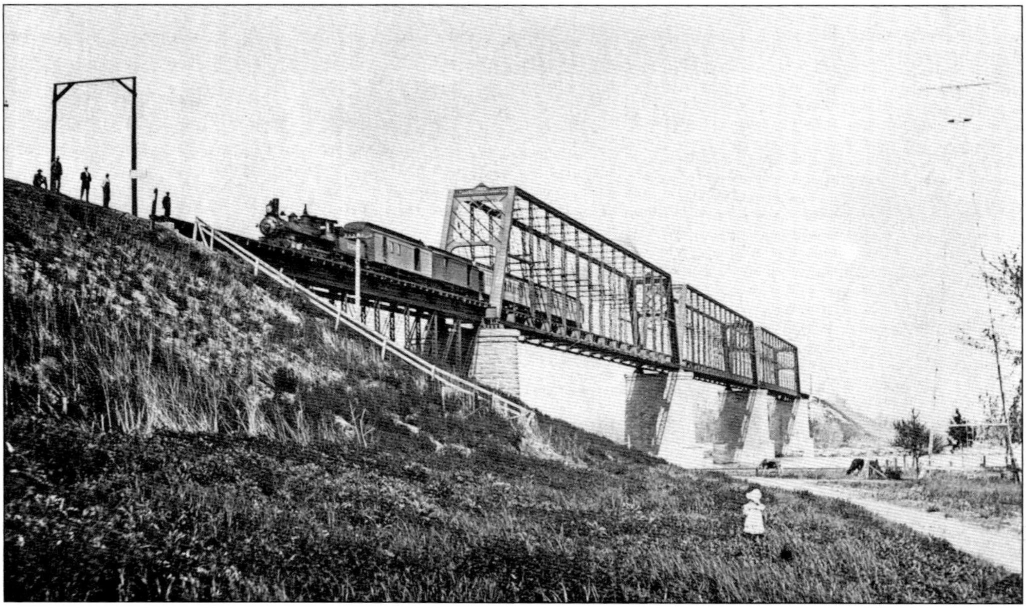

Train cars were shuttled back and forth across the Missouri River by the railroad's ferry. By the late 1870s, a bridge spanning the Missouri was a necessity. The 330-foot Whipple Truss railroad bridge, supported 50 feet above water by massive piers, took a year to build and was completed in 1883. This photograph shows a Sioux City and Pacific locomotive pulling a few cars testing the bridge's strength.

In 1881, with plans to build a bridge across the river, a 10-year period of building two- and three-story brick buildings began. Four local brickyards were turning out 1,500,000 bricks per year to meet the demands of the city's development. Two of the first buildings constructed in 1881, the Blair State Bank and Arndt's Hardware, helped to establish Blair's business district.

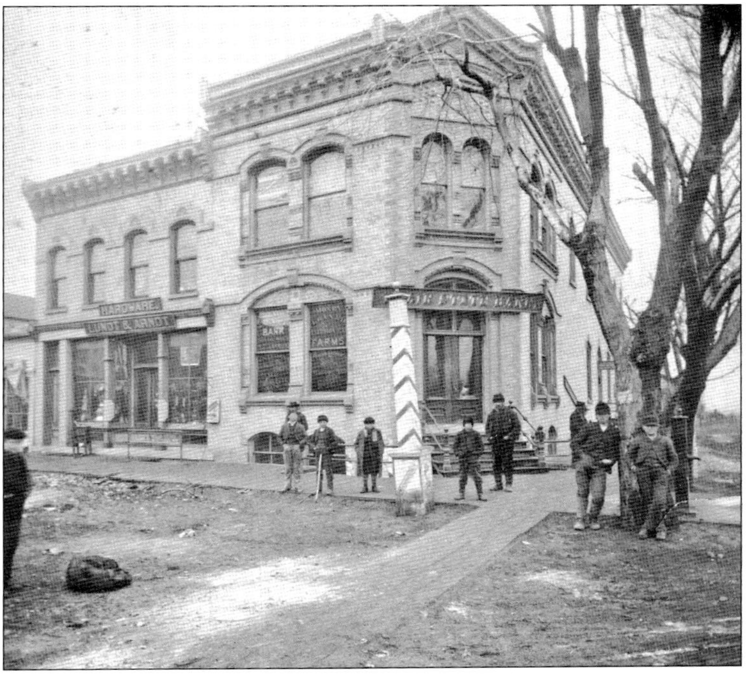

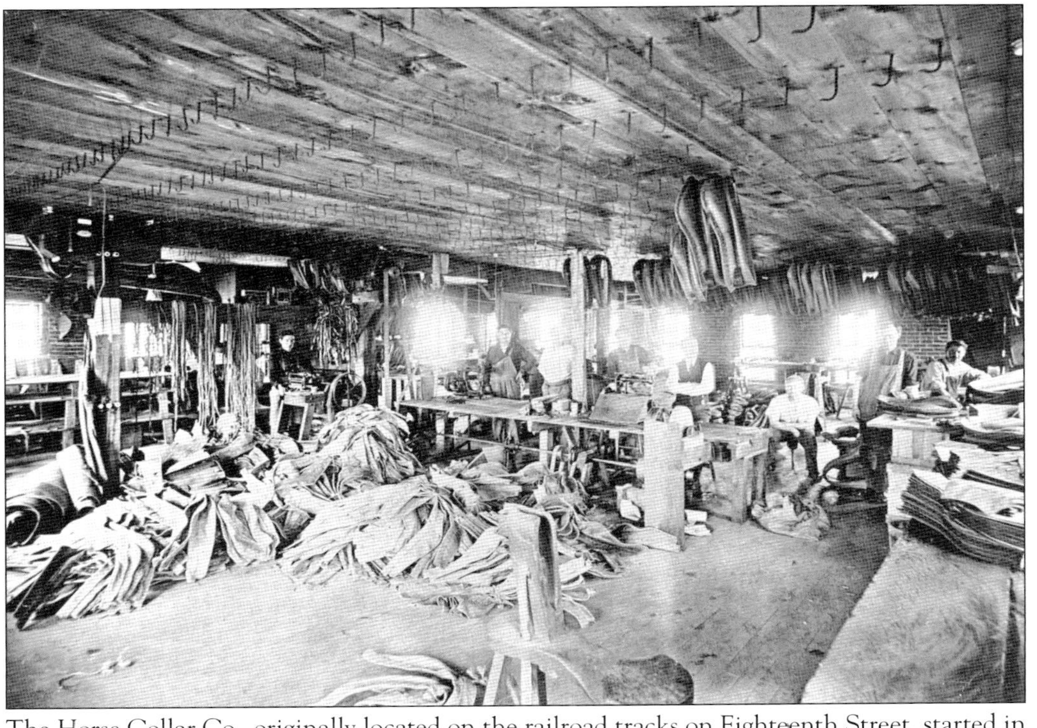

The Horse Collar Co., originally located on the railroad tracks on Eighteenth Street, started in the spring of 1888, employing 125 men. The company packed straw into leather and sewed it up making products for the use of horses. The factory was destroyed by fire and rebuilt, but as automobiles were replacing horses, there was no longer much need for a horse-collar company.

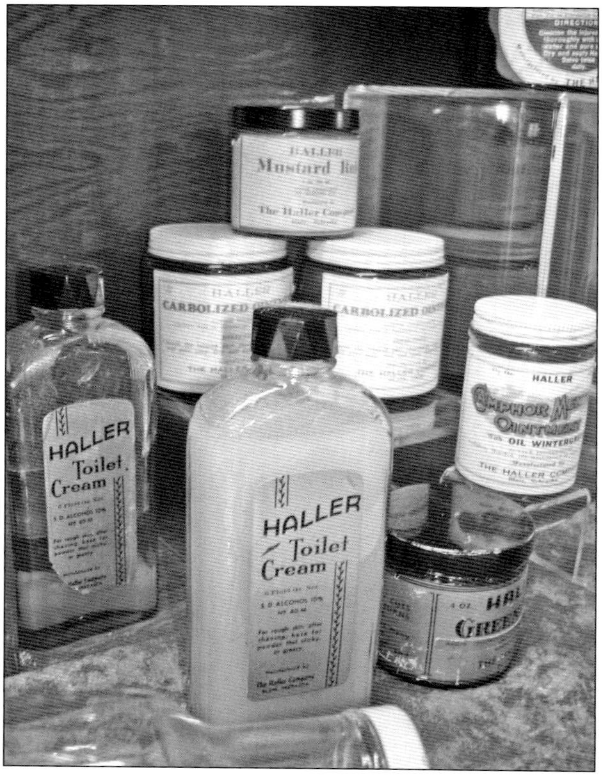

W.D. Haller founded the Haller Proprietary Co. in 1888, selling six different patented products, including Haller Pain Paralyzer. The company expanded to a line of over 100 products, including home remedies, food products, and toilet articles as well as poultry and veterinary remedies. The company salesman sold to pharmacies and farmsteads throughout the Midwest until the late 1930s and the age of modern medicine.

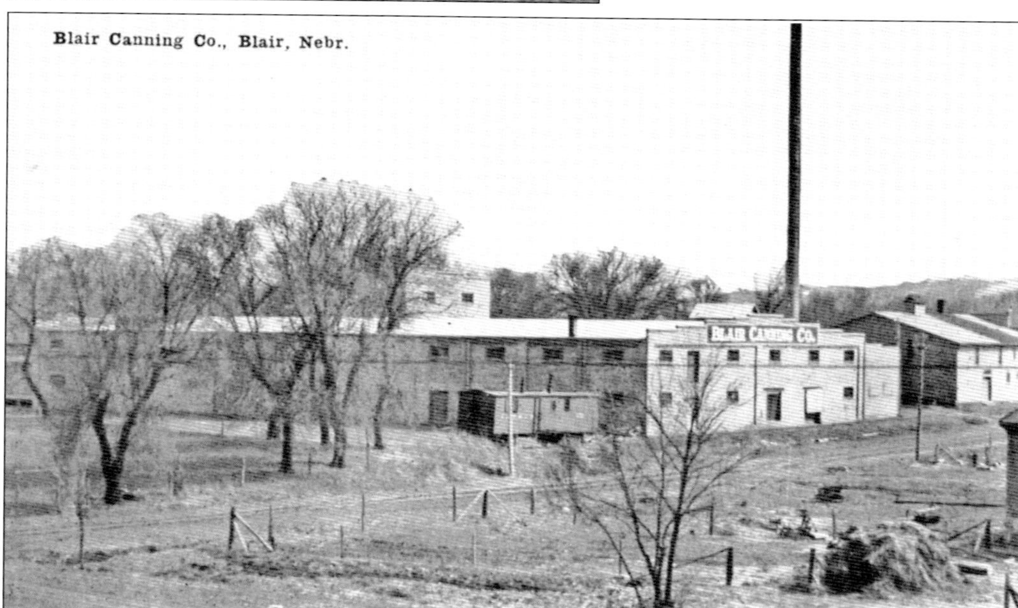

Blair Canning Factory opened its doors in the 1880s, packing corn into cans and preserving fruits. The plant provided jobs to the families of Blair and provided extra income in the summer to area farmers. At its peak, 1.5 million cans of corn were packed into cans. Poor crop seasons and a fire ended the business.

Organized in 1884, Dana College and Trinity Seminary overlook the Missouri River valley. The community, having a large Danish population, eventually established a preparatory school and a pre-seminary school. The four-story main building (pictured) was dedicated in 1886. Trinity Seminary was the oldest theological seminary among the Danes in the United States. In 2010, after 125 years, the school closed its doors. (Courtesy Blair Historic Preservation Alliance.)

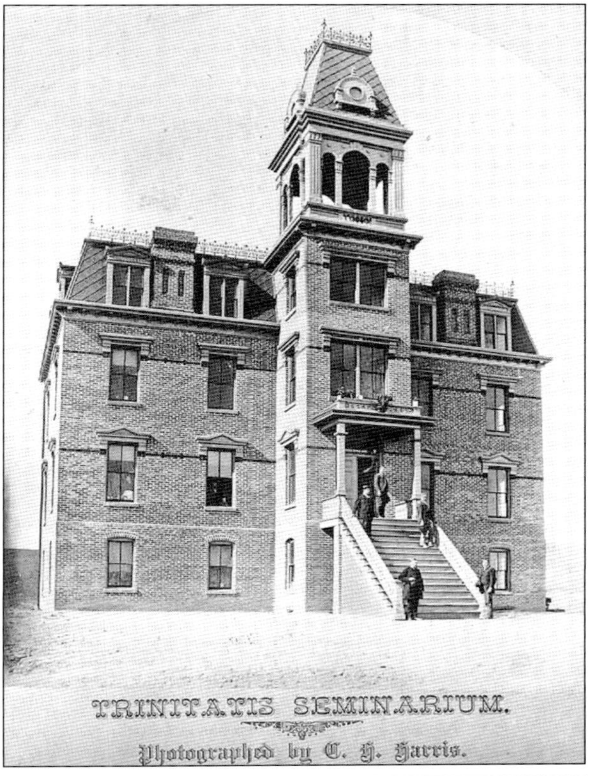

In 1889, construction of a new courthouse began, reflecting the prosperity and growth of the town. Built of St. Louis pressed brick with Warrenburg stone trim, it was completed in 1891. The courthouse square became a center of activity. Every Wednesday, the Blair band played a concert. Baseball games were a favorite pastime. Remodeled in 1936 and with a later addition, it still serves as the courthouse today.

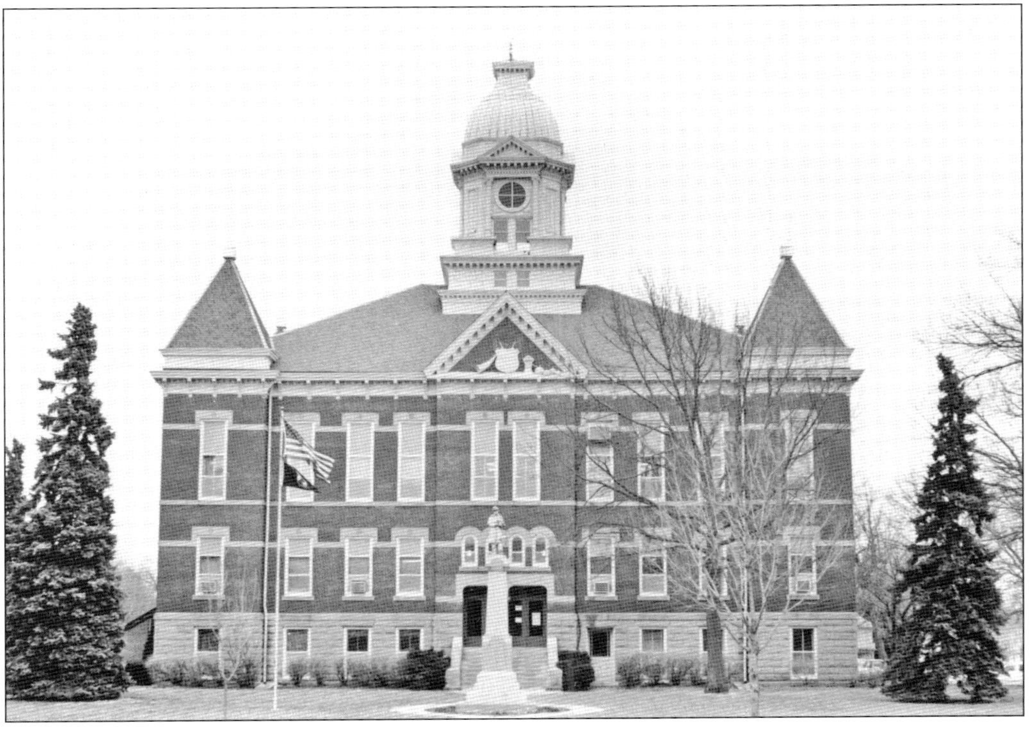

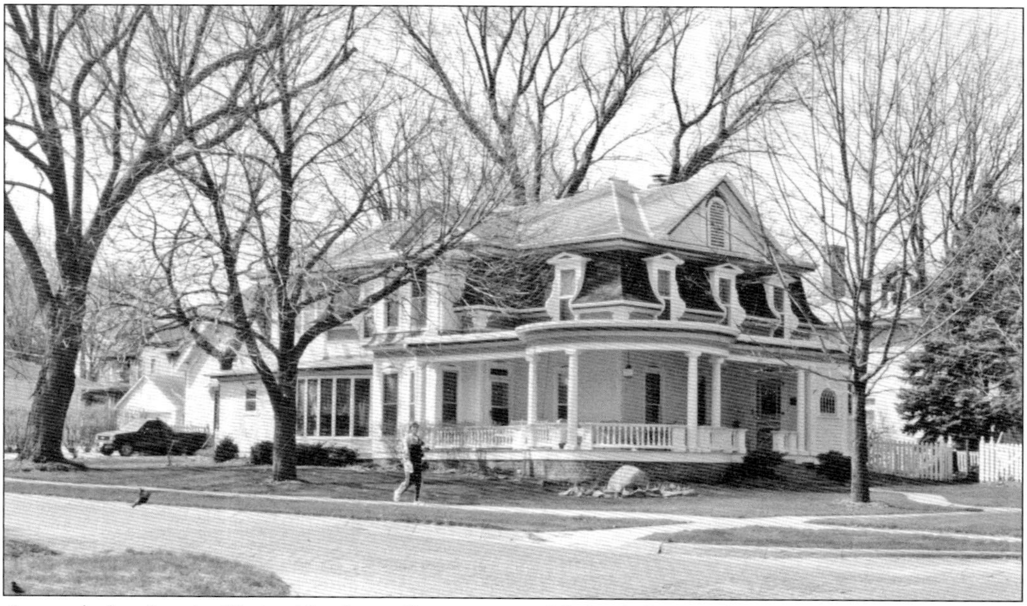

An early banker in Blair, Abraham Castetter established the Banking House of A. Castetter in 1869. Castetter's private residence was built around 1873, in the Second Empire style. Later additions were made using architectural styles that were popular during the 1880s and 1890s, resulting in an example of Eclecticism. The property remains a private residence and is listed in the National Register of Historic Places.

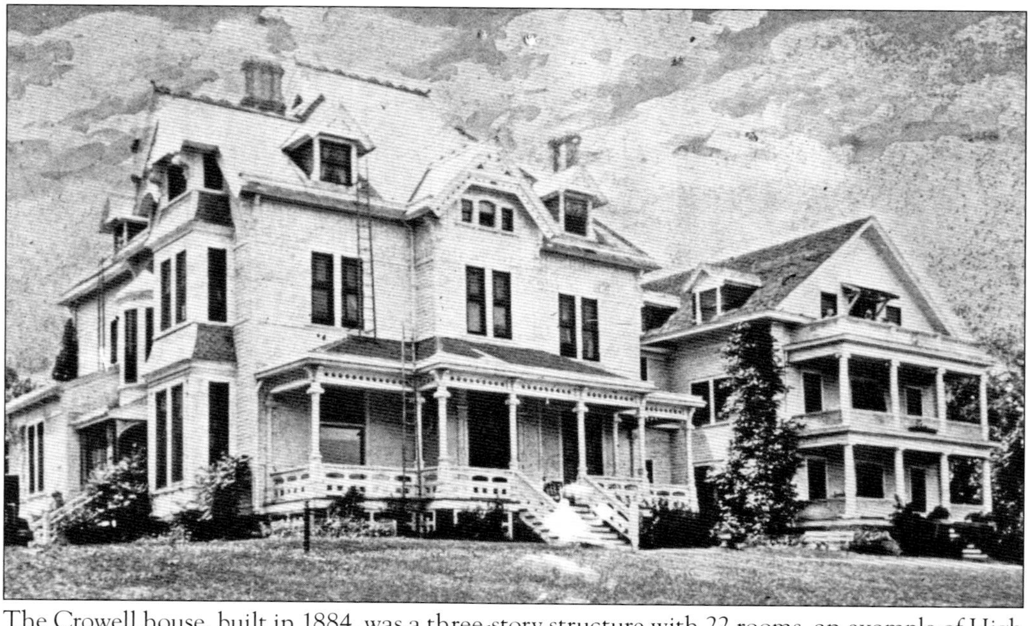

The Crowell house, built in 1884, was a three-story structure with 22 rooms, an example of High Victorian architecture of the 1880s. Complete with 10 marble fireplaces, stained-glass windows, etched glass panels, and the most modern plumbing facilities of its day, it was one of Nebraska's most elegant mansions. In 1905, it was converted into the Crowell Memorial retirement home. It was demolished in 1972, against many objections.

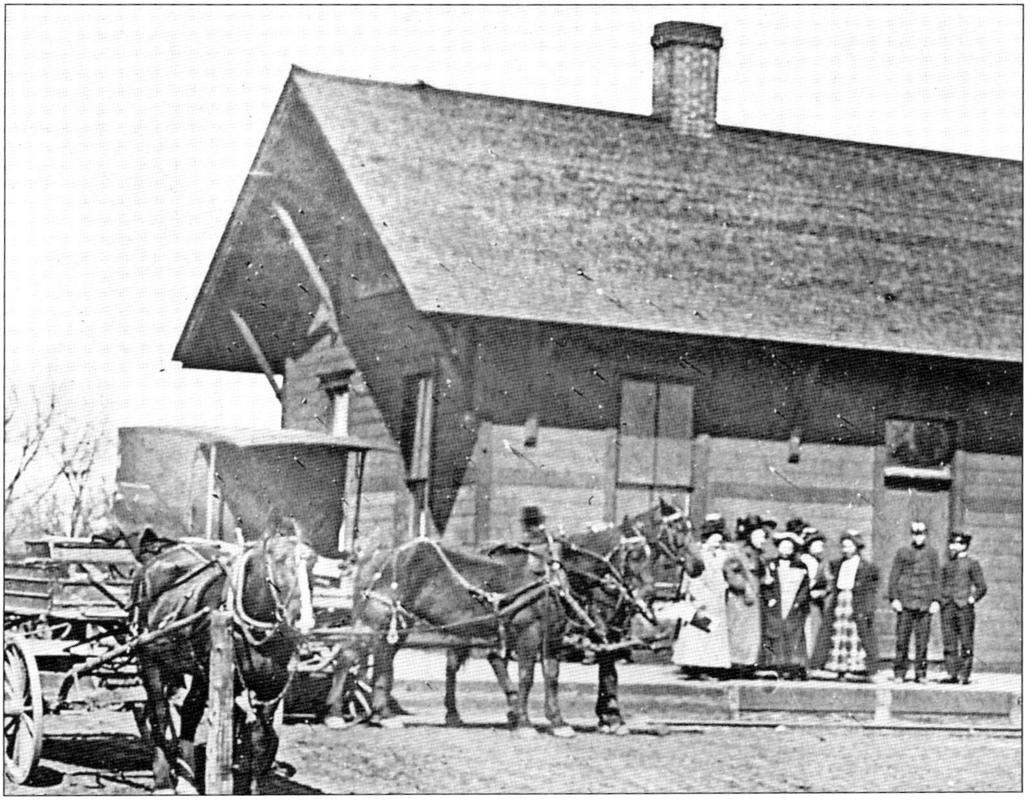

The wooden depot pictured here was built in 1880. In 1910, with the building of a new depot, the depot was moved a few blocks west and used for storage. The Blair Historic Preservation Alliance and the City of Blair have restored and refurbished the depot, and it has a new home in Lions Park.

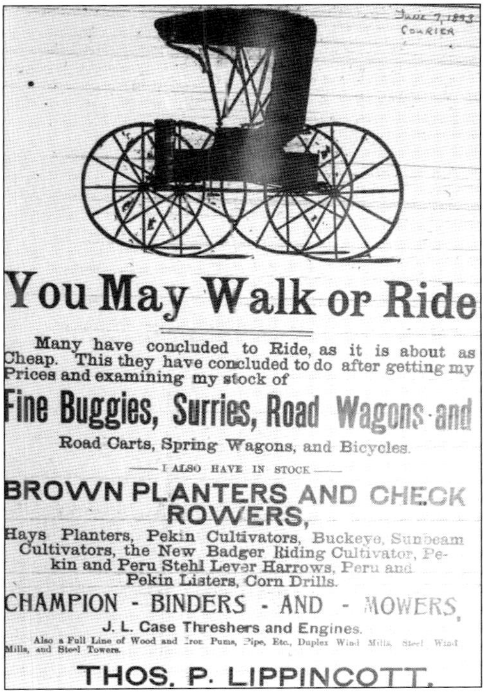

This Lippincott advertisement lists the latest in transportation vehicles and farming equipment. Posters like this were published and posted. In 1877, Lippincott went into the agriculture and livestock business and formed Thomas P. Lippincott & Co., located in Blair. He continued in the coal, wood, and implement business until his death in 1915.

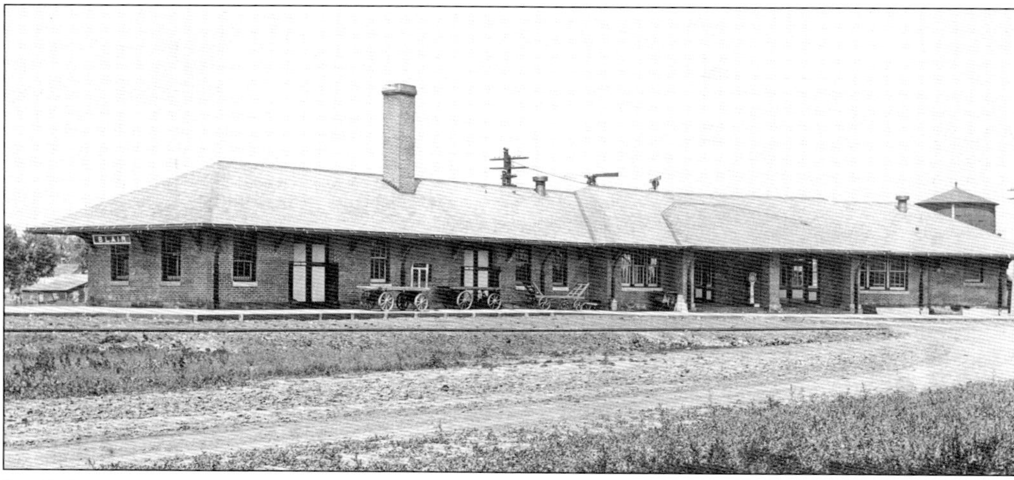

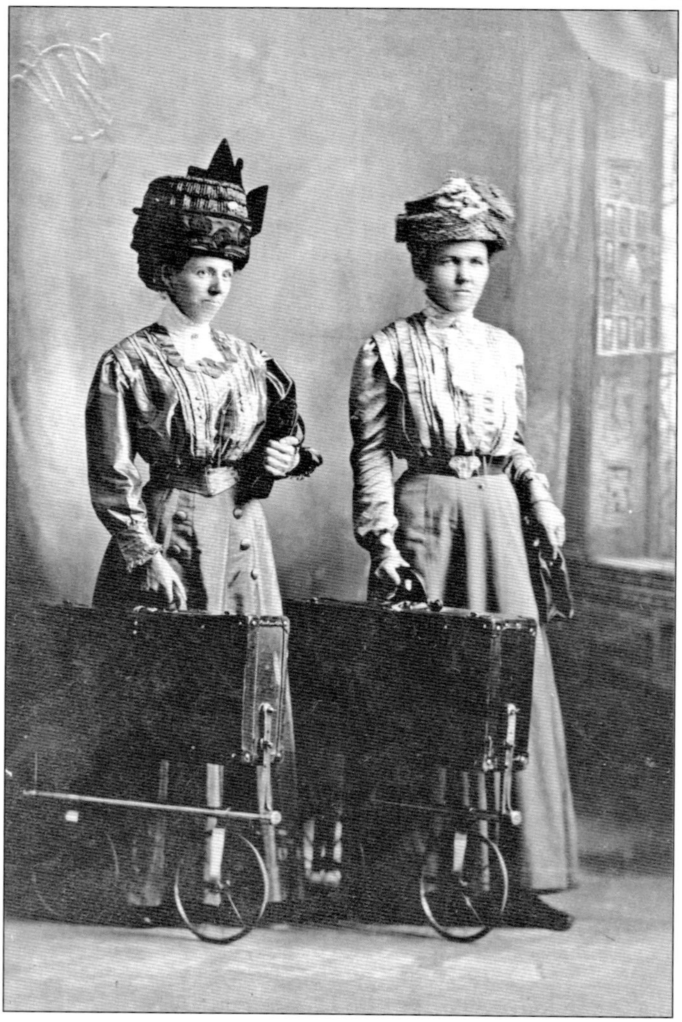

In 1910, a new larger and modern brick depot, built between the two merging railroad tracks, replaced the old depot. The last passenger train ran on June 3, 1950, and the building remained empty until it was torn down in October 1987. The railroad continues to run the same route through the county established 150 years ago.

In this gem of a photograph, Blair teacher Sarah Aronson and her friend are wearing truly exquisite hats at the Blair train station in 1911. Their wheeled suitcases reflect an innovation in travel at that time.

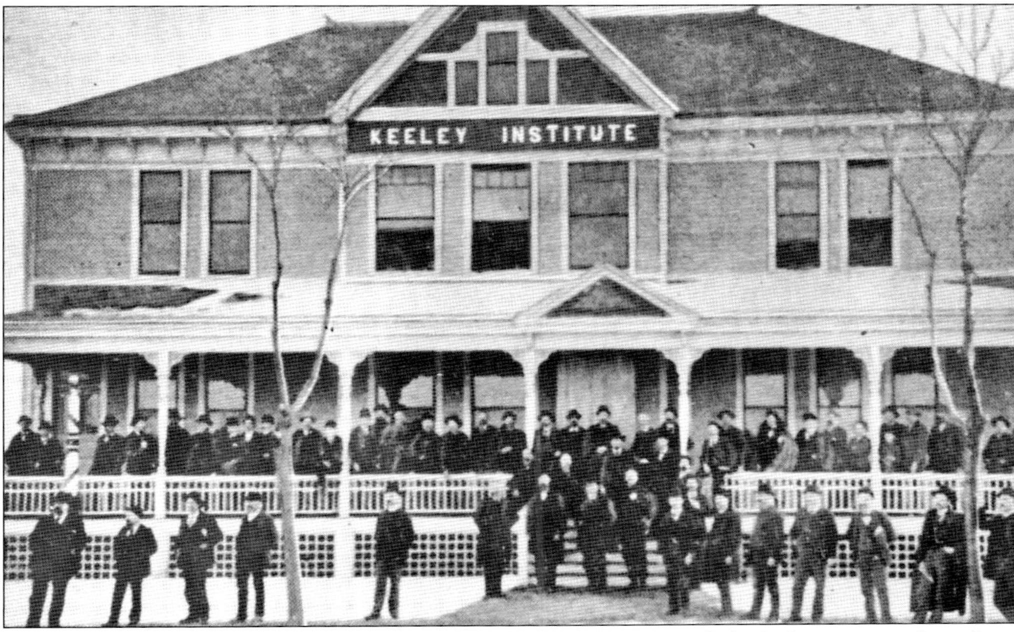

The Keeley Institute, one of many franchises for the treatment of alcoholism, opened its doors in Blair in 1891. Seeking a cure from the curse of drink, men came from all parts of the state for treatment at a cost of $25 a week. The cure business was fading by 1896, and the 28-room (4 of them with running-water pitchers) building began life anew as the Clifton Inn.

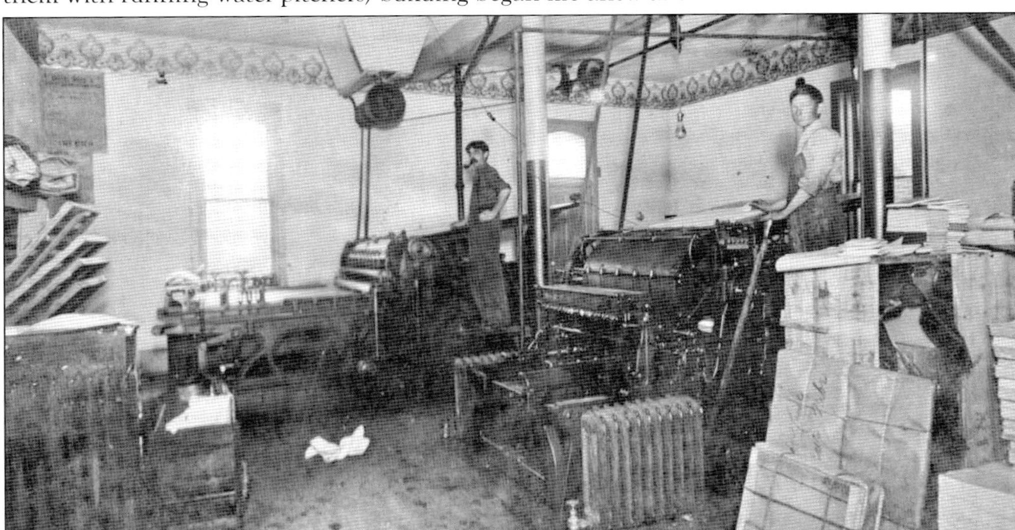

For 67 years, the Lutheran Publishing House was an institution in the community of Blair. It published songbooks, hymnals, devotional and religious books, and works of fiction in Danish and later in English. The publishing house closed in 1961. Pictured sometime between 1924 and 1929 are Elmer Johnson (foreground) and Chris Johnson, Elmer's uncle. Elmer worked in the publishing house for 50 years. (Courtesy Danish American Archive and Library.)

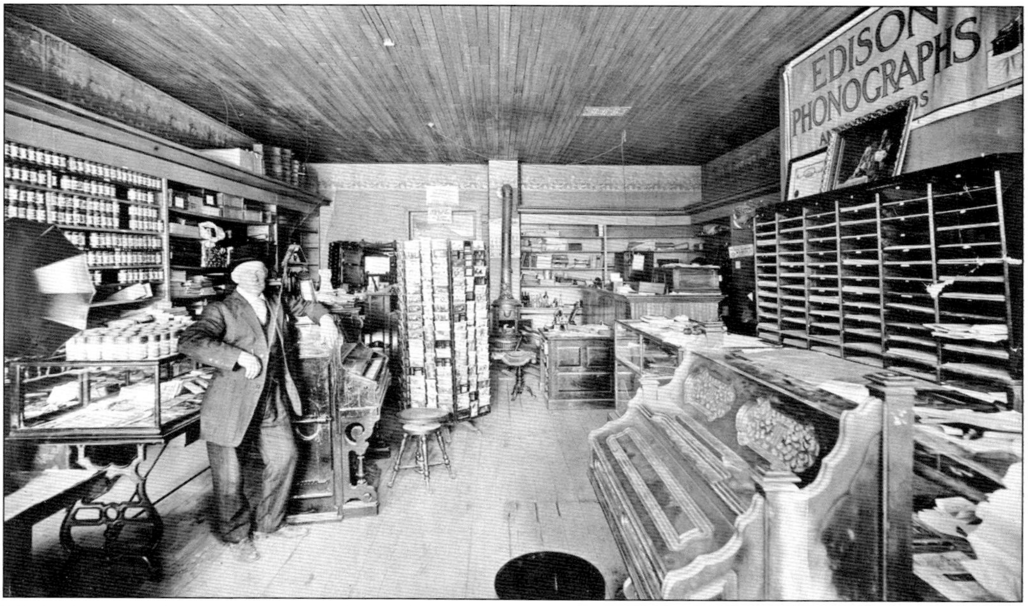

This photograph was taken inside the *Democrat* newspaper office. In 1904, the *Blair Register* and the *Blair Times*, which became the *Blair Republican*, combined, becoming the *Democrat*. The paper absorbed the *Tribune* in 1917. In 1929, the *Tribune* and the *Pilot* became the *Pilot Tribune*, which remains a weekly newspaper. The *Blair Enterprise*, having its origins dating back to 1869, is one of the oldest and largest weekly newspapers in the state.

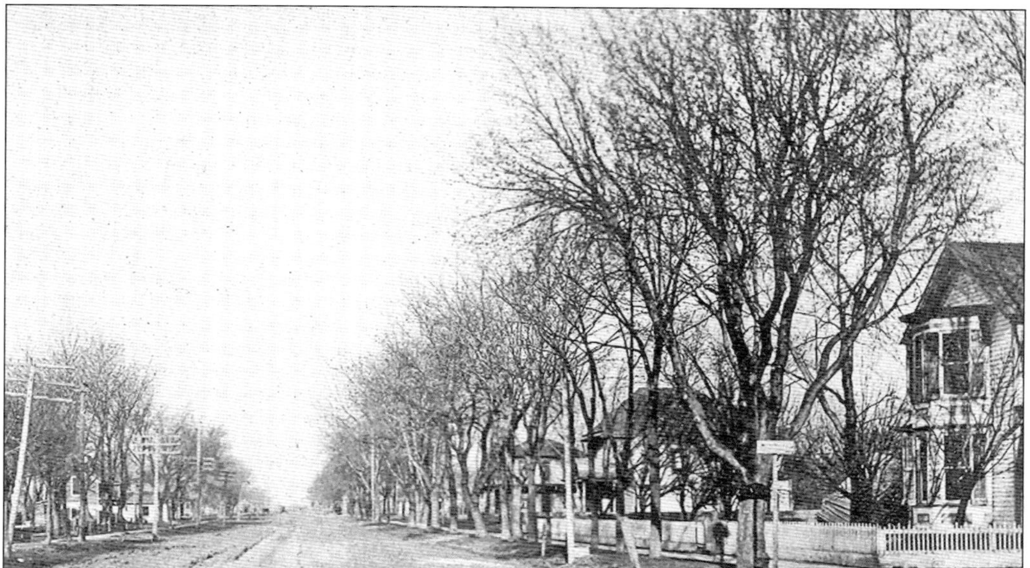

Located along the Elkhorn River near the southwestern border of Washington County, the town of Arlington takes its roots not from the river but from the railroad. Arlington, originally named Bell Creek, was platted in 1869 by the Sioux City and Pacific Railroad, the railroad line having reached the Elkhorn from the town of Blair. The town was divided into lots that were sold for $40 to $150 each.

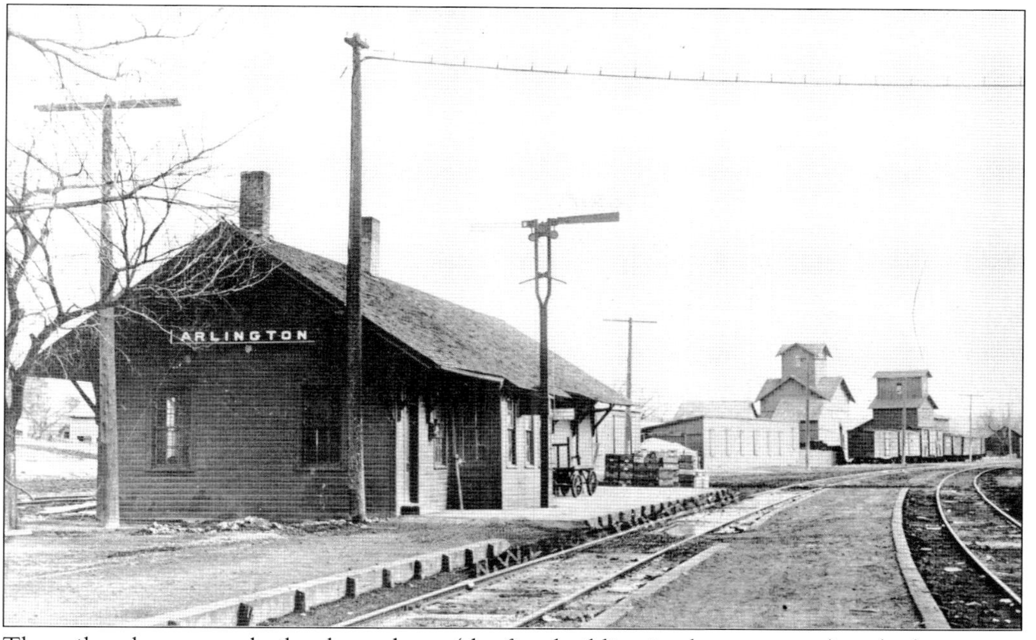

The railroad company built a large depot (the first building in the new town) and a large store building, which were quickly followed by several dwellings, a lumberyard, a grain warehouse, and a general merchandise store. Aware of the significance of a railroad town platted on the opposite side of the county, merchants and settlers were moving to the new village.

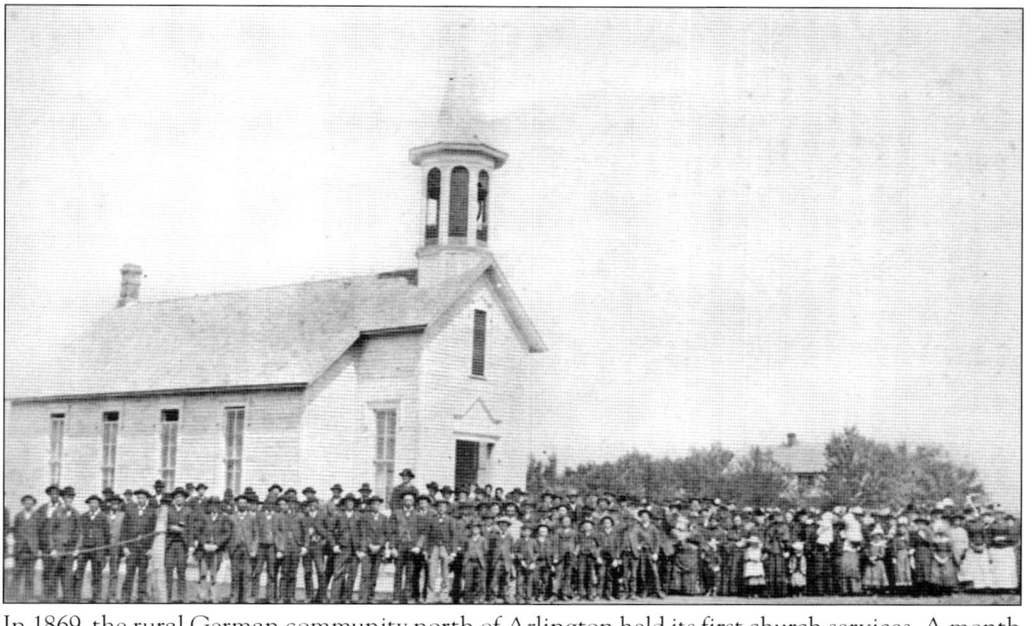

In 1869, the rural German community north of Arlington held its first church services. A month later, the first Lutheran pledge card in Nebraska was made by these pioneer families. In 1877, the first wood-frame church was built, named St. Paul Lutheran. Note the men flanking the left side in this photograph and the women and children on the right. (Courtesy Janine Carlson.)

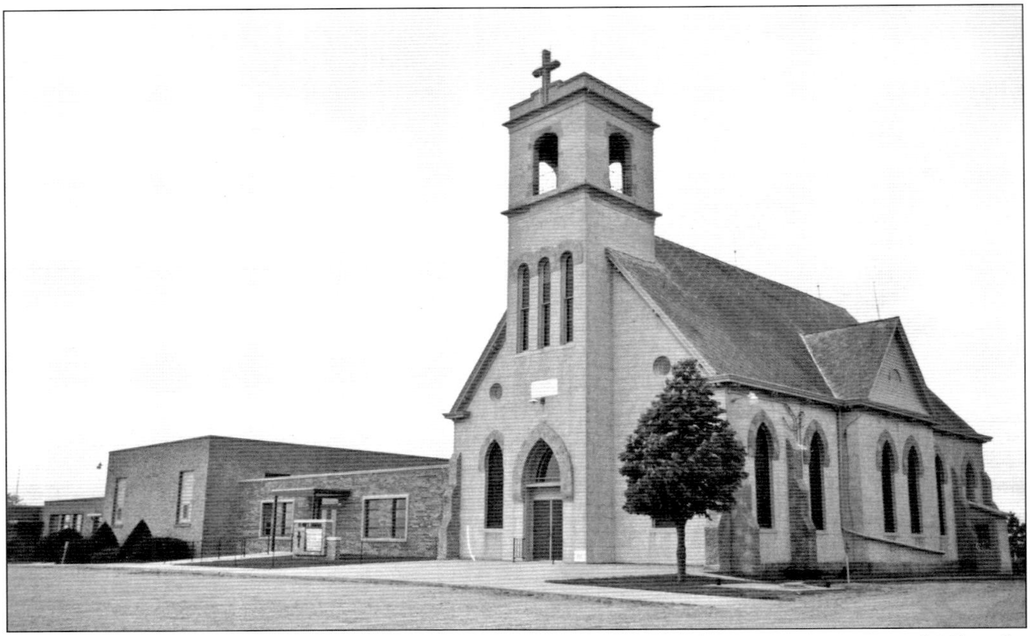

In 1890, St. Paul's congregation built an impressive brick church with a seating capacity of 475 and a 100-foot tower visible for miles and holding a 1,200-pound bell. In 1890, the old church was converted into a school. Today, St. Paul's has the only Lutheran parochial school in the county.

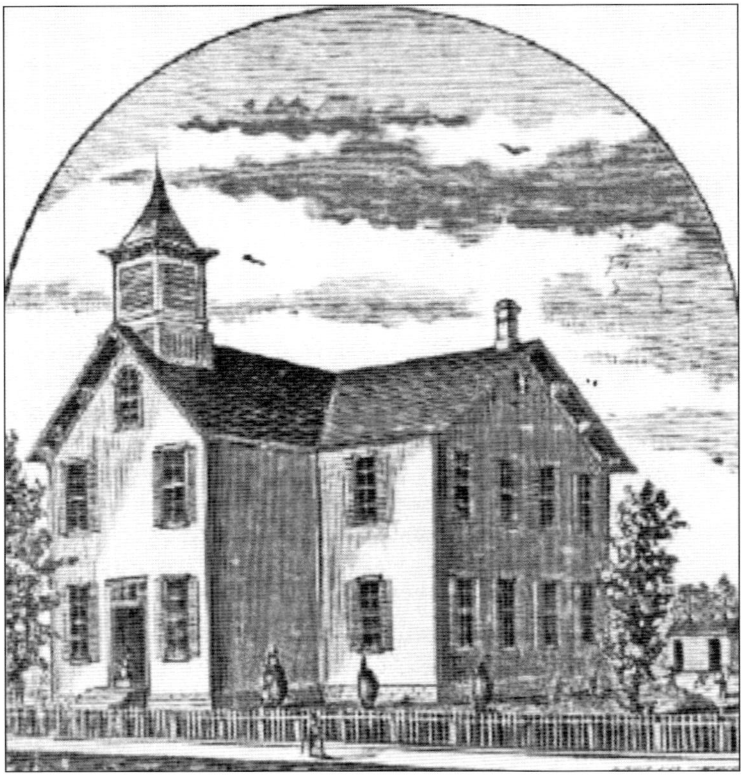

Educational classes were held in private homes until a two-story frame school, located at Fourth and Elm Streets, was built in 1879 at a cost of $5,000. The school served the community for 30 years before a larger one was built in 1907. The old schoolhouse began life anew as the city hall building.

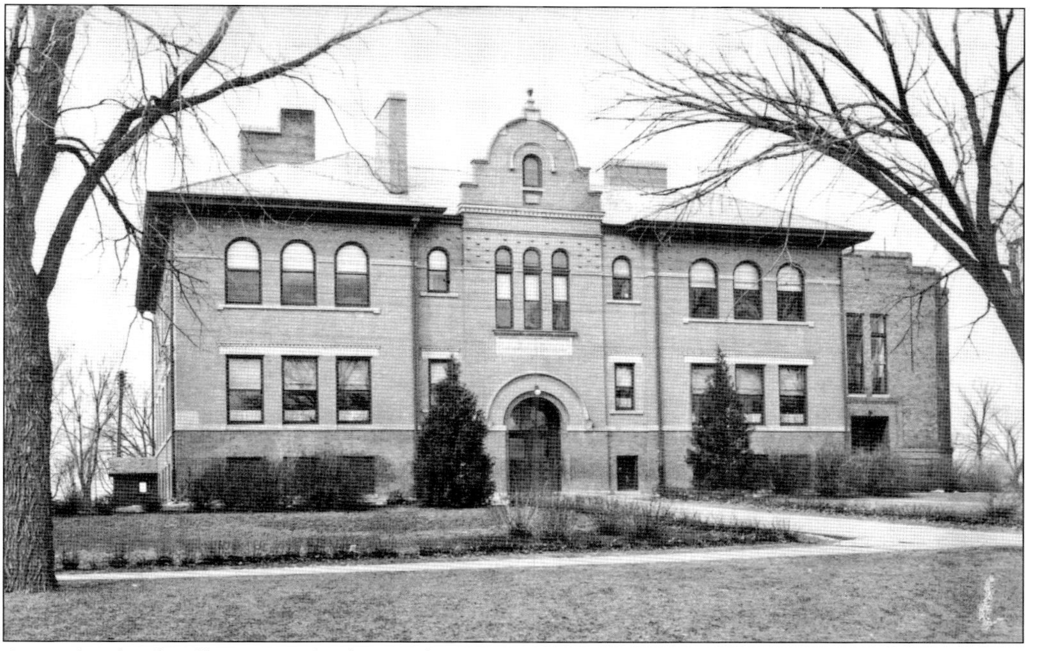

A new brick schoolhouse was built in Arlington on Quality Hill and dedicated in September 1907. This brick structure contained six recitation rooms and was equipped with the latest in modern technology, with steam heat, a water supply system, and a ventilation system.

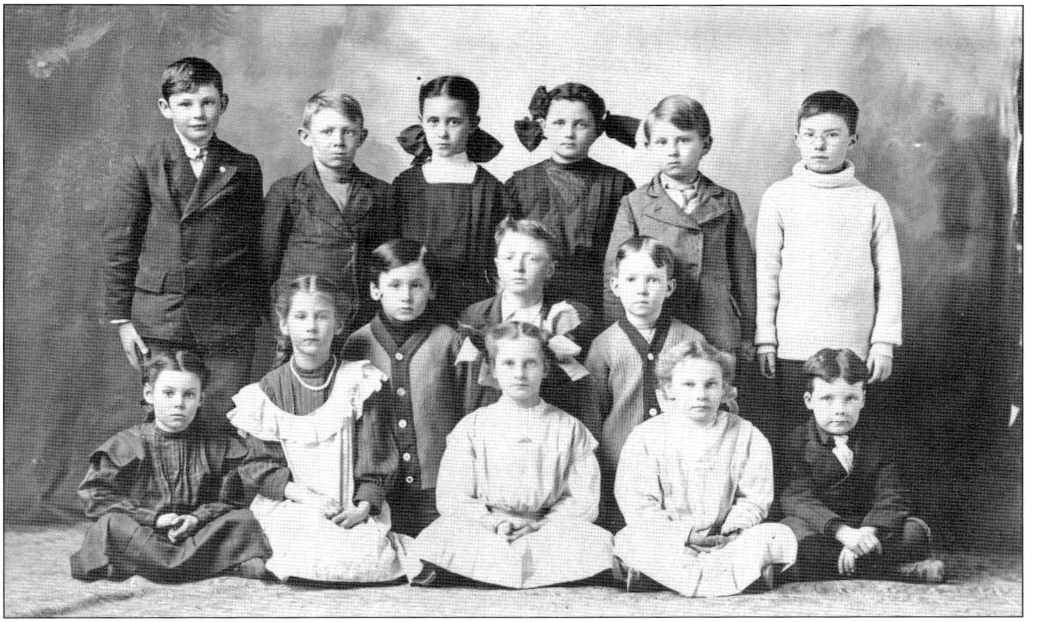

In 1910, three years after the new Arlington school opened, students pose for a class photograph. From left to right are (first row) Erma Antrim, Luella Reckmeyer, Violet Lockman, Bertha Brinkman and Donald Dailey; (second row) Vernon Pfeiffer, Joe McKillis, and unidentified; (third row) Wilfred Gilfry, Raymond Kruger, Verna Hadley, Mildred Ludwig, unidentified, and a young Mr. Melbrand.

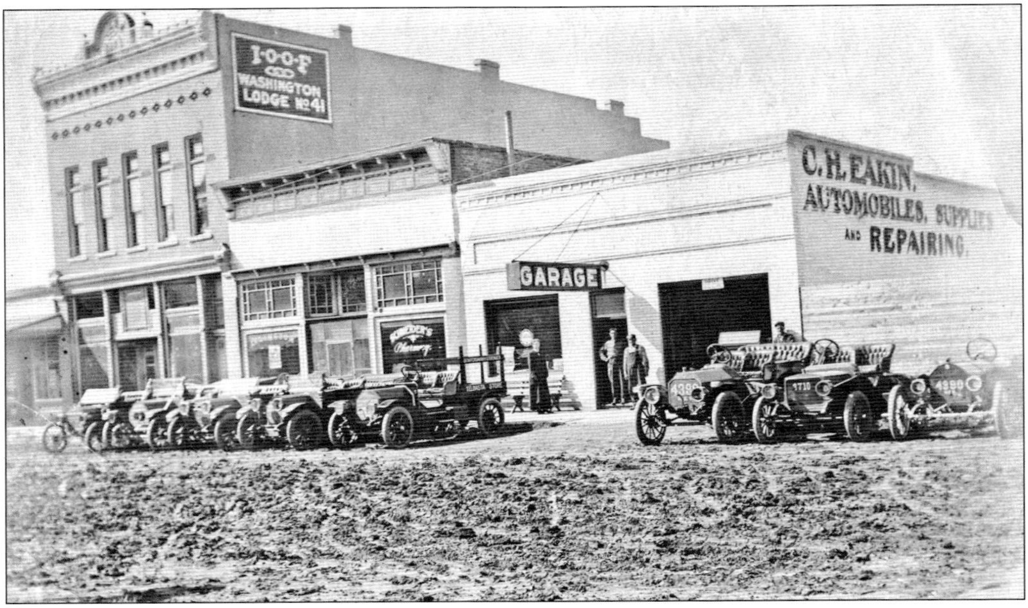

Clarence Holland Eakin owned the automobile dealership in Arlington, seen in this c. 1915 photograph. Automobiles were replacing horses, and garages and service stations were taking the place of livery stables and blacksmiths. In for repairs, Telbasta's store truck sits near the garage. A sharp businessman could make a good living in the automobile business.

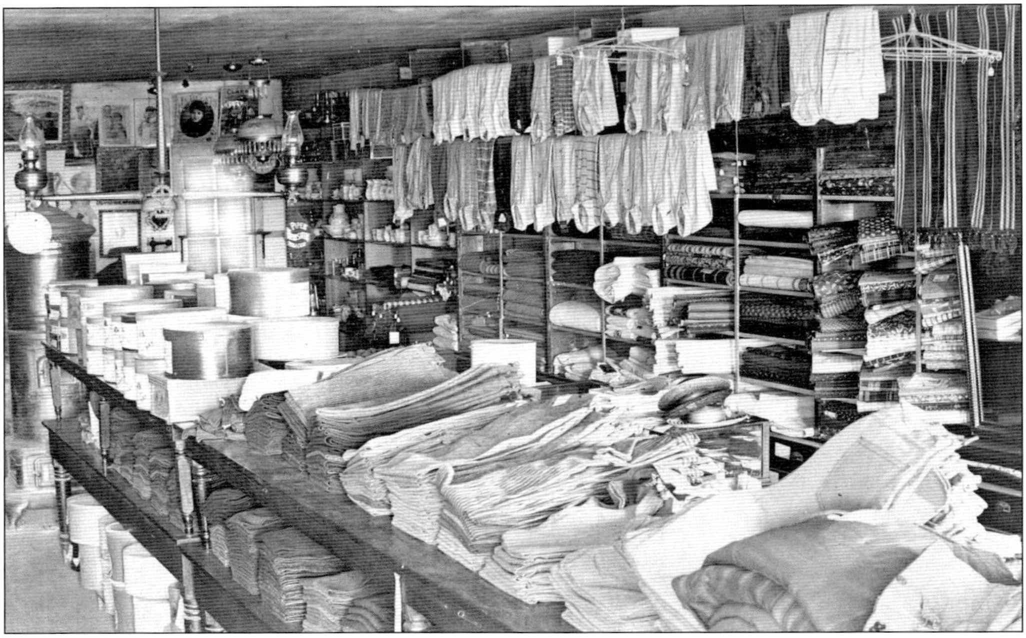

Paschal Z. Wilson opened his store, P.Z. Wilson, in Arlington, with a stock of general merchandise in 1879. By 1900, the company was carrying a large inventory of linens and shoes. In 1901, a store was opened in Blair, incorporated under "P.Z. Wilson, The Shoe Man." In 1903, the company bought the store in Telbasta. The Blair store operated until 1928; the Arlington store closed in 1935.

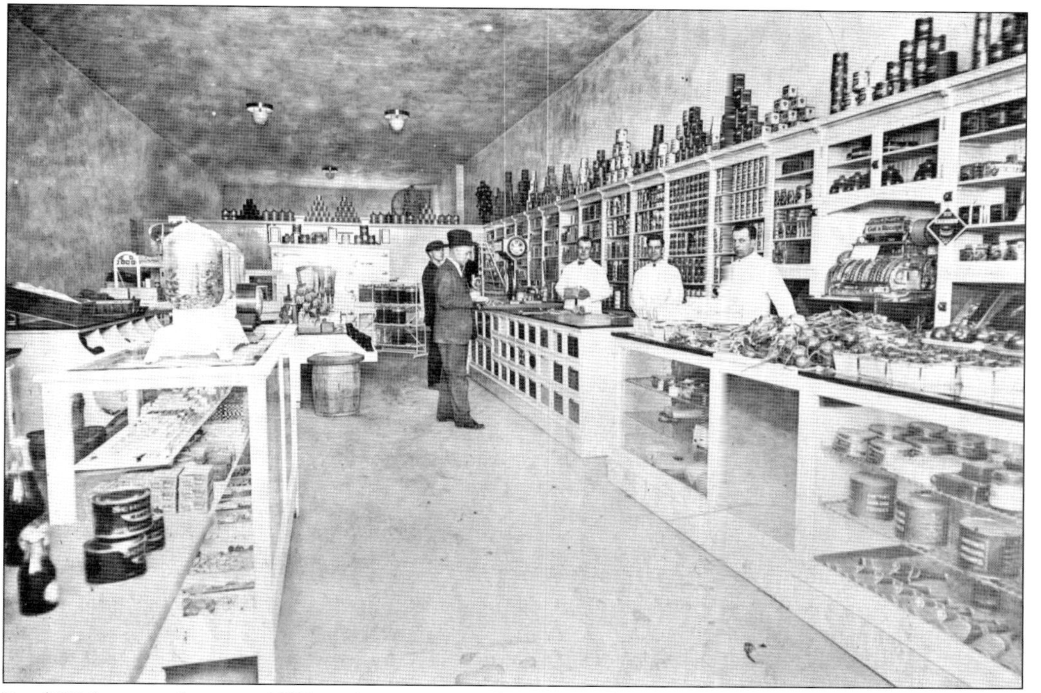

Fred Weber was born in 1871 and grew up in the town of Arlington. He began his career in the retail business as a salesman in the general merchandise business and later was selling ladies ready-to-wear clothing.

The eldest son of Johann Herman Hilgenkamp's 21 children, Wilhelm Heinrich Hilgenkamp arrived with family, settling north of Arlington by 1870 and speaking little English. He married Caroline Wilkening and set up housekeeping with a determination to succeed. He was a successful farmer of 2,300 acres of farmland and very involved in St. Paul Lutheran Church. Many Hilgenkamp descendants live in the Arlington community today. (Courtesy Janine Carlson.)

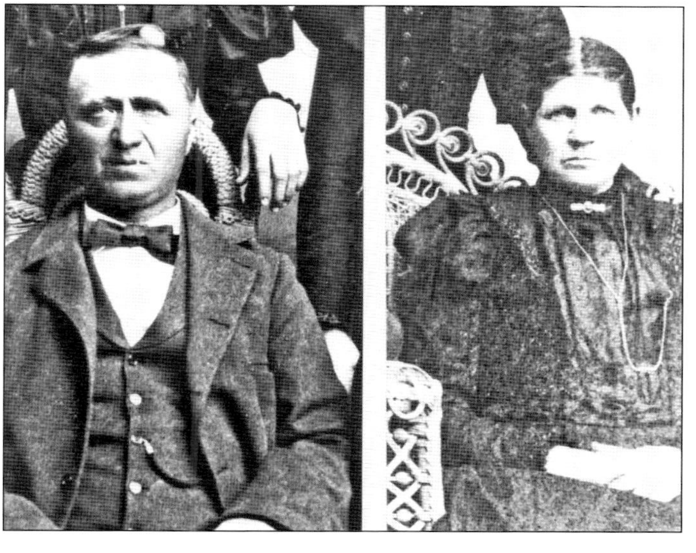

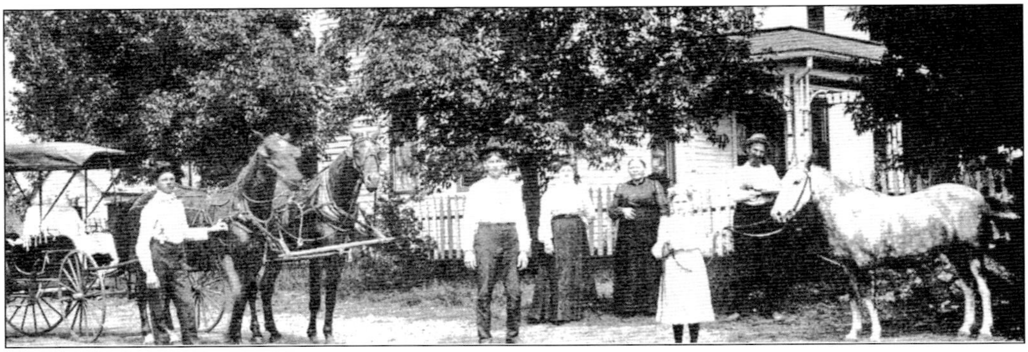

Zacharias Dunklau arrived in Arlington with his wife, Johanna, and infant child in 1869. Customary of the time was to be photographed with prized possessions. Zacharias and his family, Rudolph (left), Louis, Emma, wife Johanna, and daughter Johanna are surrounded with their horses and buggy in front of their home.

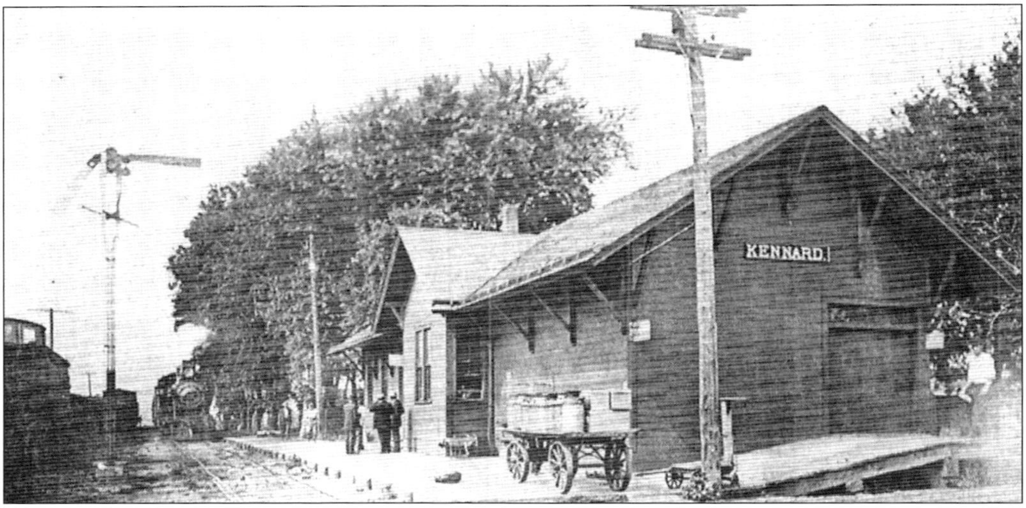

Kennard was established by the Sioux City and Pacific Railroad and named after the Honorable Thomas P. Kennard, secretary of state, but was not incorporated until 1895. It is located between Blair and Arlington along the then Sioux City and Pacific Railroad line. The depot, among the first buildings in Kennard, sat near the east road going into town.

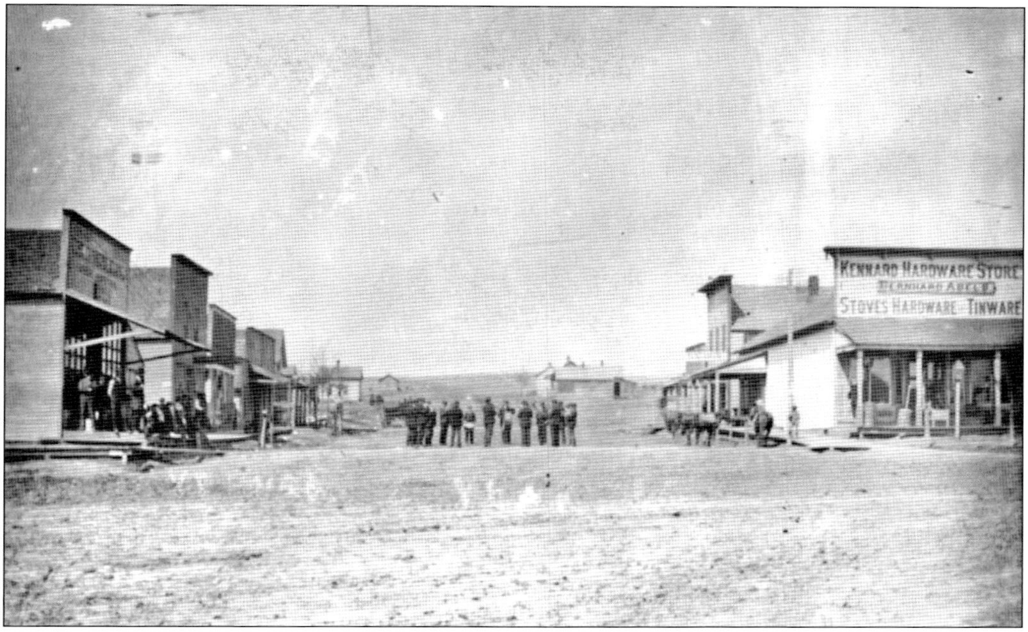

Bands reflected the pride of the towns and residents attended concerts; watched bands in parades, social events, and political celebrations; and requested them to play at dances. One of Kennards' first social organizations was its band, as seen on Main Street in this early photograph of the town.

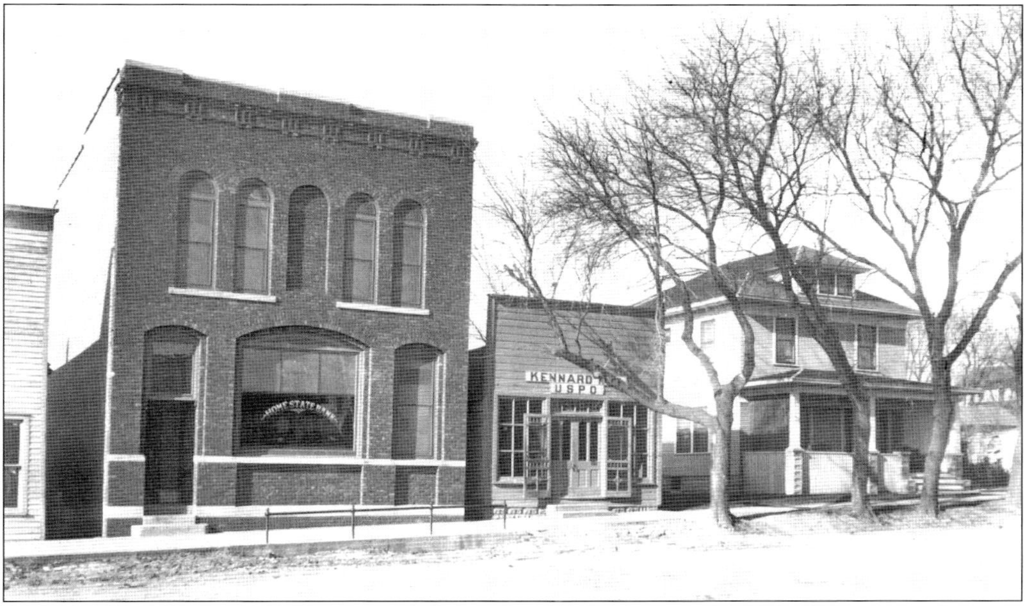

Originally the home of the State Bank, built in 1915, it became a hardware store when the bank moved into the Farmers and Merchants Bank in 1929. In 1960, it became the post office location. The first post office location was next door where the jewelry store was located, until 1922. The house on the end belonged to Charlie Weed, proprietor of the jewelry store. (Courtesy Dixie Lambert.)

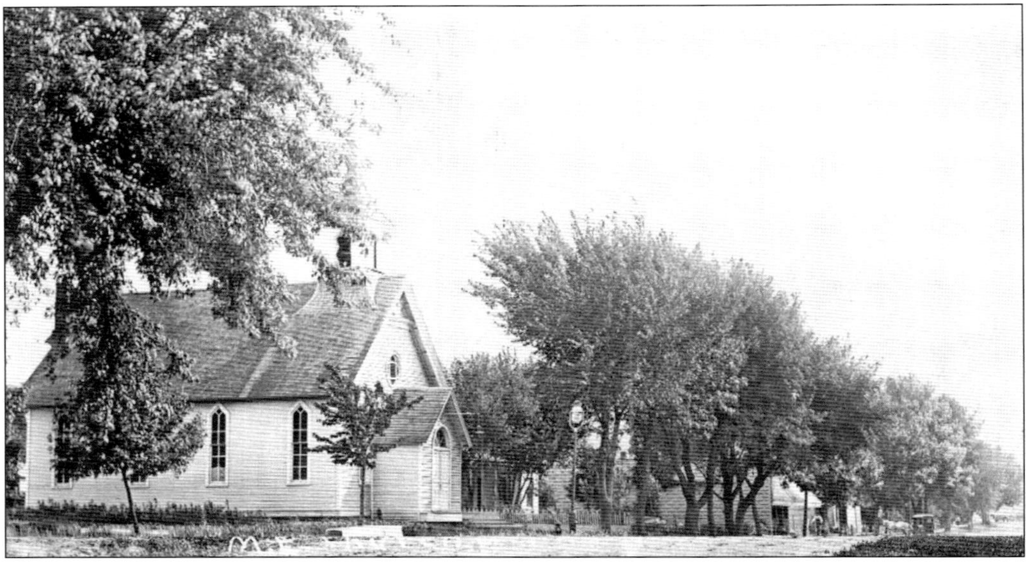

Kennard Methodist Church was dedicated October 10, 1888, with 500 people attending the ceremony. In 1988, activities were held throughout the year to mark its centennial. Now known as Grace United Methodist Church, it is one of the county's oldest continuous Methodist congregations holding services in its original church. (Courtesy Dixie Lambert.)

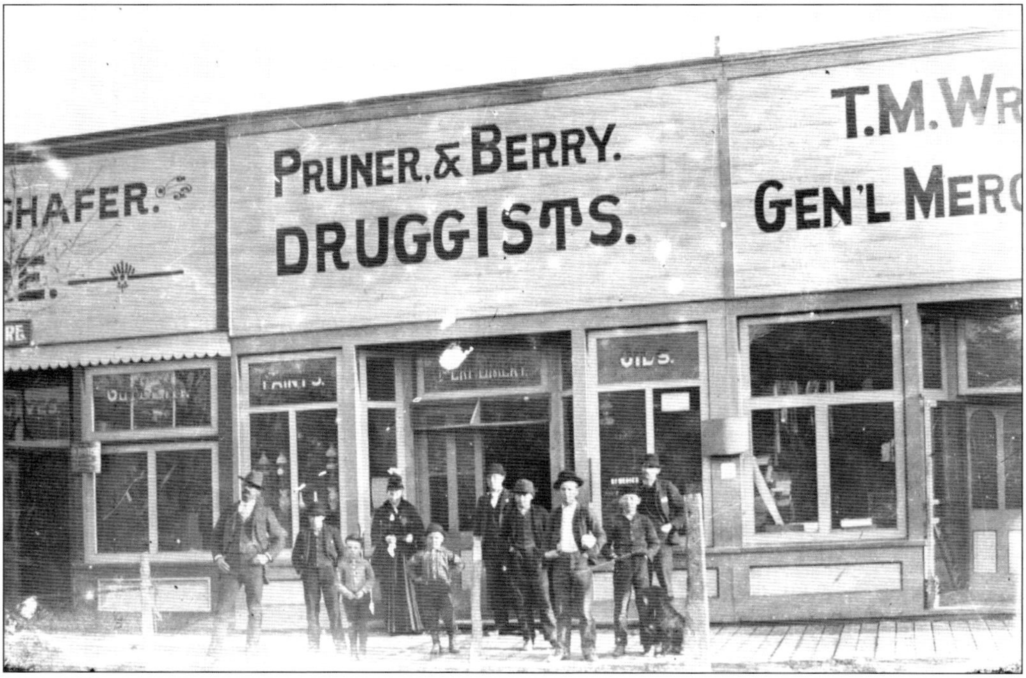

Dr. William H. Pruner migrated west with a group of Virginians settling in Kennard about 1890. He was the town doctor for 25 years until his death in 1915. On the day of his funeral, businesses closed for an hour, the school closed, and over 1,300 people from communities all over came to pay their respects. Mr. Berry was the druggist. (Courtesy Dixie Lambert.)

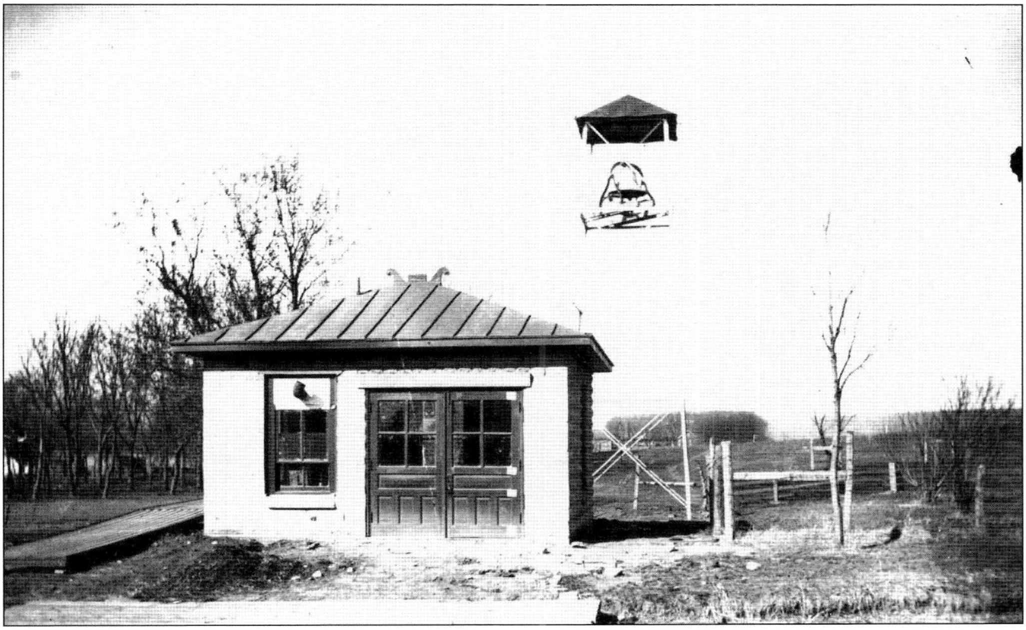

The Kennard VFD was organized in 1909 and named the Kennard Hose Company. The department had a hose cart and two hoses pulled by hand to fight fires. In 1923 a model T flatbed truck was obtained to hull the hoses and equipment. In 1947, a front pumper was bought. A new fire barn was built in 1972, and the fire and rescue squad was formed in 1976. (Courtesy Dixie Lambert.)

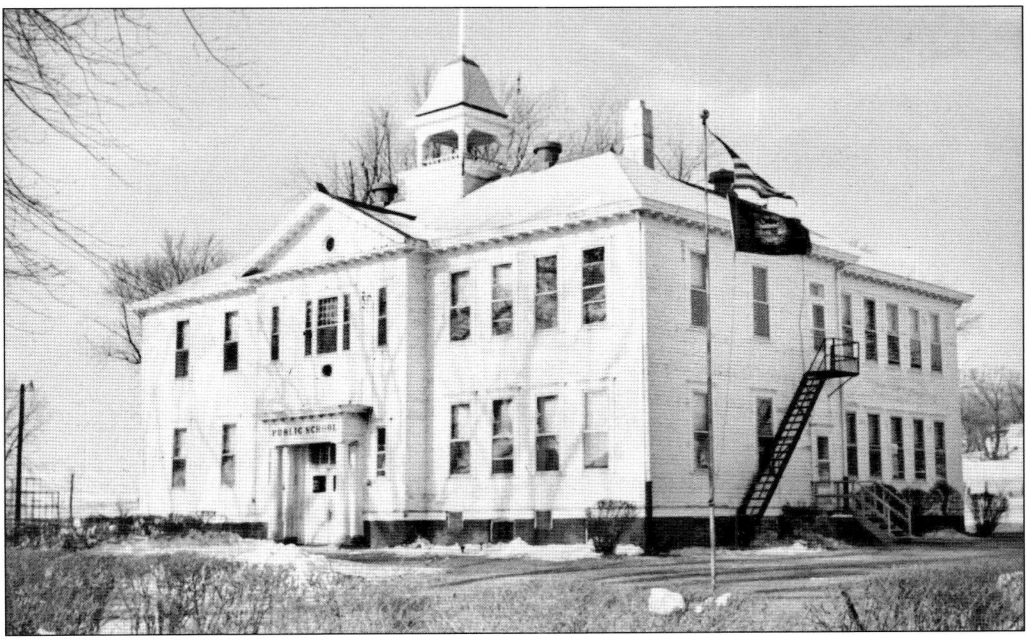

The Kennard School was formed in March 1884. In the 1920s, a $16,000 frame schoolhouse was built to house both elementary and high school students, furnished with modern desks and the modern conveniences of newer schools. The last high school graduation was held in 1960; the grade school closed following the 1972–1973 school year.

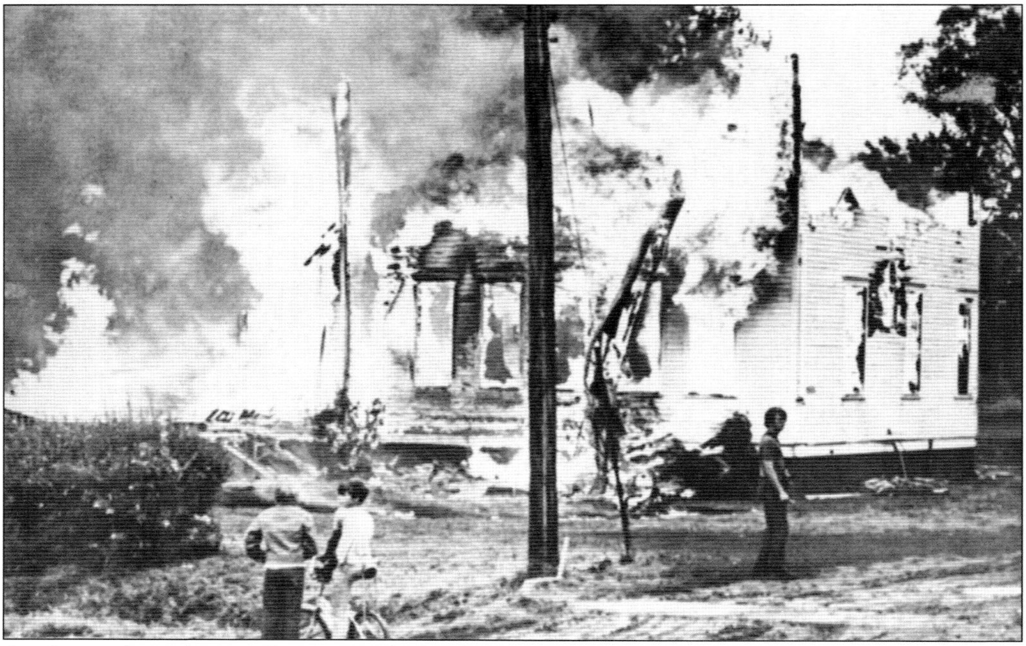

On September 15, 1973, the Kennard school was burned as an exercise by the Kennard Volunteer Fire Department.

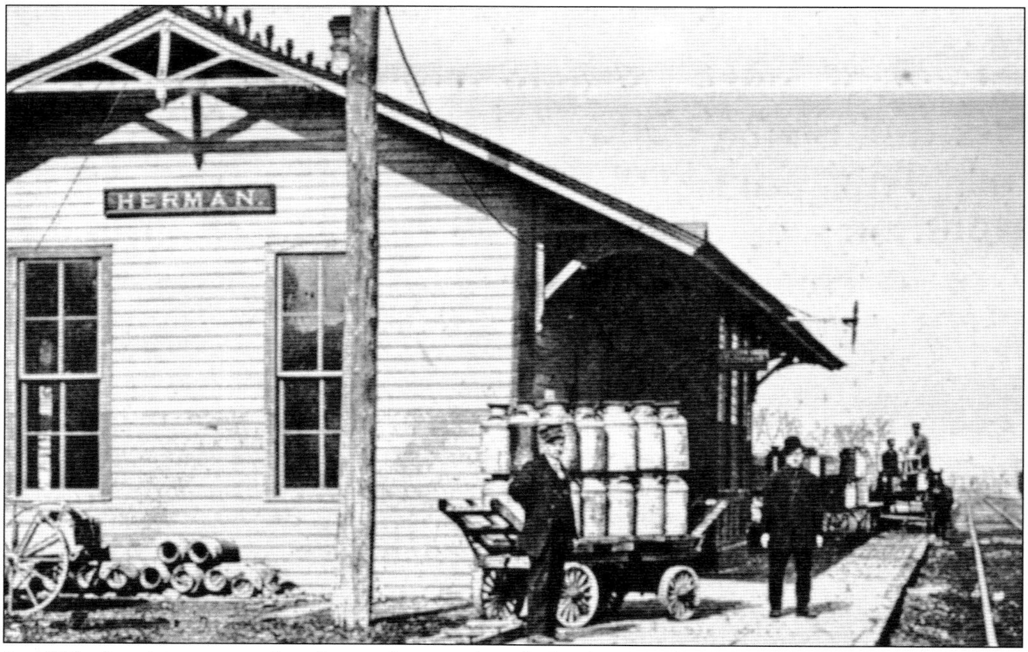

In 1870, the citizens voted in favor of raising bonds for the Omaha & North Western Railroad to lay track north through Washington County. In 1871, this line was completed to a small farming community along the northeastern portion of the county and named in honor of Samuel Herman, a conductor on the North Western Railroad. The Herman depot was destroyed by the tornado of 1899. It was promptly rebuilt.

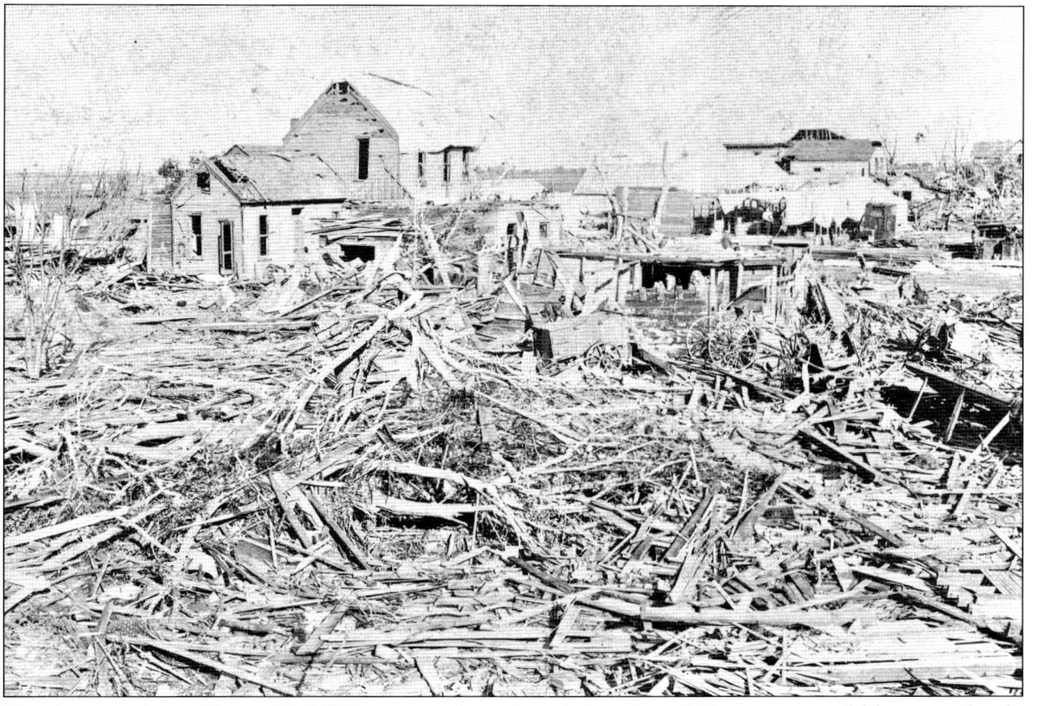

On the evening of June 13, 1899, a tornado reduced the city of Herman to rubble, completely demolishing the business section and killing 13 residents and injuring many more. The citizens of Herman were undaunted and quickly rebuilt their town.

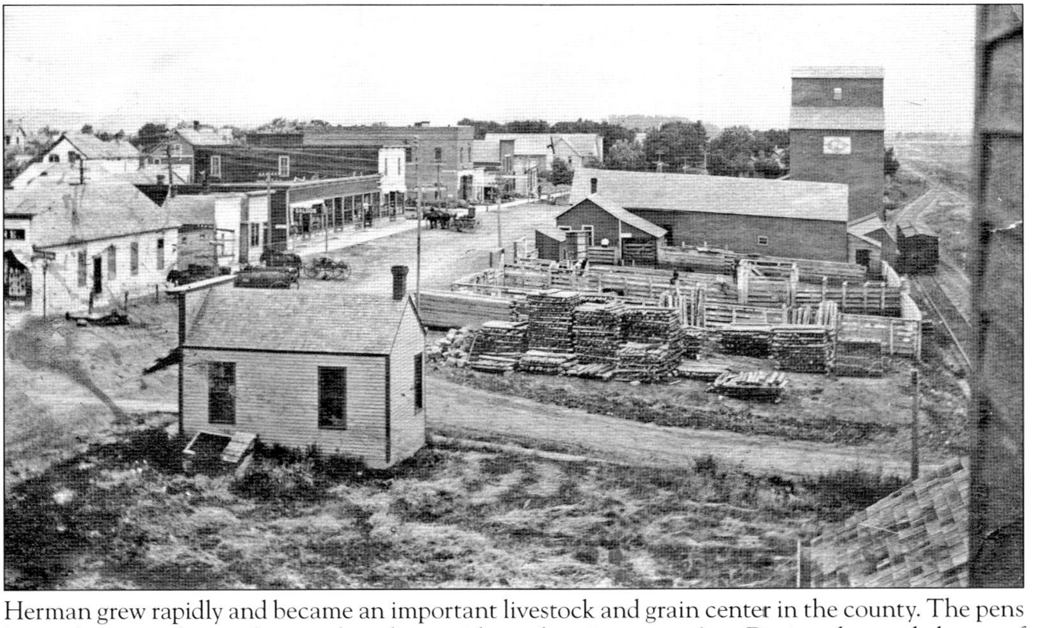

Herman grew rapidly and became an important livestock and grain center in the county. The pens located next to the tracks were kept busy with cattle going to market. During the cattle boom of the 1880s, the Frontier Cattle Feed Co. was sending 4,000 steers to market annually, keeping the pens next to the track busy. (Courtesy the Bordic Collection and Jonnie Andrew.)

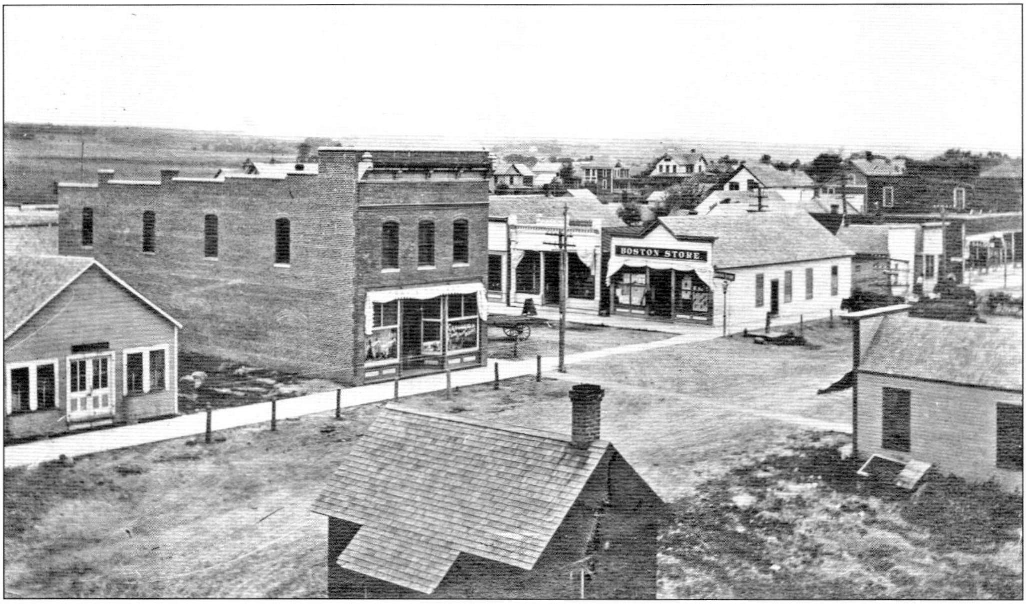

The town of Herman had three churches, a grain elevator, newspaper (the *Herman Independent*), grocery, lumberyard, hotel, bank, pool hall, dentist, doctor, and veterinary office. This photograph, taken about 10 years after the tornado of 1899 wiped out the town, shows no sign of the damage. (Courtesy Jonnie Andrew.)

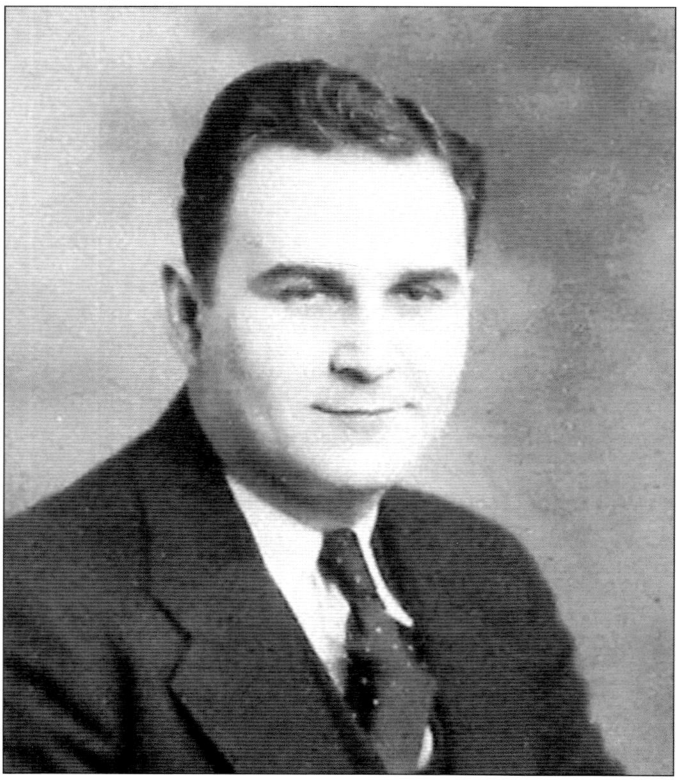

Forrest Shrader, pictured around 1938, was the superintendent at Herman High School from 1929 to 1940. Aside from the fact that he was a beloved and respected administrator, Shrader must be noted for writing *A History of Washington County, Nebraska*, published in 1937. (Courtesy Jonnie Andrew.)

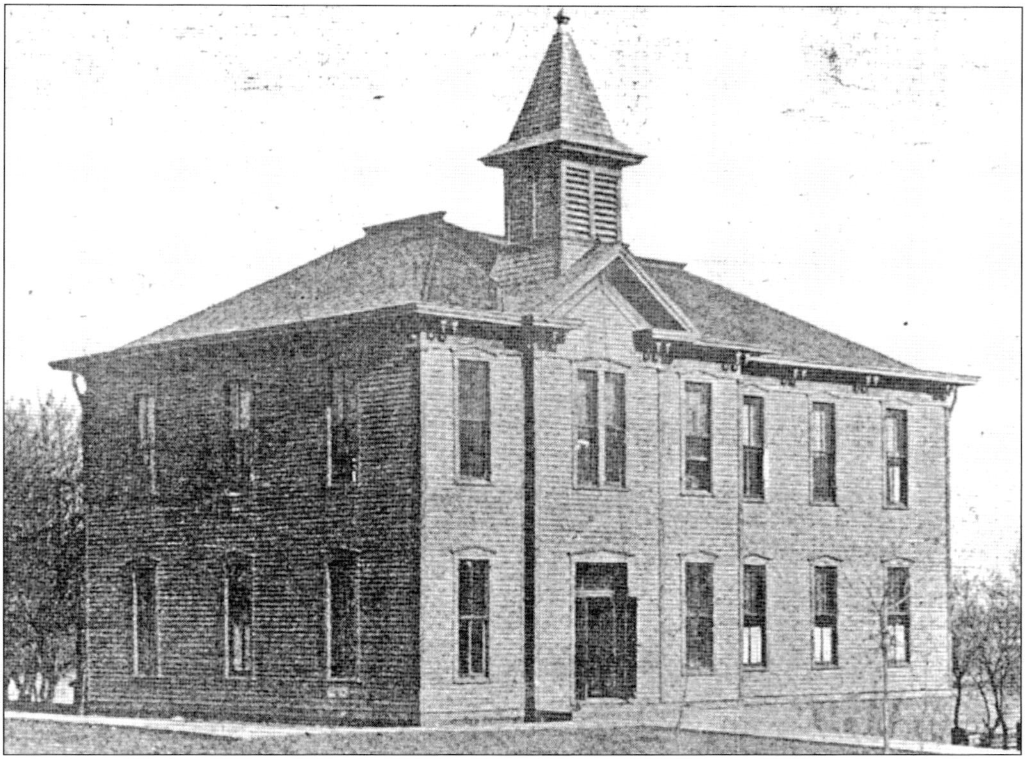

The Town of Herman built a school in 1874, three years after the railroad arrived and the farming community was officially a town with a name. It was torn down in 1911 to make way for the new school.

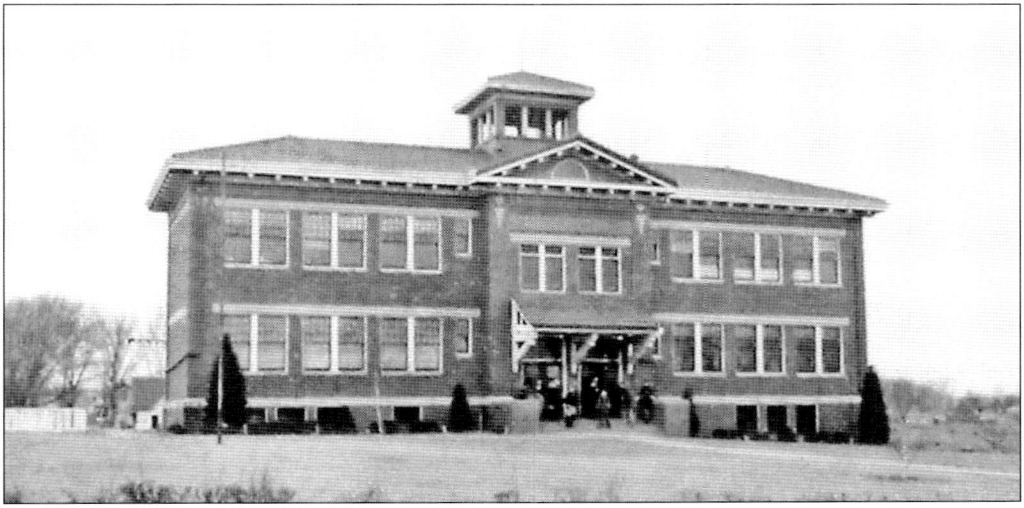

The new Herman School was built in 1912. In 1961, a new structure was built next to it and contained the new cafeteria, gym, and classrooms. In 1969, the high school consolidated with Tekamah's school in Burt County and the gym became home to the elementary grades. The school was torn down in 1973. In 2016, Herman lost its school when the elementary classes moved to Tekamah. (Courtesy Jonnie Andrew.)

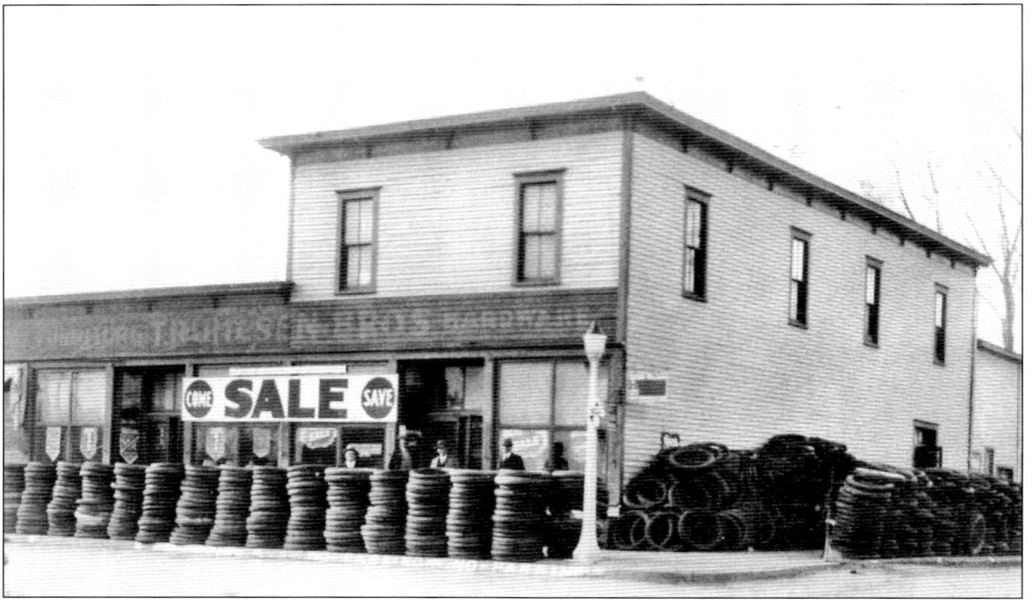

In October 1910, Niels Truhlsen and his son Chris bought the hardware and undertaking business. One year later, Chris went into partnership with his brother Henry. The Truhlsen Bros. Hardware building, the name barely visible in this photograph, was also home to Potadle's Grocery and the Herman Market. It later burned, and the new Volunteer Fire & Rescue building was built on this spot. (Courtesy Jonnie Andrew.)

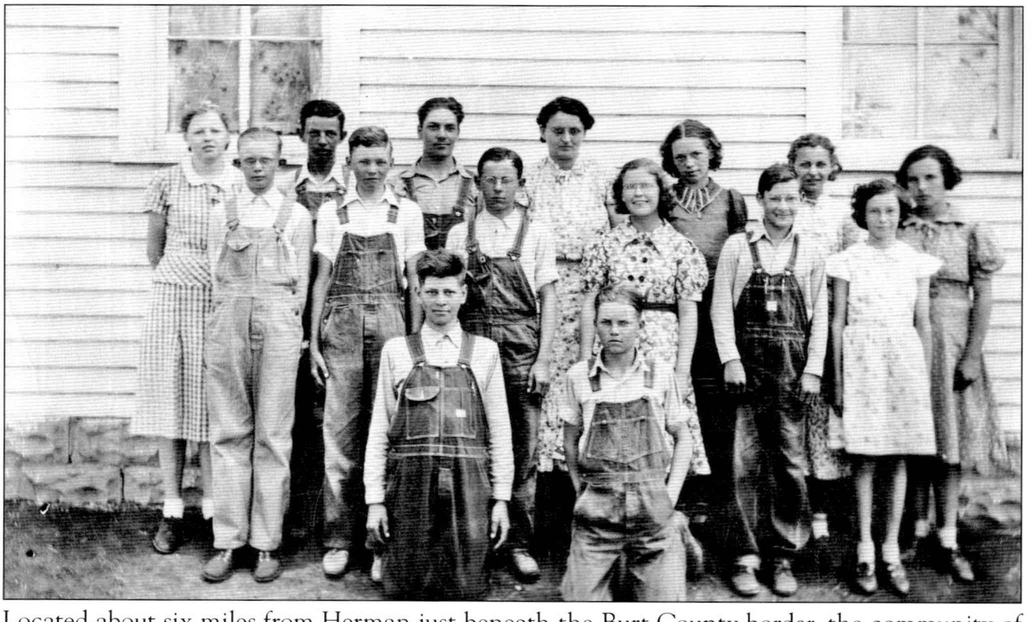

Located about six miles from Herman just beneath the Burt County border, the community of New England sprang up in the late 1860s. A group of unidentified students poses for the camera in front of the Fletcher/New England School in 1937. Built in 1882, it operated until the mid-1950s and was auctioned off in 1966. The New England Cemetery is the only sign left that a village existed.

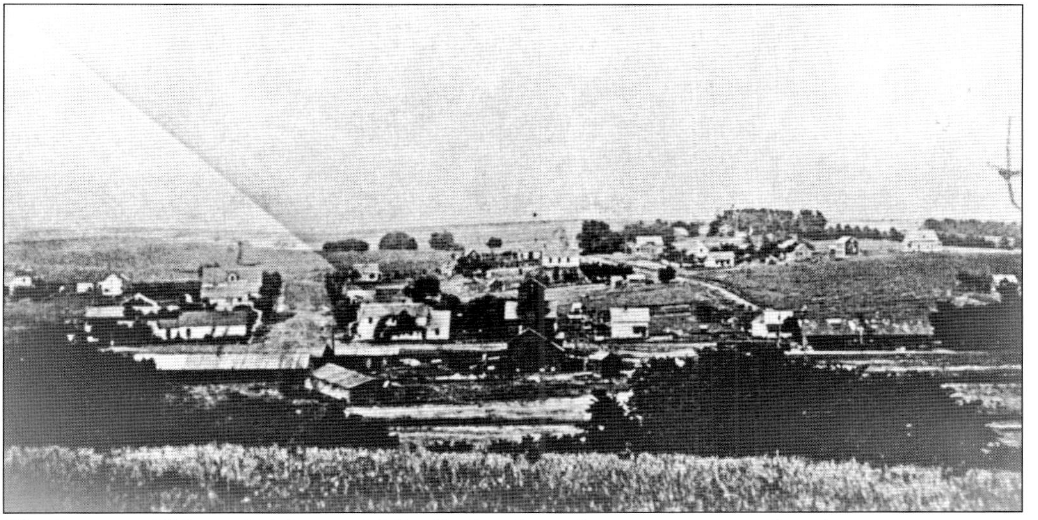

The Fremont, Elkhorn & Missouri Valley Railroad, needing a new station, bought a quarter section of land in 1887, on the southern county line, on which to build a depot. The name Washington was chosen by the Pioneer Town Site Company, with streets named for Revolutionary War heroes. Washington was the last city to be formed in Washington County and was incorporated in 1915.

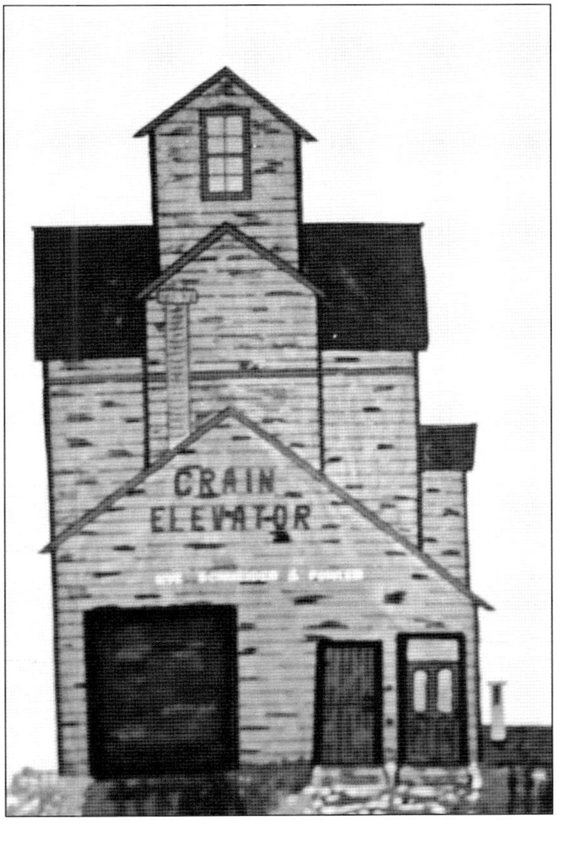

Passenger and freight trains ran daily. Near the tracks were two grain elevators, cattle pens, loading chutes, and a lumberyard and coal yard. George and Joe Wardell were large cattle feeders west of town who sent their steers to market by rail. Eventually, cattle were shipped by truck and the elevators torn down. The depot was demolished in the 1950s and the tracks taken up about 1970. (Courtesy LeMara Eicke.)

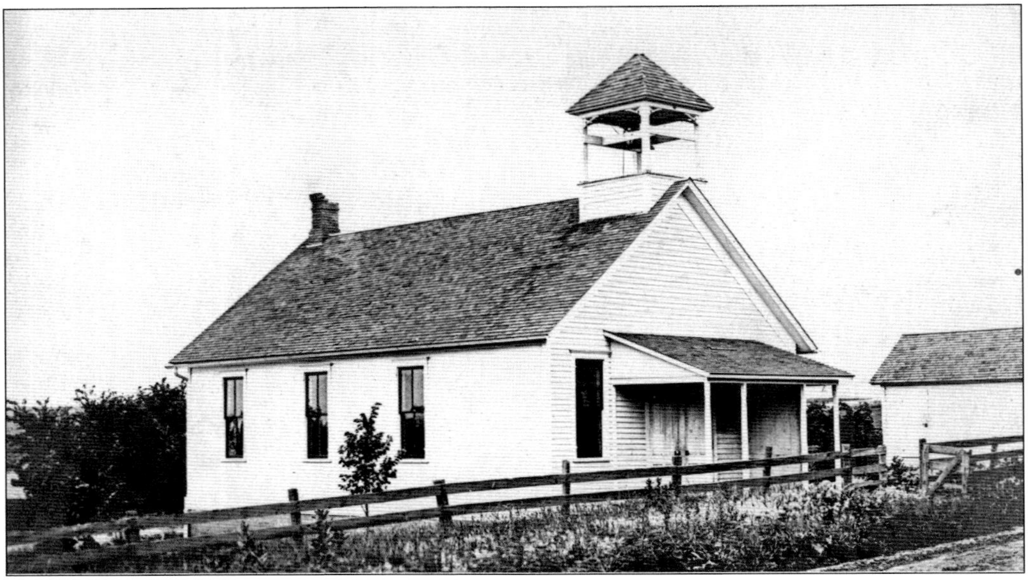

Children attended Rispin School two and a half miles north of town, and a buggy service was provided by a Jaszkowiak boy until 1895, when classes were held in the Jaszkowiak Store. In 1897, a school was built on the corner of Jefferson and Putnam Streets. Through the years, a basement, furnace, electricity, and running water were added. In 1956, the Rispin and Washington Schools merged.

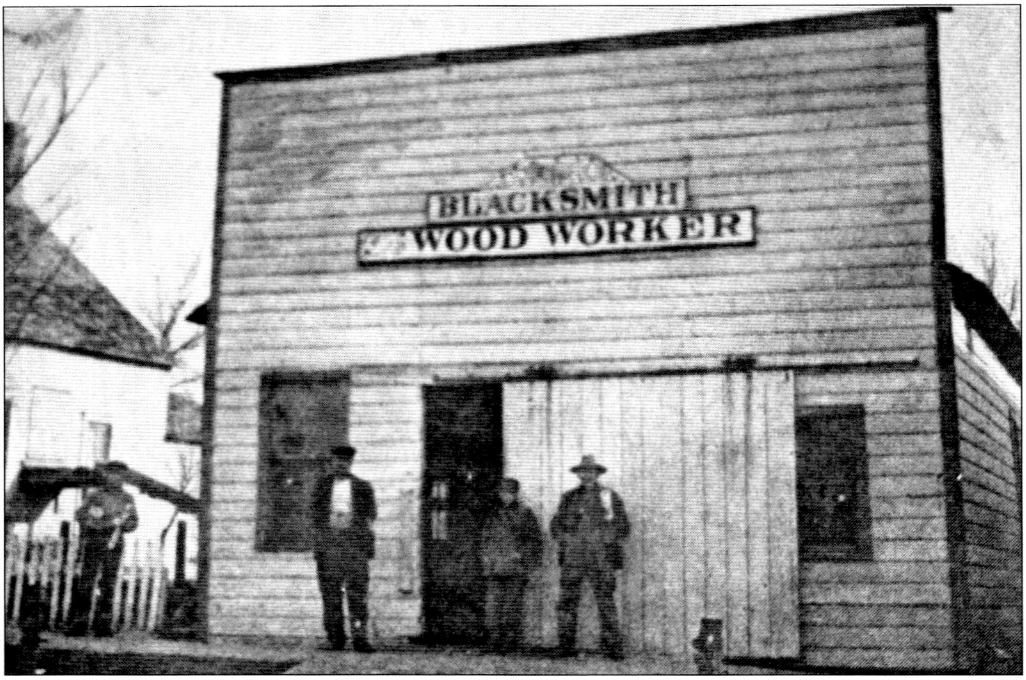

The first blacksmith shop in Washington town began in 1890. Soren Rosenkilde bought the blacksmith shop in 1899 and continued in business until 1942, making it the longest continually operated business in Washington under the same management. (Courtesy LeMara Eicke.)

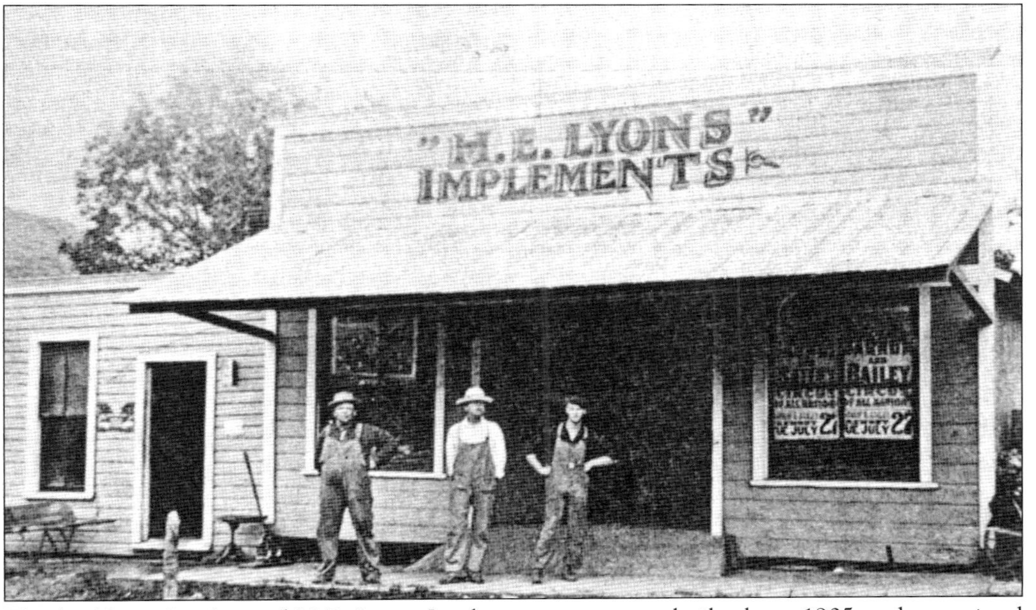

The building that housed H.E. Lyons Implements store was built about 1905 and contained inventory for both John Deere and McCormick implements. Hal Lyons was one of the largest implement dealers in this area of Washington County. He was also the town auctioneer and in demand at box socials and church events. Hal is standing on the far left in front of his store. (Courtesy LeMara Eicke.)

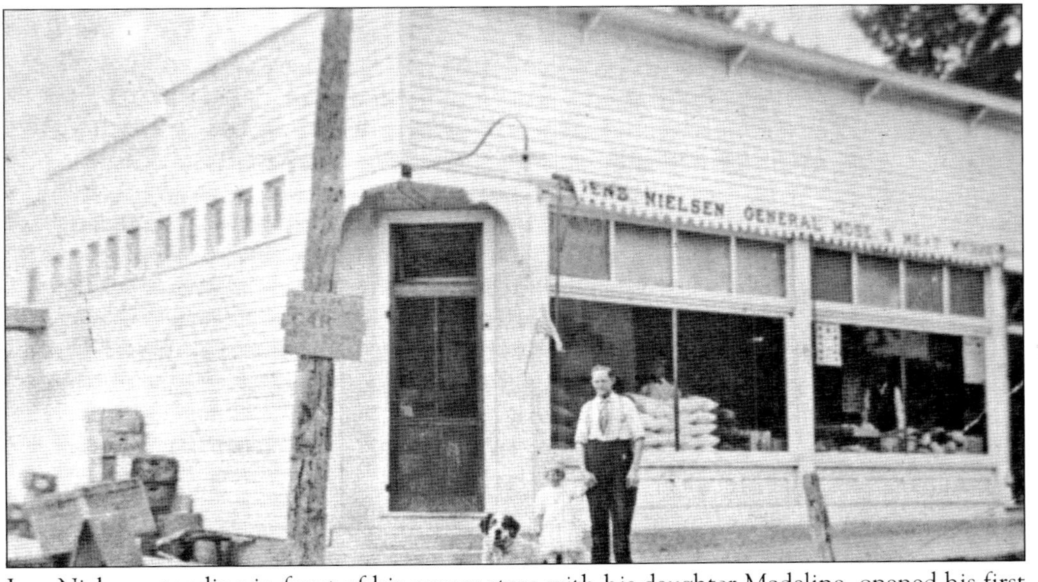

Jens Nielsen, standing in front of his corner store with his daughter Madeline, opened his first general merchandise store in 1911. In 1917, Nielsen constructed a larger store on the corner, attaching it to his original business, known as the Corner Store. The store had a walk-in cooler for fresh meats and was considered quite modern for its time. It lasted through the 1950s. (Courtesy LeMara Eicke.)

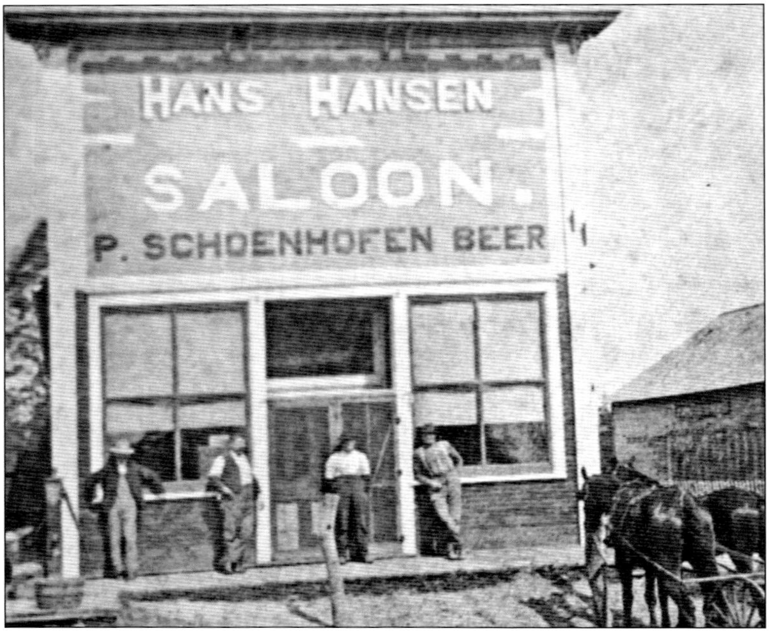

Hans Hansen built the saloon in 1894, complete with a card table and pool tables. Hansen offered a take-home service, charging a quarter if the patron brought his own pail. Around 1903, he sold the establishment to Herman Busch. Busch operated the business until Prohibition, at which time his wife turned the saloon into a variety store, selling fancy hats and silk stockings. (Courtesy LeMara Eicke.)

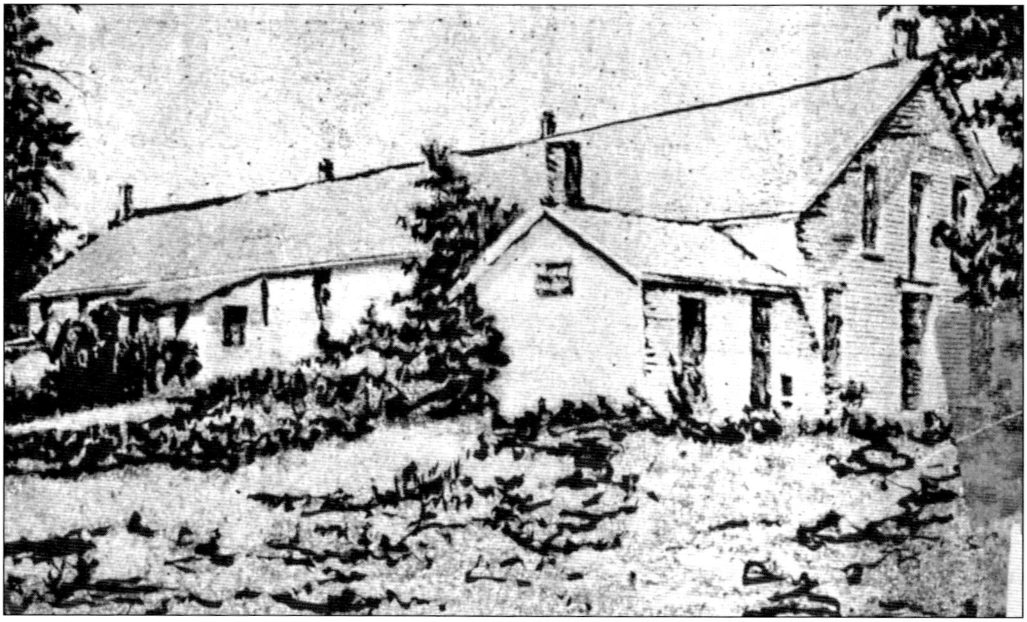

In 1876, a group of 44 farmers in a German settlement east of Washington, located near the border of Douglas County, purchased materials to build a hall to serve as their social center. The hall grew in popularity and three additions were built, including a balcony rooms upstairs where children would sleep while parents entertained themselves downstairs. Dutch Hall Road serves as a boundary between Washington and Douglas Counties.

Three

AGRICULTURE

BACKBONE OF A COUNTY

The rapid settlement of the farming territory began as settlers pushed westward and northward into Washington County. The pioneers who settled in the northwestern part of the territory were immigrants and homesteaders engaged in farming, many having obtained a tract of land through the Preemption or Homestead Acts and along neither a railroad line nor the rivers. They came to farm. The farmers arrived often with little money, sometimes a cow, and plenty of grit and determination. Wild game—fish, wild turkey, prairie chicken, quail, and pheasant—was plentiful. Wildflowers, gooseberries, plums, and strawberries were for the picking. Sorghum was used for sugar and butter, and cornmeal for flour. Water was found by digging an average of 30 feet down.

Agriculture rhythms have changed little. Corn is still king. The farmer still listens to hear the weather forecast, but machinery has made much of the actual work in the fields easier. At the turn of the 20th century, corn sold for 10¢ a bushel to $2.50; a bushel of wheat 27¢ to $3.30.

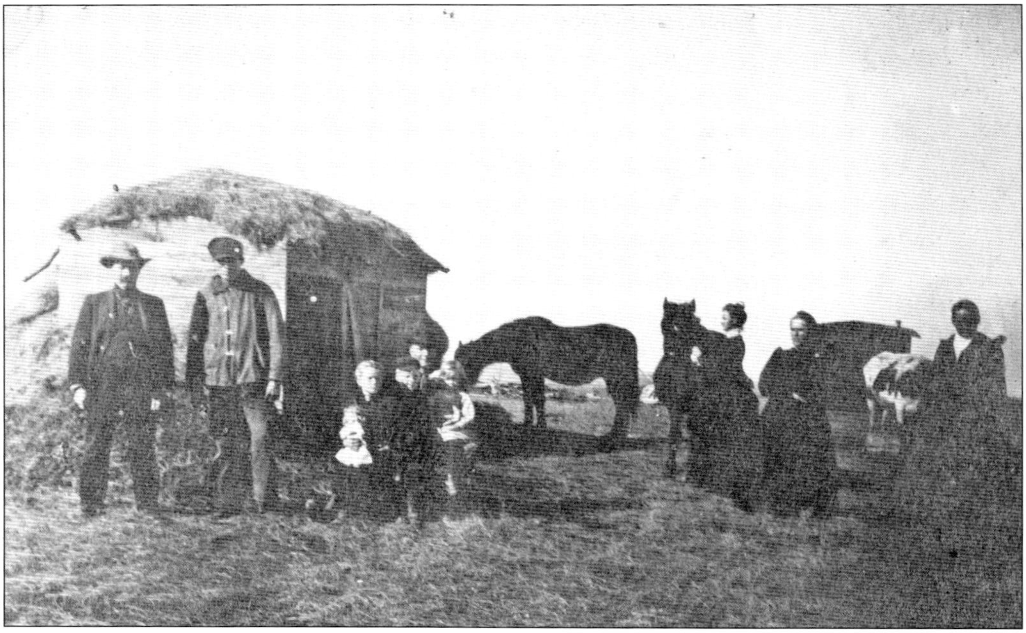

The prairie lacked building materials of wood or stone. The prairie grass with its thick root structure provided an inexpensive and quick form of building material to erect a temporary home, sheltering a pioneer family staking its claim. The sod homes were well insulated but vulnerable to weather conditions.

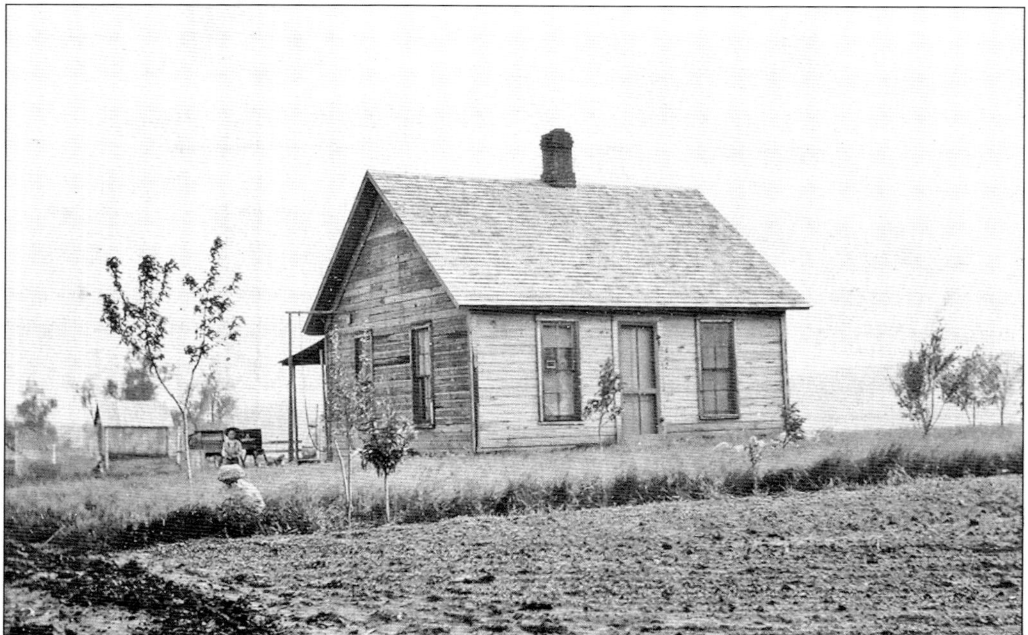

A more permanent structure was built and the rich prairie sod was broken with a large prairie breaker. Oxen were used instead of horses as power to pull the plow. The first crops consisted of buckwheat, raised until about 1875. By 1880, corn, soybeans, and alfalfa were the main crops.

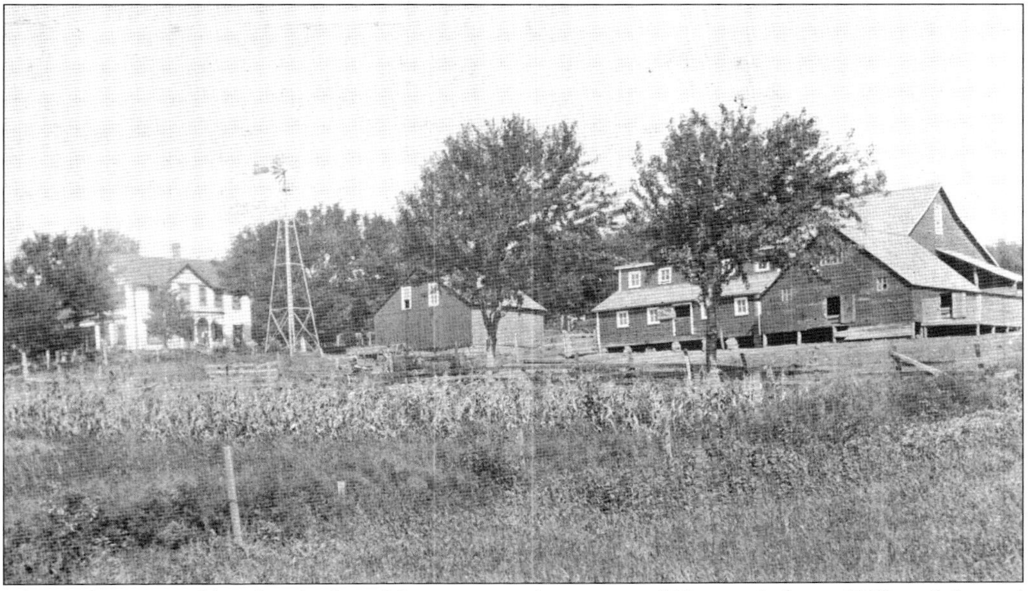

John Eakin moved his family from Virginia to a farm west of Kennard about 1879 and farmed until his retirement. Windmills, as on the Eakin place, started to appear in considerable numbers during the 1870s through the 1920s and were synonymous with farmsteads. John and his wife retired to Arlington.

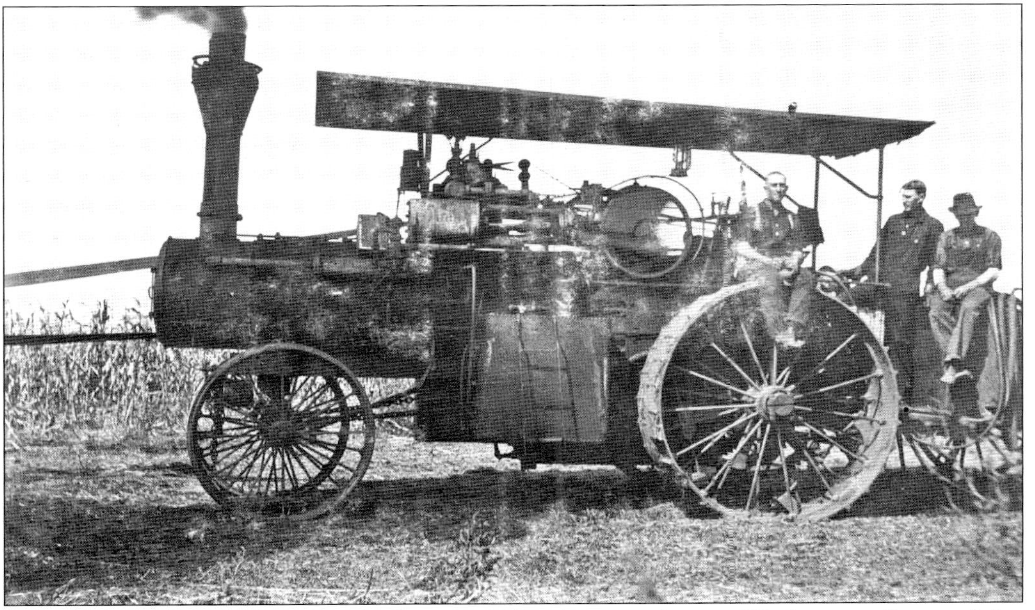

The McDonald brothers bought the first steam threshing machine in Washington County. John and Anna McDonald married in 1885, settling on 40 acres south of Blair. They grew alfalfa, wheat, corn, and oats in rotation. McDonald operated a threshing business in and around Washington County for 45 years and saw the shift from horse-powered to steam-powered threshing machinery. Their farm is listed in the National Register of Historic Places.

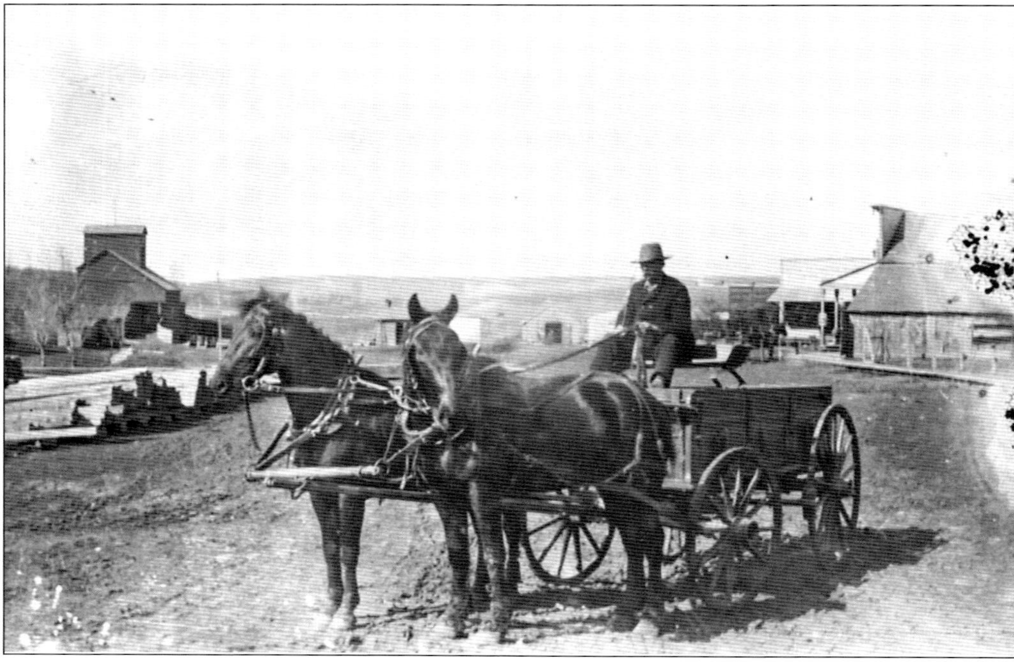

Albert Miller is pictured in Kennard on Second and Main Streets. A pair of good horses and a sturdy cart were essential. (Courtesy Dixie Lambert.)

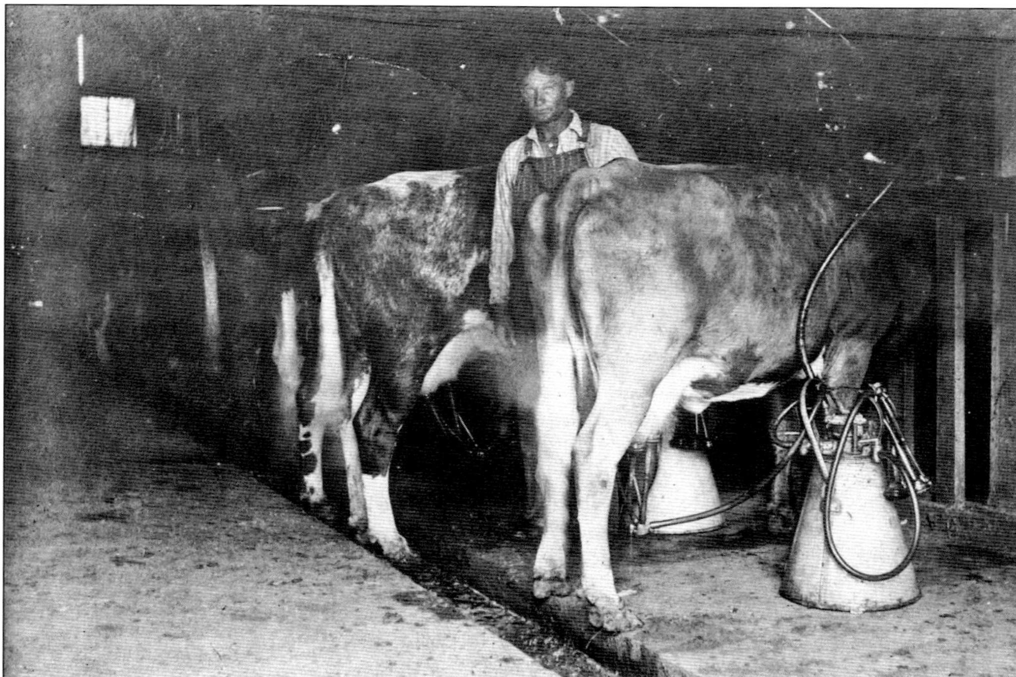

Mark Slader is pictured in 1908 with his milking machine. In the early 20th century, milking was done by hand. The introduction of milking machines changed that. Technology kept improving farm equipment.

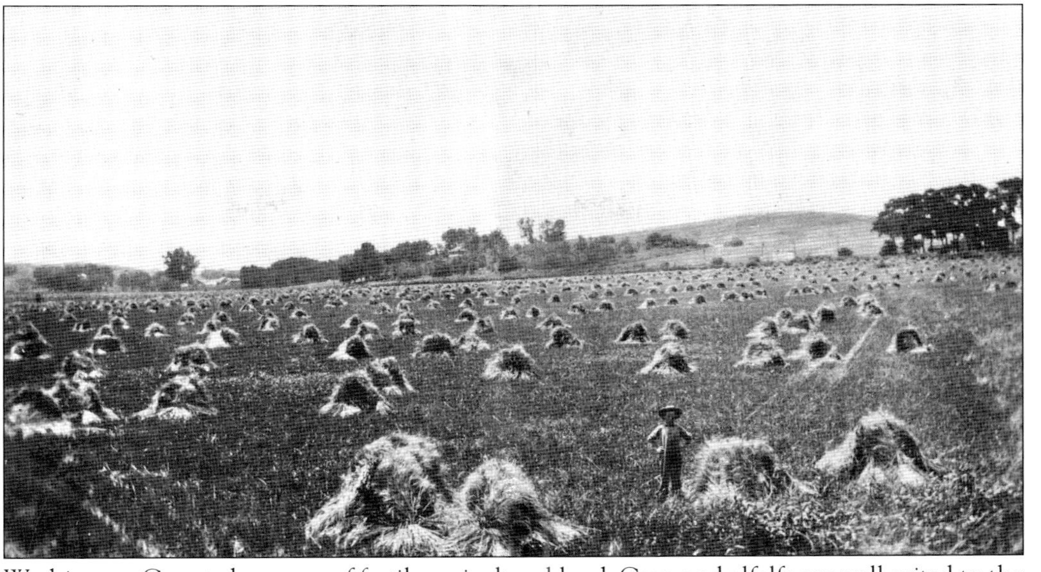

Washington County has acres of fertile agricultural land. Corn and alfalfa are well suited to the loess soil found in the county. Grain was cut and bound by a horse-drawn reaper-binder and put into shocks by hand. Later models were tractor-drawn. Note the little boy next to a haystack.

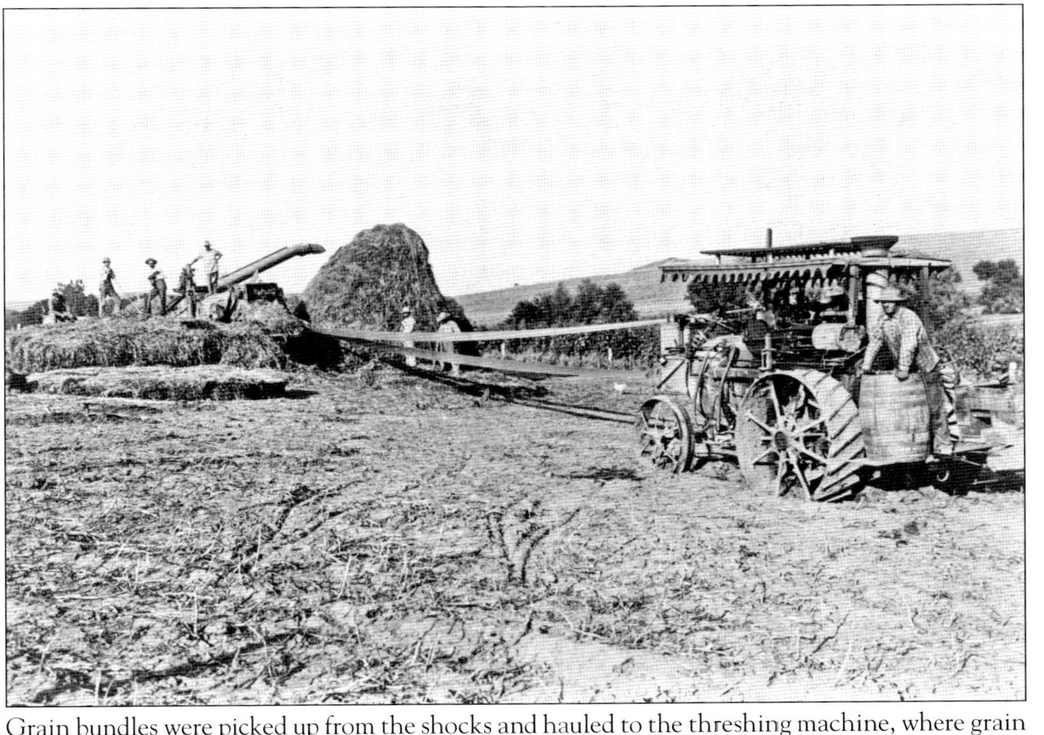

Grain bundles were picked up from the shocks and hauled to the threshing machine, where grain was separated from straw. During harvest season, when the wheat or alfalfa was dry, threshing crews traveled from farm to farm spending a couple of days at each farm working long hours in the summer heat. The first man to quit for the day was the first man to start in the morning.

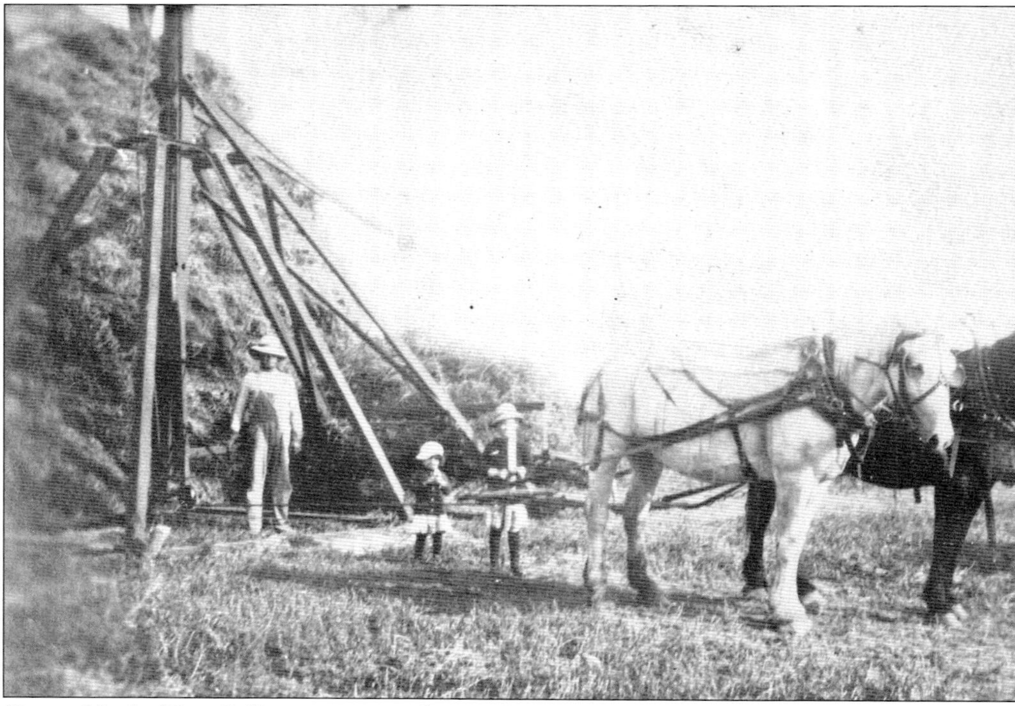

George Neal of Fort Calhoun is pictured around 1913 taking a break from stacking hay while two girls dressed in their Sunday best, believed to be his daughters Mabel and Eleanor, stopped to say hello. By the 1900s, machines powered by horses began to replace hand-powered labor. Alfalfa was introduced around 1875 in Washington County.

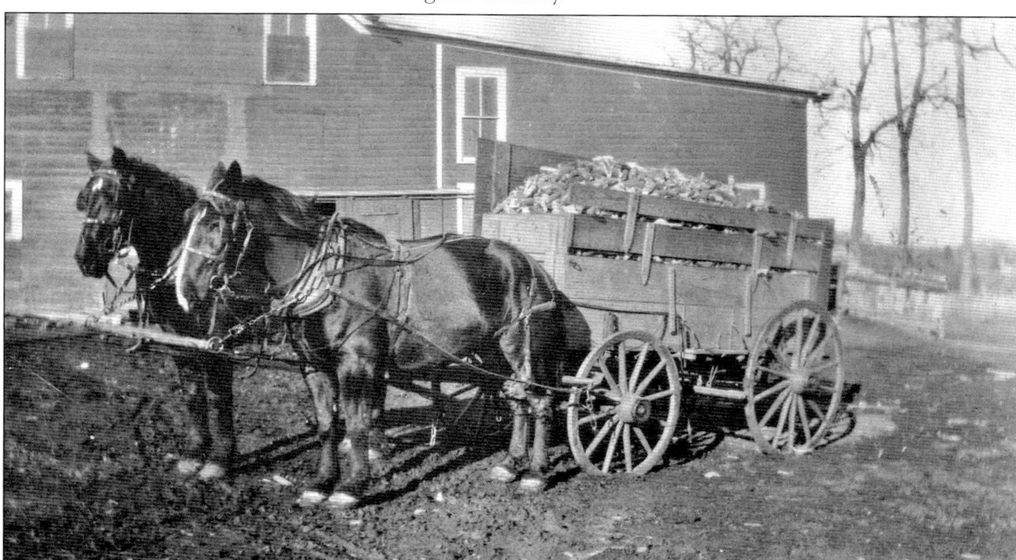

A horse-drawn corn-hauling wagon is waiting to be moved. Husking corn by hand was slow work. The high board on one side is called a bangboard. As each ear was picked, it was tossed into the wagon, hit the board, and dropped into the wagon. Yellow corn is a mainstay crop and is used for both feed and market.

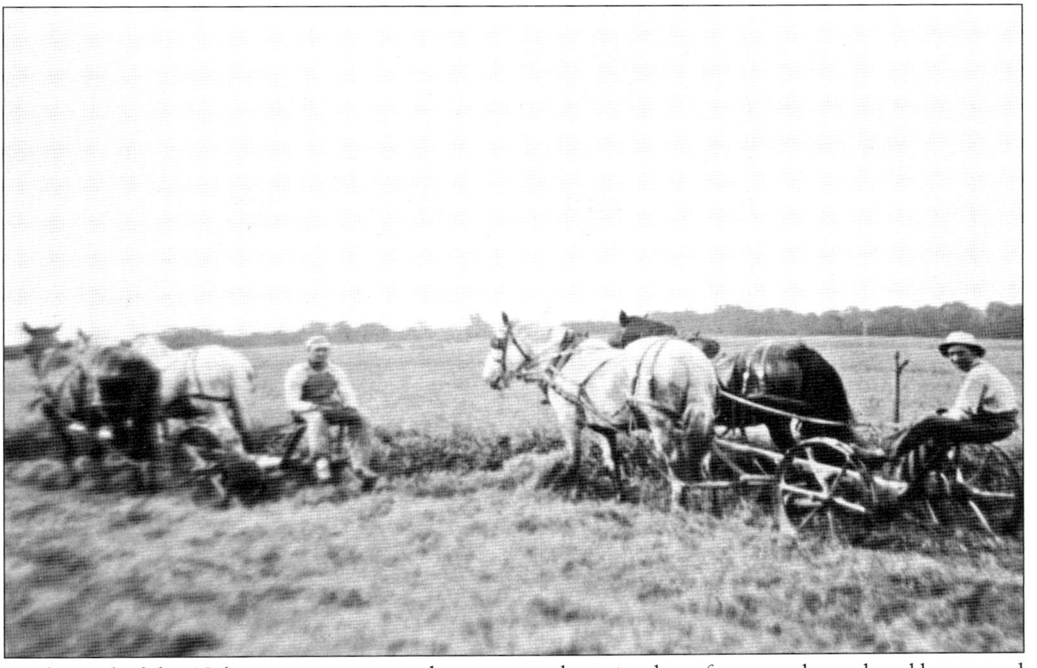

By the end of the 19th century, new machinery was changing how farmers planted and harvested crops. A sulky plow, pulled by two horses and with a seat, allowed the farmer to plow up to six, seven, maybe eight acres a day. Roy and Mark Slader, pictured around 1916 mowing hay with their sulky plows, welcome the opportunity to farm sitting down.

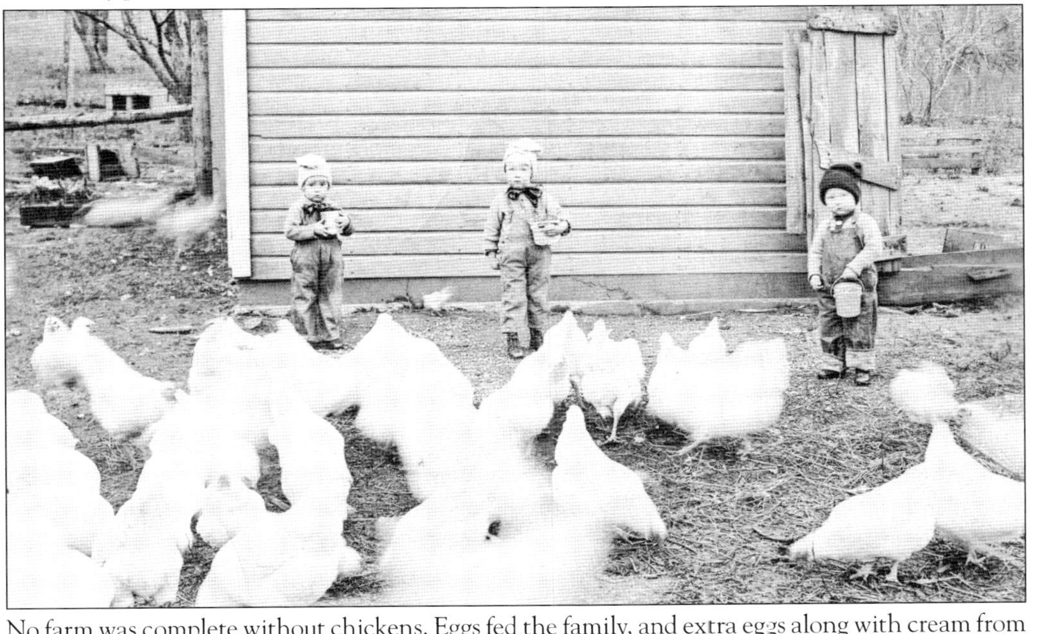

No farm was complete without chickens. Eggs fed the family, and extra eggs along with cream from the family cow were sold or traded for groceries at the local store. During the Depression, many families survived off their chickens and trading eggs for groceries. The three youngsters—Milton, Clarence, and Ray Hitchcock—are feeding their chickens on the family farm.

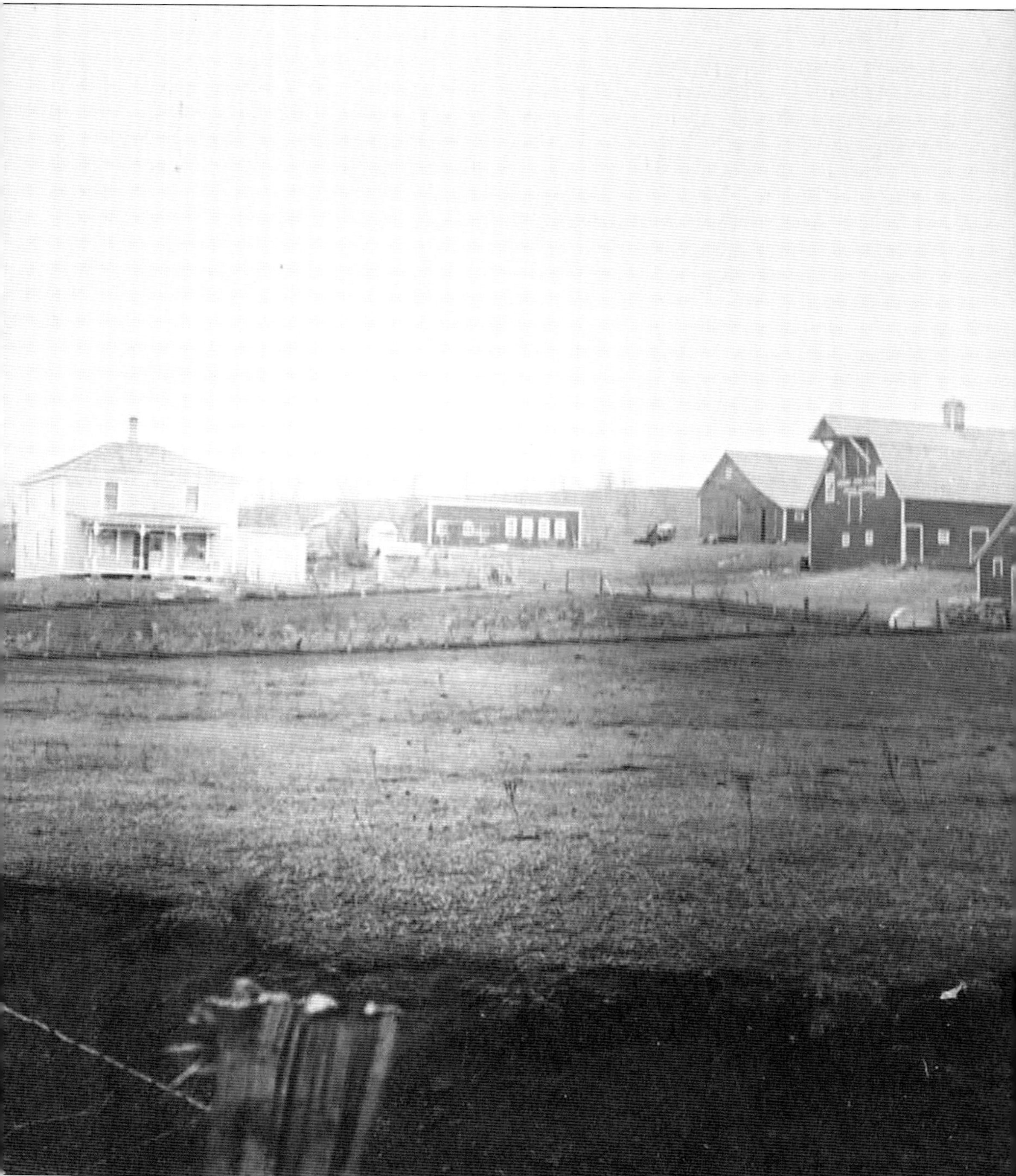

Frank Jahnel was born in Holstein, Germany, in 1851. He arrived in the States as a young man, married, and moved his family near Kennard, where he bought his farm about 1883. Interested in politics, he also served two terms as a member of the legislature. His son Fritz took over the farming operations when he retired in 1909, and it remained a family operation. Their farm was

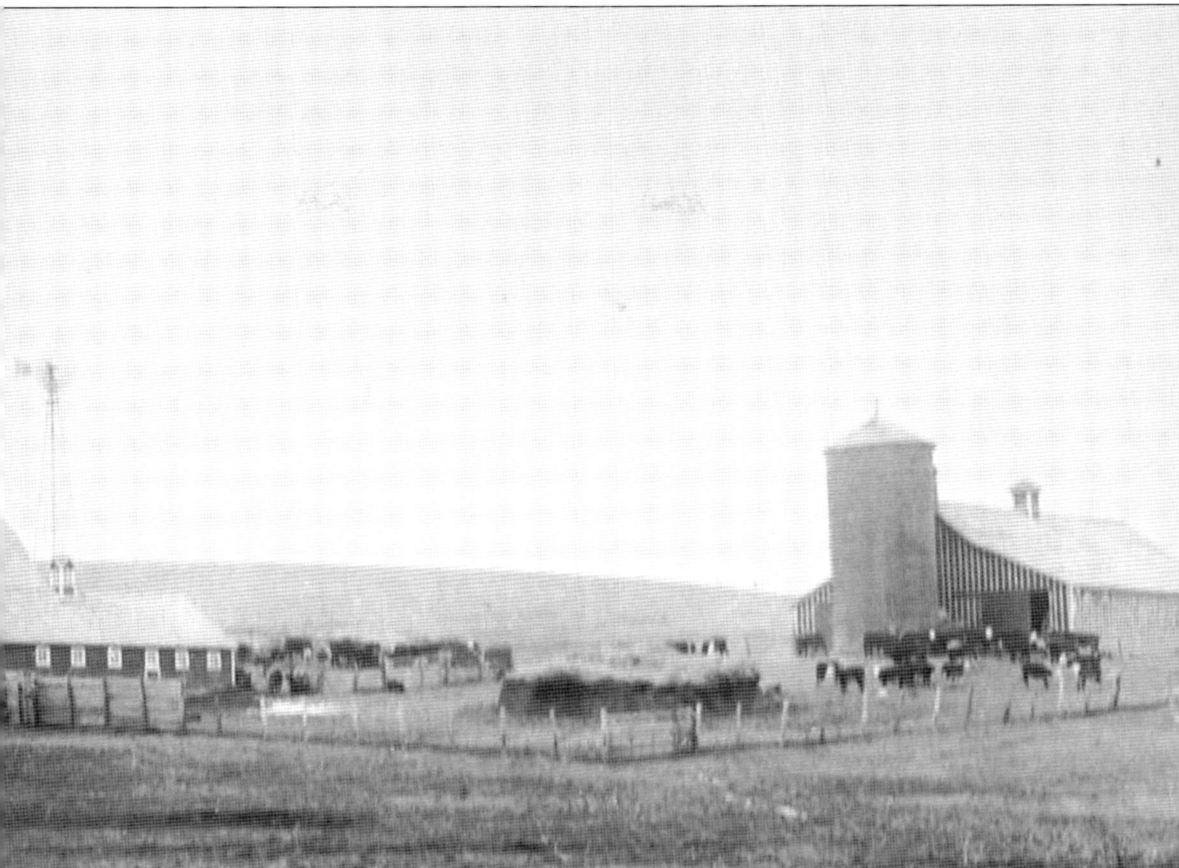

typical of the two-story balloon farmhouses and barns that dotted the countryside. Houses were painted white, but outbuildings and barns were painted red, as the cost of paint was cheaper. Washington County is a rural county. The Fritz Jahnel farm represents farms that have been in the family for generations and reflect the pride of farming operations.

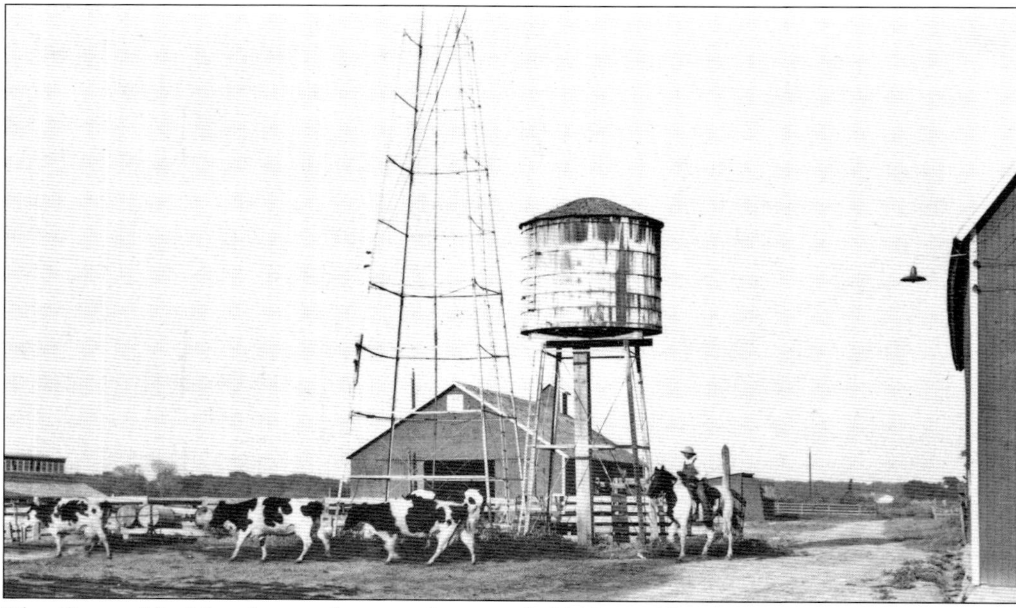

The George Neal family raised corn, wheat, and alfalfa; and bred cattle, hogs, and sometimes sheep. In 1920, George bought his first tractor. A few years later, he was the first one in the area to own a grain combine that threshed grain in the field. The family farmed through the Depression and survived droughts, dust storms, grasshoppers, and floods.

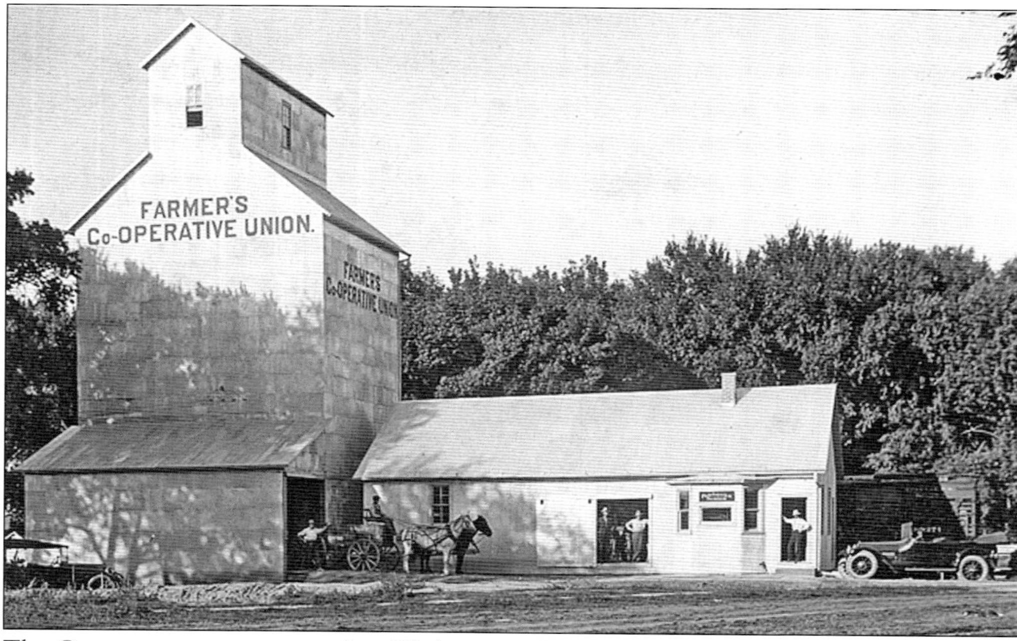

The Granger movement started in Washington County in 1873 when the City of Fontanelle organized Washington Grange 130. By 1874, there were 17 Granges in the county, averaging 30 members in each lodge. A farmers' co-op was the first step for farmers to unite in owning their own joint-stock stores and grain warehouses and controlling their own grain marketing. (Courtesy Blair Historical Preservation Alliance.)

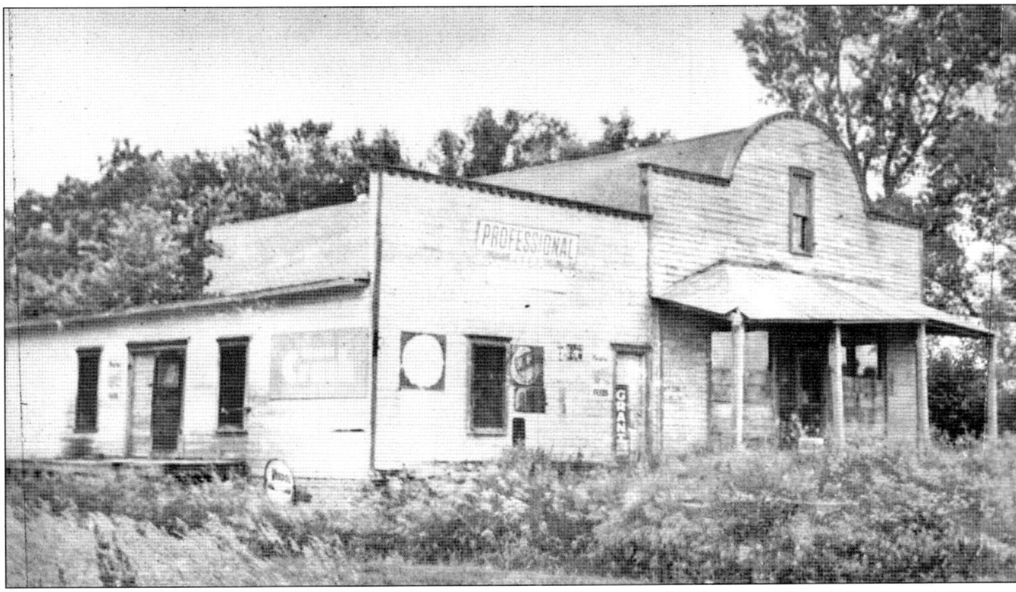

Three names of early settlers were placed in a hat: Christian Holstein, Elias Mars, and Samuel Spiker. The town would be christened with the name from the winning draw. The Spiker store (pictured) not only stocked necessities the community might need, but also hosted social events, dancing, boxing matches, elections, and various activities held above the store. In the fall of 1963, the store closed. It was torn down in 1970.

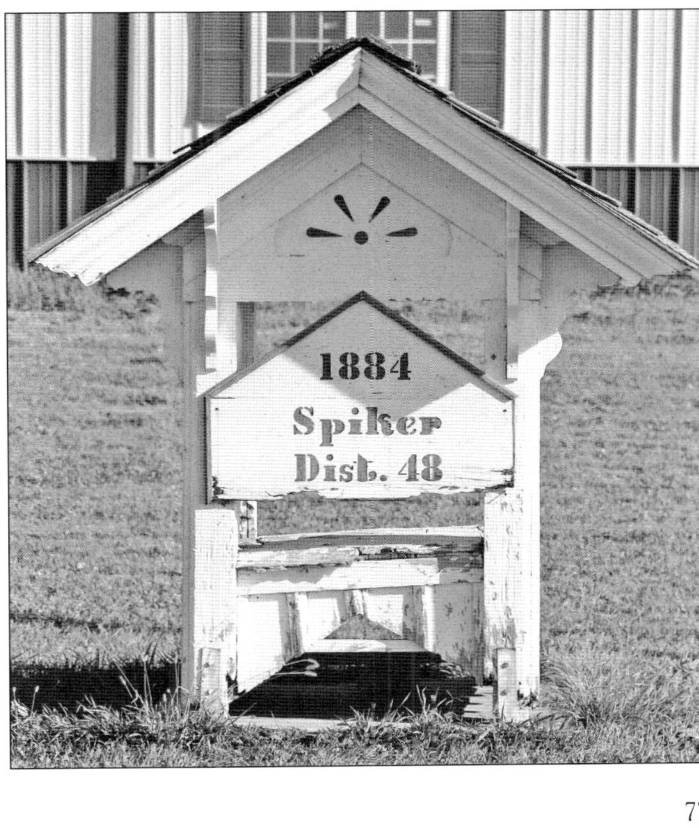

Bob Rasmussen, the grandson of Rasmus and Petrina Karstad Rasmussen (immigrants from Denmark and pioneers in Spiker), bought the school property when the school closed. He recycled the lumber, constructing two additional rooms onto his home. The belfry was repaired, painted, and moved to the exact spot where the schoolhouse sat, proudly relating its history. Today, remnants of the old gas station and a few houses are all that remain of the town.

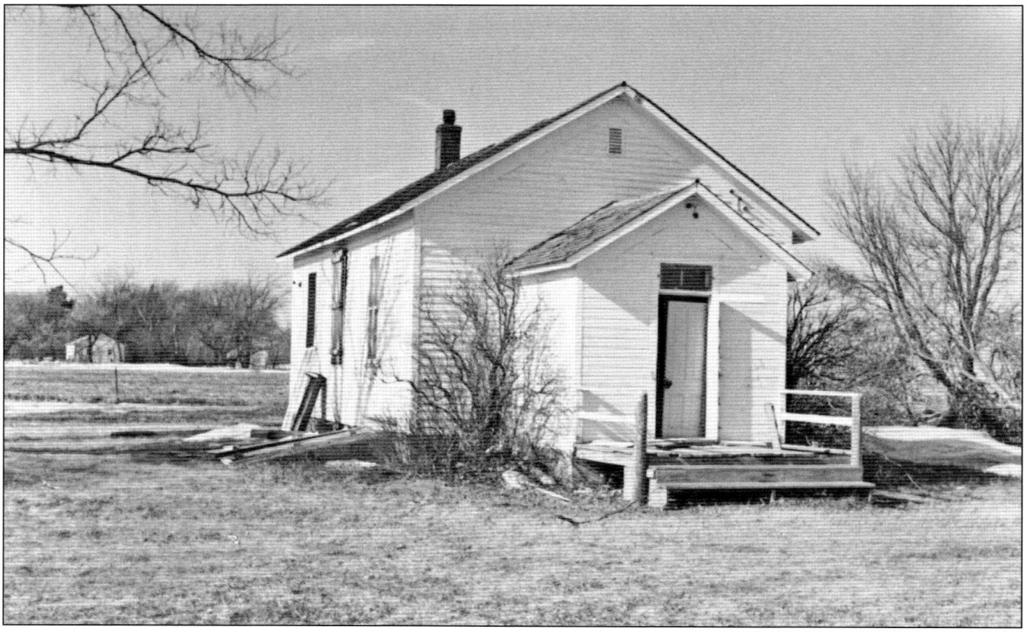

Vacoma was a village located about nine miles southwest of Herman and a few miles west of Spiker. It took its name from the first letters of the names of three early settlers: James Van Valin, Vital Coupal, and Malcom Cameron. The Vacoma School, built in 1874, continued as a rural school, teaching area children for nearly 100 years and long after the village was gone, before it was disbanded in 1970.

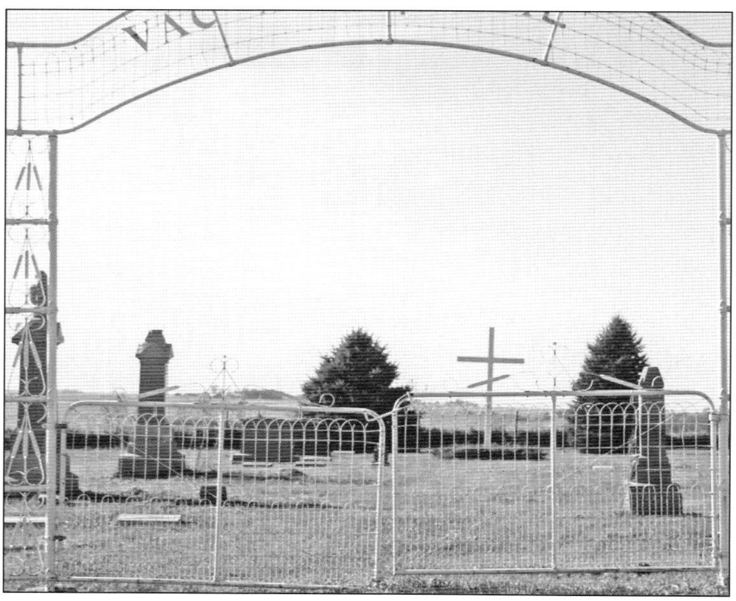

St. John's German Evangelical Lutheran Church of Vacoma was started in the home of Ernest Meier in March 1893, after the original church burned. The church officially closed on February 12, 1963, and was later razed. Today, the cemetery remains as the only testimony of this early settlement's existence.

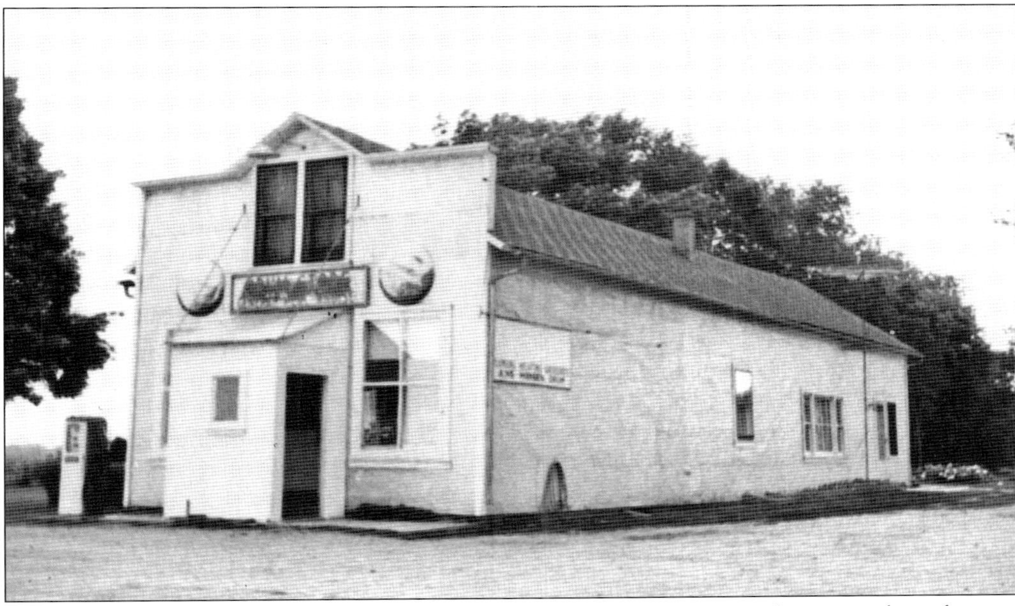

Shortly before the community of Orum was established, there was a settlement eight miles west of Blair, in the neighborhood of present-day Orum, called Andersenville. By this time, Neils Anderson had established a store, and a blacksmith and a few settlers had moved in. In 1890, Andersen sold his business to Robert Orum, a post office was established, and the name Orum was recorded. The Orum store closed in the 1980s.

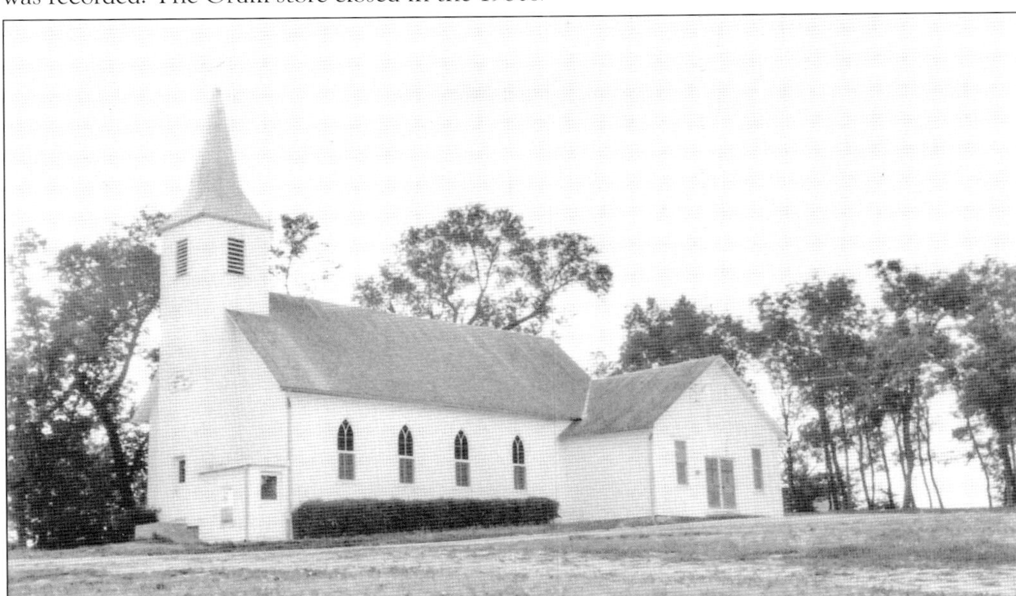

St. Paul's Lutheran Evangelical Church was built east of the church cemetery in 1882. In the 1890s, a dispute over whether Christians should belong to secret lodges caused some parishioners to organize a new congregation, building a church west of the cemetery. In 1953, with a name change to Immanuel Lutheran, the church was moved to St. Paul's and attached, combining the two parishes. The church still serves the rural community.

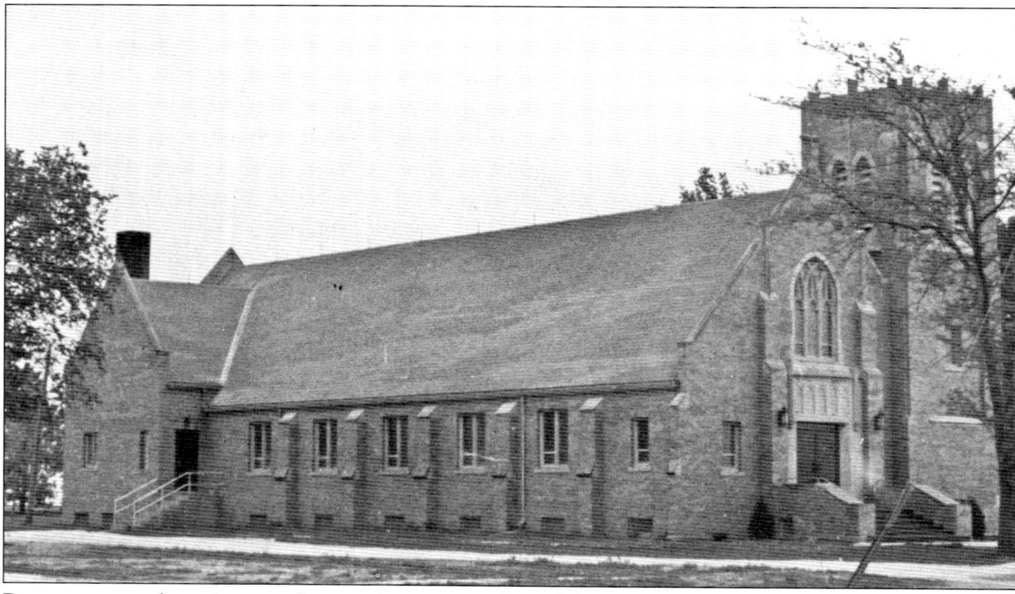

Pioneers were locating on the rural western edge of the county bordering with Dodge County by 1866 and were being visited by Lutheran missionaries in private homes as early as 1869. In 1876, the Immanuel Lutheran Church was organized and a church built. On May 11, 1952, a new church (pictured) was dedicated. Immanuel Lutheran continues to serve parishioners in the surrounding two counties.

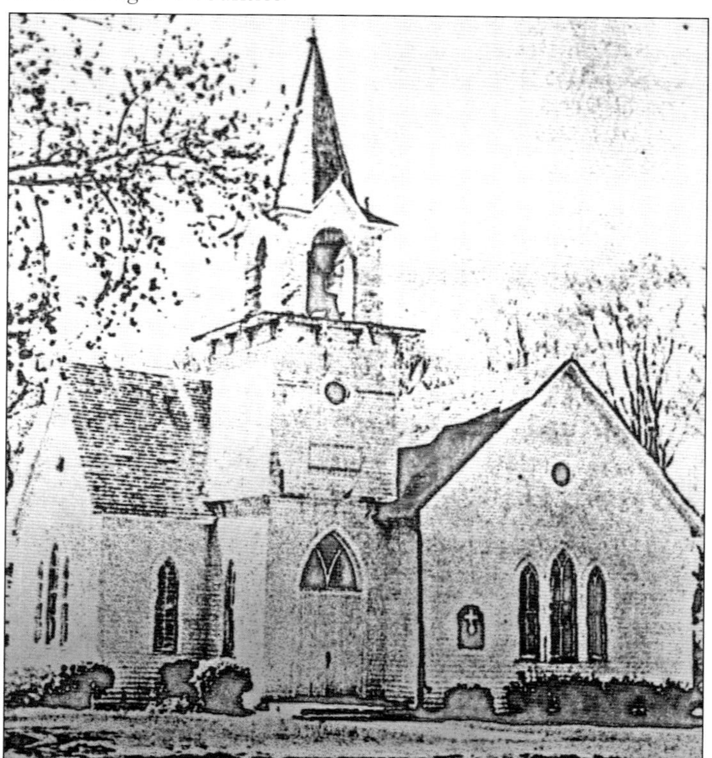

Telbasta, located north of Arlington near Fontanelle, was established in 1880, when a store was opened by Conrad Fulrodt. The Salem Congregational of the Evangelical Alliance was formed in 1876, and a church was built in 1880. In 1968, the church merged with the Methodist church. The congregation celebrated its 95th anniversary in 1971. In 1973, the congregation disbanded. The church that adjoined the cemetery was later torn down.

Telbasta's school opened in 1870. In 1961, a new modern school was built one mile south of the old school and opened with 38 pupils. The school was the last country school to be built, and by 1981 it was one of six country schools remaining in the county. A dozen houses and cemetery stand as testimony to the village's existence.

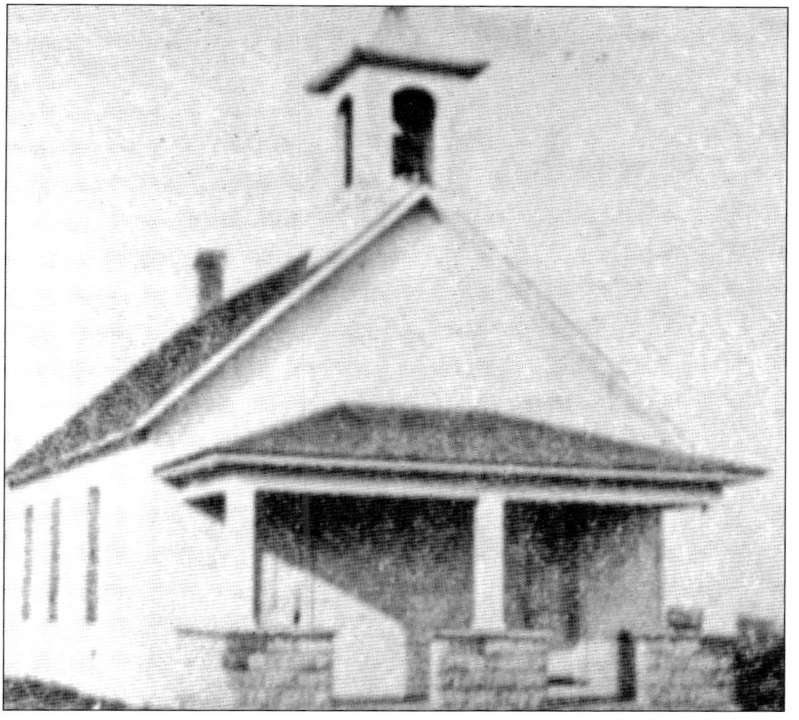

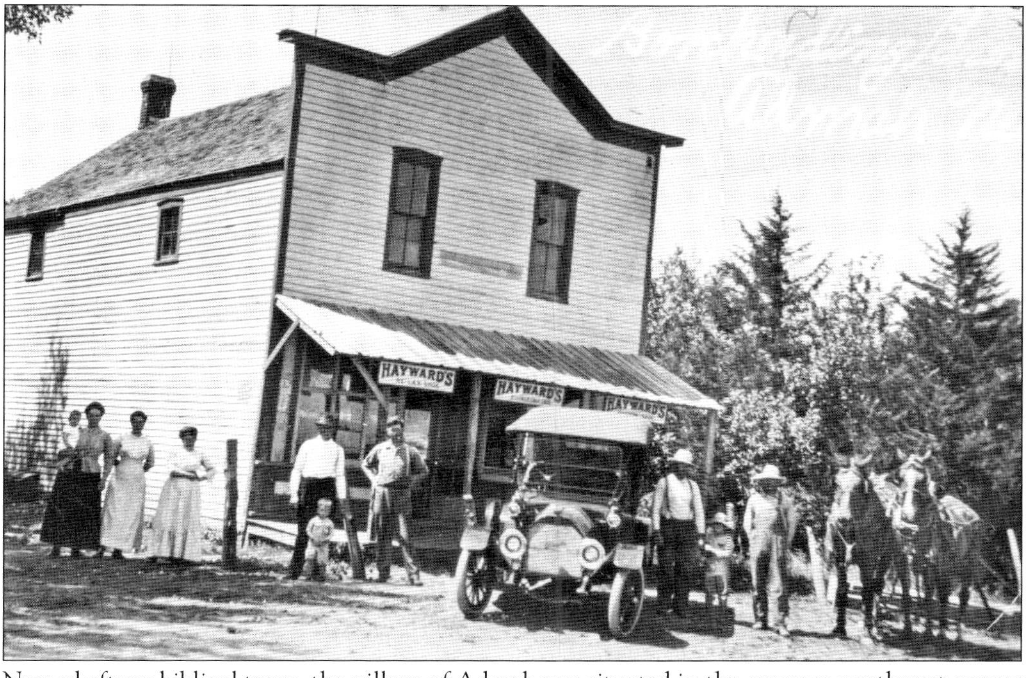

Named after a biblical town, the village of Admah was situated in the extreme northwest corner of Washington County. The village dates to 1867 and had a general store, blacksmith, creamery, a good schoolhouse costing $700, a Presbyterian and a Lutheran church, one physician, and 100 inhabitants. The store was a center of activity and entertainment until it closed in 1922.

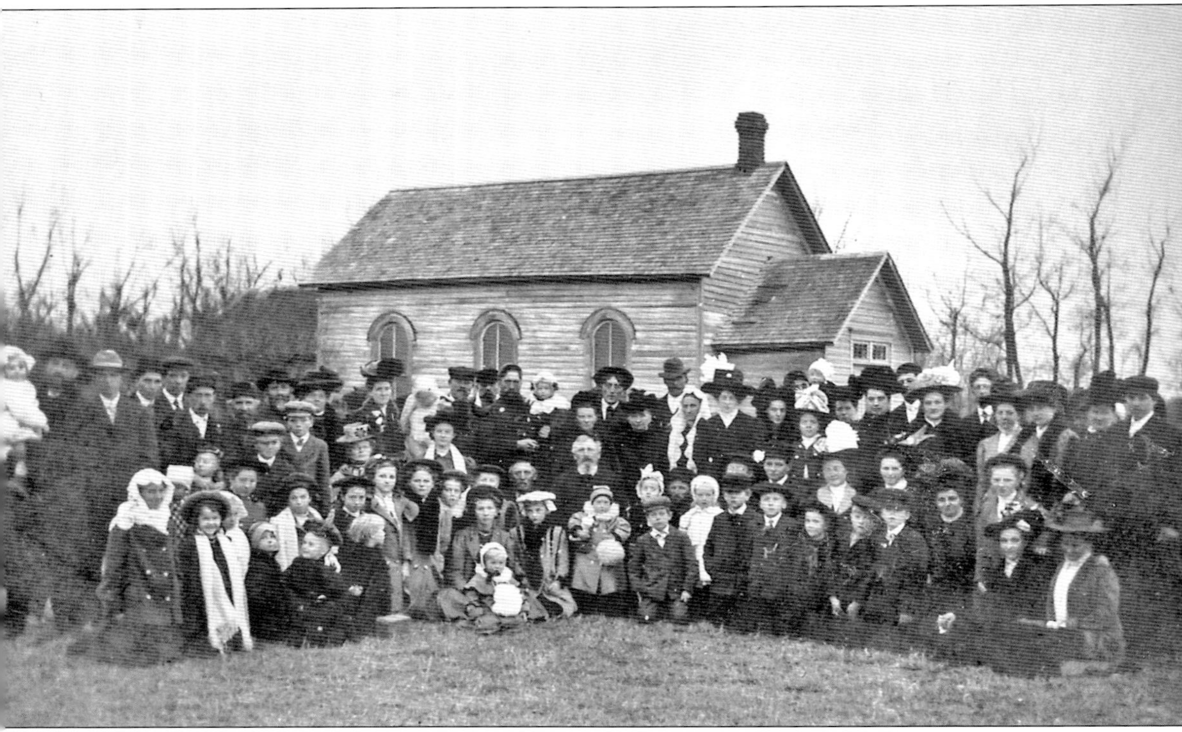

According to the book *Washington County History*, the early pioneers who chose to make Admah their home were the Cook, Hayes, Brokaw, Hewett, Peterson, and Dams families. Gustave Pegan was the first settler. By 1874, the little village had grown and the St. Johannes Danish Evangelical Church was organized. George Simpson built the church as well as the schoolhouse. Services were held once a month by a visiting pastor who came from the nearby railroad towns. The parish established a cemetery west of the village in 1879, and in 1909 an addition was built onto the church. In a common story to be told across the prairie, the village was not to last. The original pioneers were gone, families were moving away, and no one was moving to the community. The last church service was held in 1929, and the congregation disbanded. The Admah and the West Admah Cemeteries are the only visible signs of this community's existence, paying tribute to the families who settled in this area.

Four

Pride of a Community

From Hardships to Prosperity

People came. They settled. And they prospered. By 1900, the American frontier was a thing of the past. Washington County grew and by 1870 had 4,452 people, with nearly 12,000 by 1890. As the calendar flipped over marking a new century, local communities were moving into their golden anniversary. In 1900, Washington County had 13,000 residents. Brick paving of streets began in 1921. Dirt roads were graveled in 1927. The first paved road in Washington County was the highway that extended from the Douglas County line to Fort Calhoun and to Blair in 1933 and north to Herman and the Burt County line later in the year. Business establishments were no longer built of wood but of brick. Model Ts were a new mode of transportation. Electricity and street lights illuminated homes and towns. Telephones aided communications. Residents built grand houses and parks and spared no expense for schools in educating their children. Washingtonians were a blend of nationalities who united and were proud of their communities.

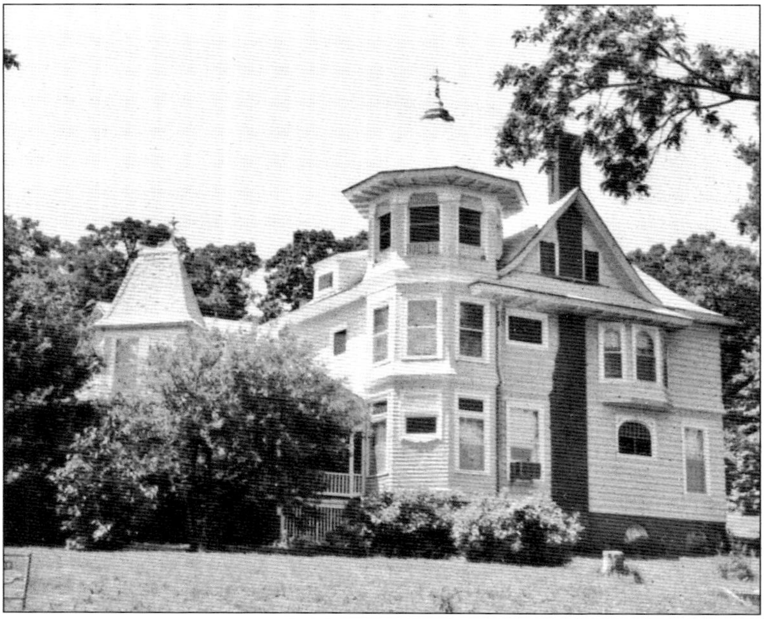

The sod and hewn houses gave way to sturdy frame and brick homes and working farms graced the fields. By 1910, many farmers and prosperous townsfolk had built beautiful homes. The three-story, 21-room J.E. Markel home, built on 300 acres in 1887, overlooks the Missouri River. Many young people earned their first wages working on the estate. The house was sold in 1916.

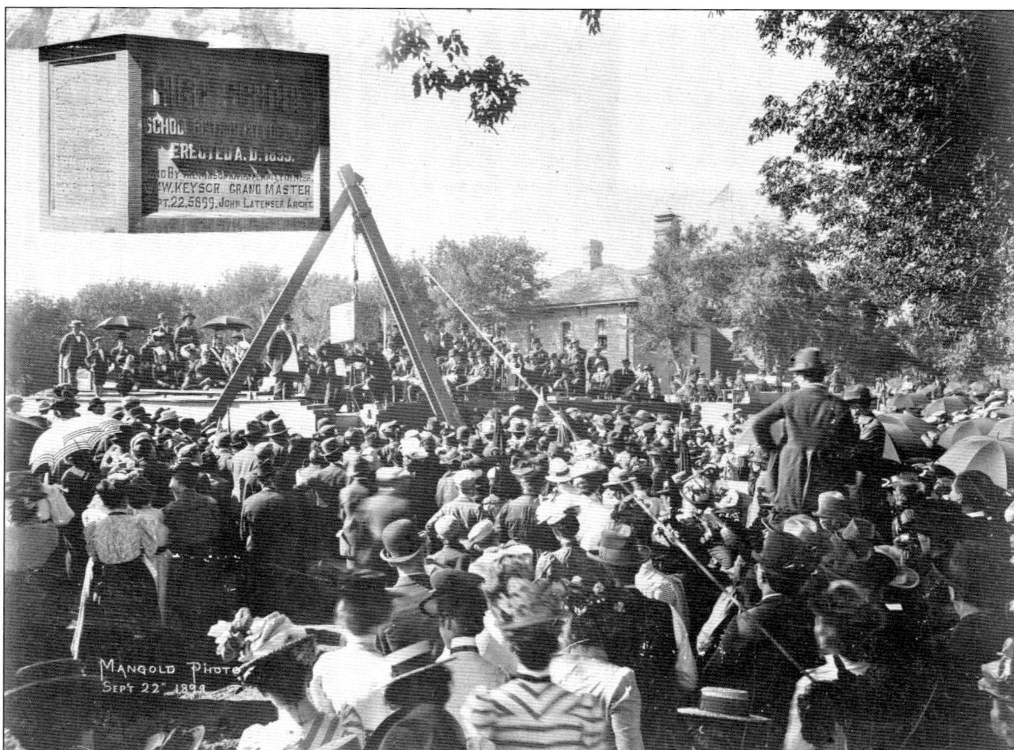

On September 22, 1899, the citizens of Blair dressed in their Sunday best and gathered to witness the social event of the day—the laying of the new high school's cornerstone. The school, built across from the courthouse, was completed in time for the next fall term and christened Central High School.

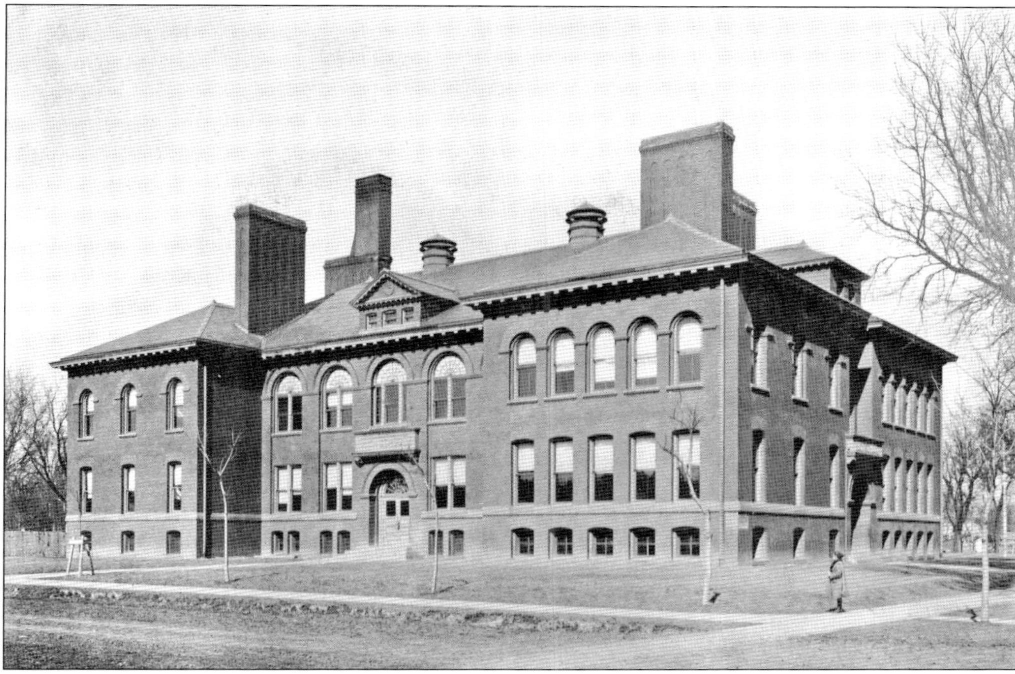

The new Blair High School was constructed in the Richardsonian Romanesque style of hard burned red brick and red sandstone trim for about $40,000. A large assembly hall on the third floor required a roof span of 60 feet and a metal ceiling that included an ornate cornice. Over the years, the school campus would have many face-lifts.

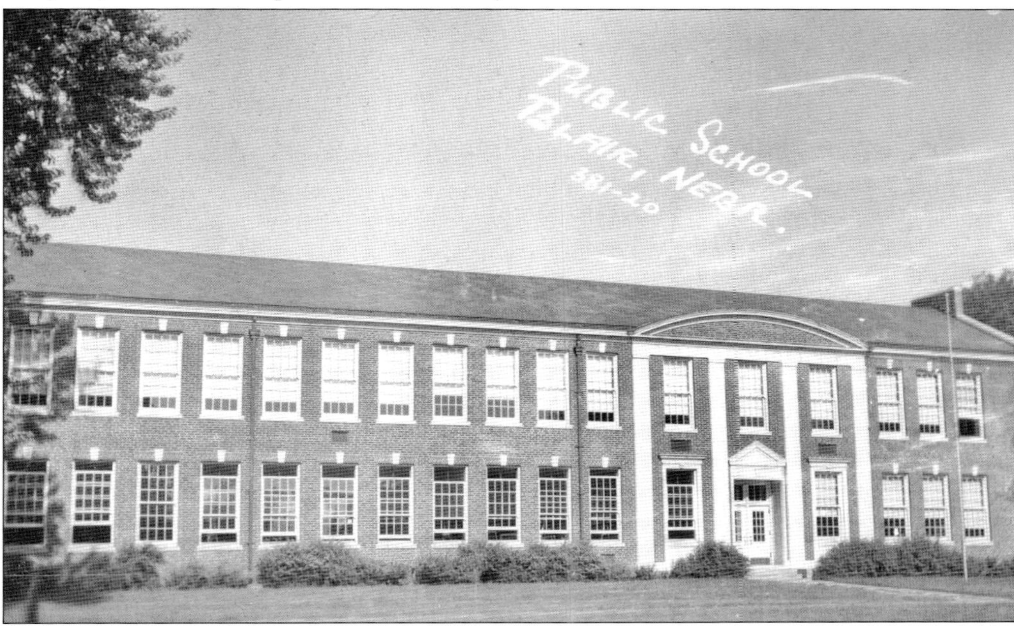

In 1929, a new modern Colonial Revival–style high school was built just north of the 1899 Blair school. The last class graduated in 1970 and this became a lower grade school until it was closed and sold at auction. The school has been refurbished as an apartment building.

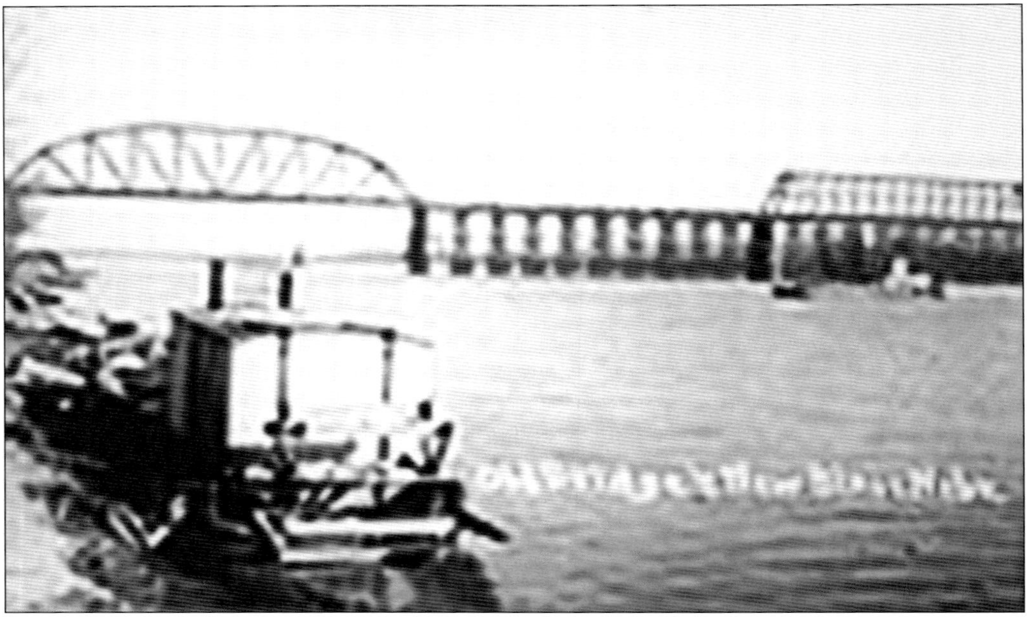

The crossing over the Missouri River between the states of Iowa and Nebraska, in Blair, has been a railroad crossing since the pioneer days. In 1924, the railroad bridge spanning the river and built in 1883, was replaced and a more rounded trestle was used, as shown in this photograph taken during construction.

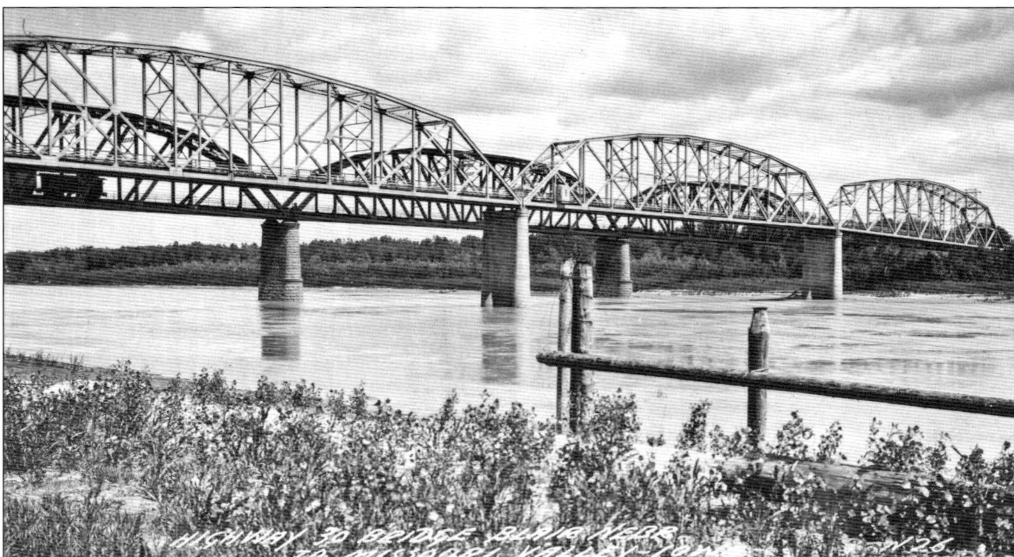

By 1925, with the completion of the new railroad bridge, the City of Blair began serious talk of building another bridge crossing the Missouri River. Since the founding of the town, Blair had no vehicle or pedestrian bridge crossing the river into Iowa. One of the most expensive bridges ever constructed over the Missouri River opened for traffic on June 29, 1929. The new Pennsylvania truss bridge shortened the route of crossing into Iowa—and without the need of a ferry. The photograph shows the two new bridges.

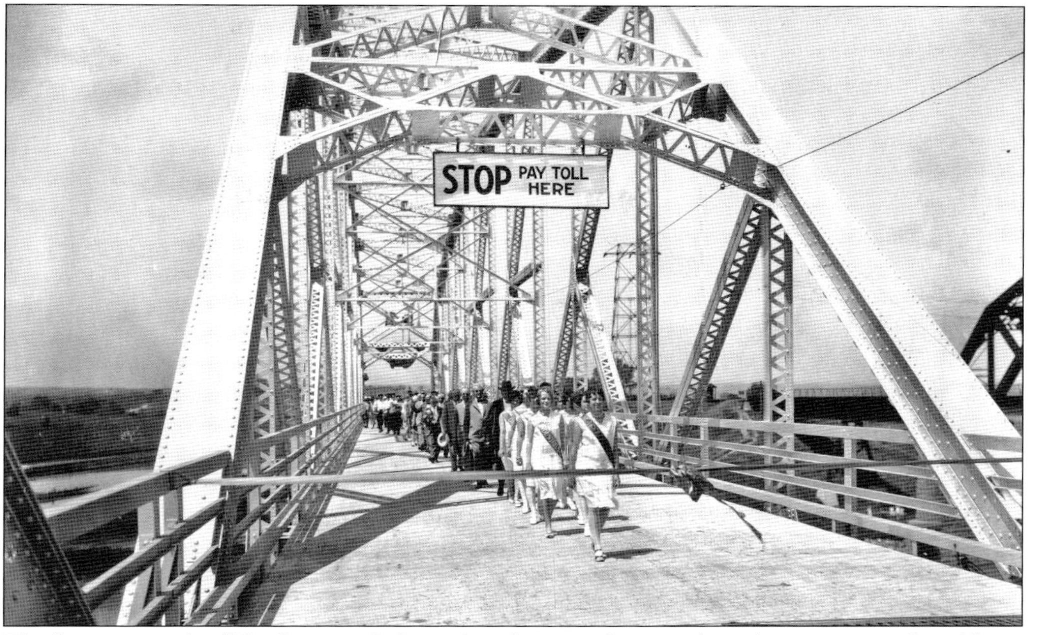

The long-awaited toll bridge was dedicated with a parade, speeches, dignitaries, and a ribbon-cutting ceremony. The tolls were later removed and, in 1991, the bridge was demolished and a new, modern one built.

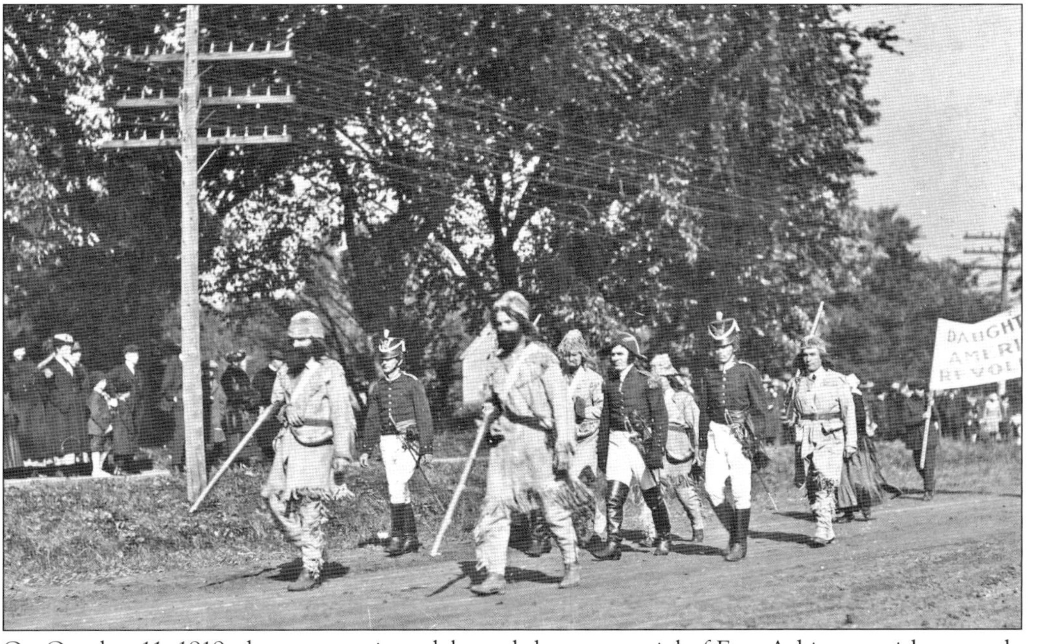

On October 11, 1919, the community celebrated the centennial of Fort Atkinson with a parade and reenactments of soldiers and fur traders. With a crowd of 5,000 spectators, it was the largest celebration held in the county. Thousands came from outside the county, including Army regiments from Fort Crook in Omaha.

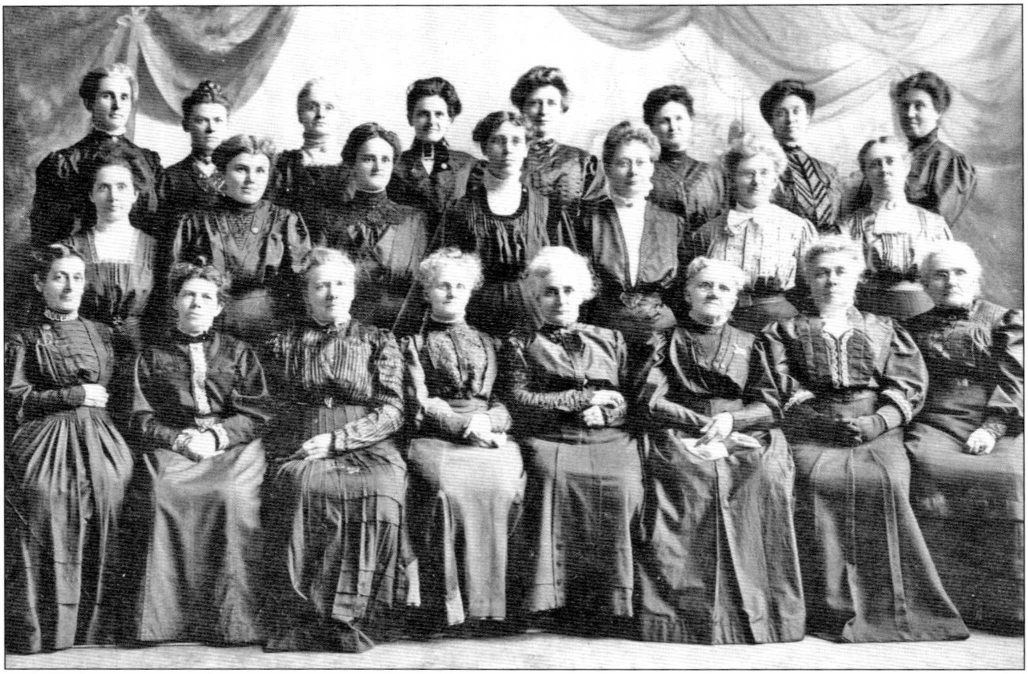

Believed to be the oldest cultural club in Nebraska, the Monday Afternoon Club of Blair first met in late 1876. Although begun as a study club leaning toward book and play reviews, the club evolved to include discussions of current events and important issues facing the country. With membership declining in the 2000s, the club voted to disband in April 2009, one hundred thirty-three years after its founding.

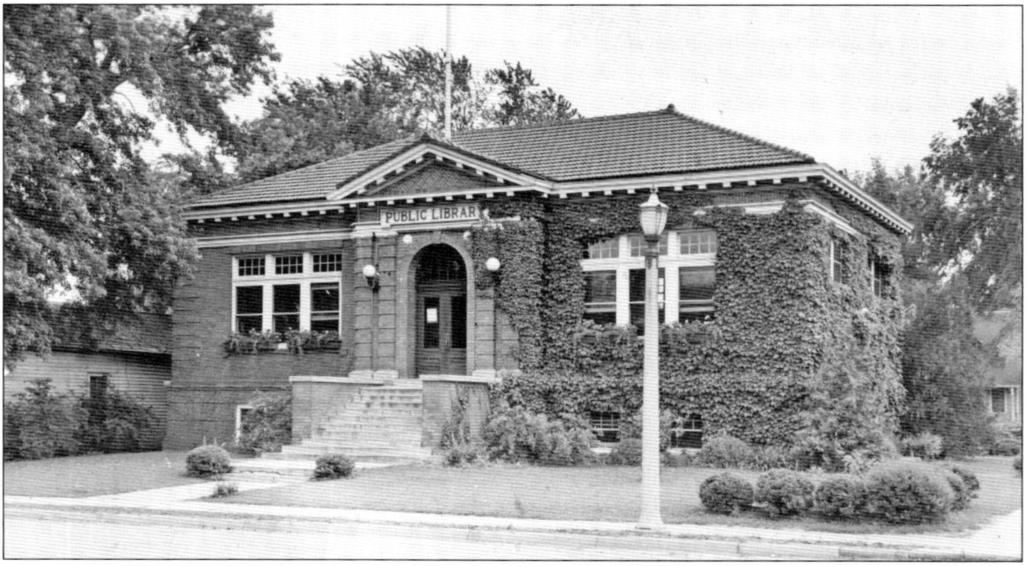

In 1877, the Ladies Library Association was formed in Blair. The Monday Afternoon Club waged a campaign to have a permanent library. In 1916, the cornerstone of the Carnegie library was laid and the first building purposely built as a public library opened on October 16, 1917, with an inventory of 5,000 books. Fire destroyed the library in 1973, and in 1976 a new library was built.

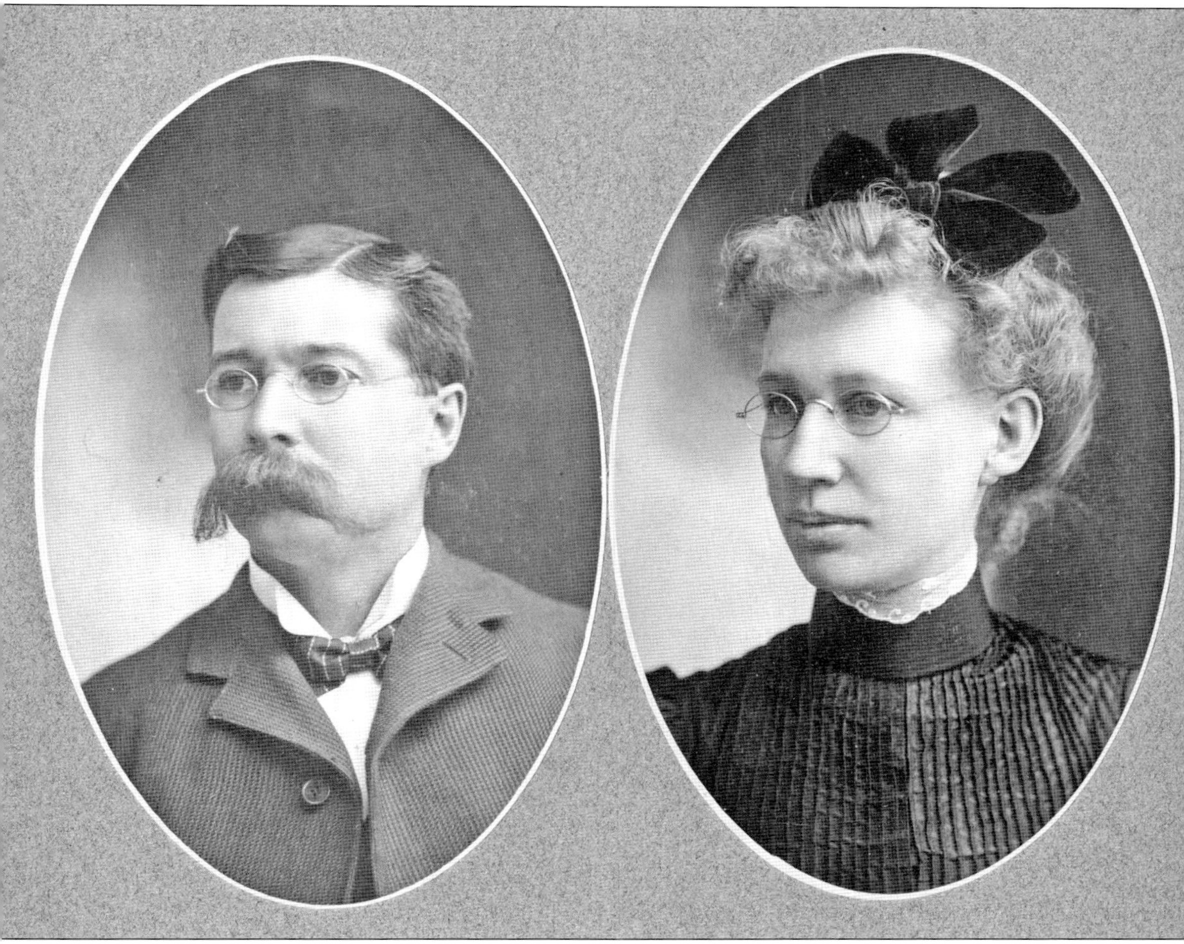

In 1890, Clarence Vail, self-schooled, started a business repairing watches and jewelry in Weber's Drug Store, expanding his services to include the testing of eyesight. In 1900, he established a photography studio. In his studio, Vail ran a telephone switchboard that he built himself, stringing a phone line from his home to other residences in the community. This evolved into the Arlington Telephone Company in 1902. In 1908, a large commercial switchboard and phones were purchased and installed in Vail's home. Phone lines were strung to rural customers. Clarence Vail's determination to better the town of Arlington continued with the founding of the light plant. Viola Vail operated the photography studio on the second floor of their home and was known for traveling the community and surrounding area taking pictures of people and events.

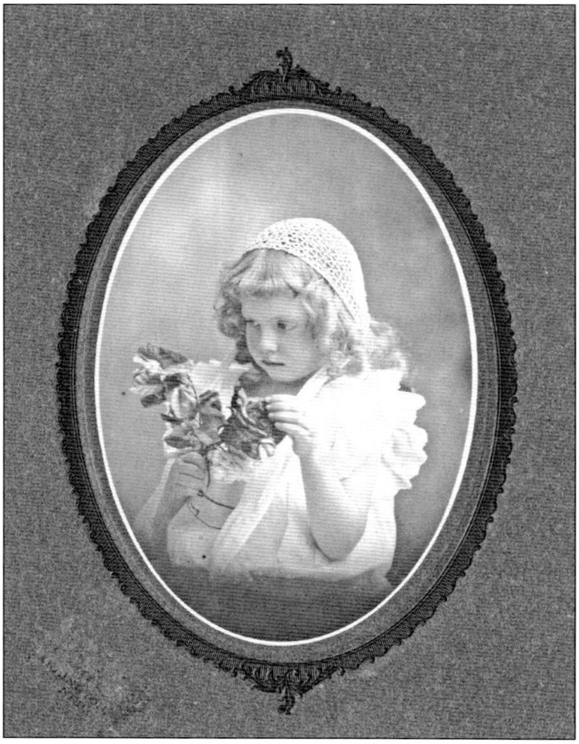

Viola Vail especially enjoyed photographing children. Many homes had family pictures displayed that were taken in her studio. The image at left depicts Bernice Vail, photographed by her mother.

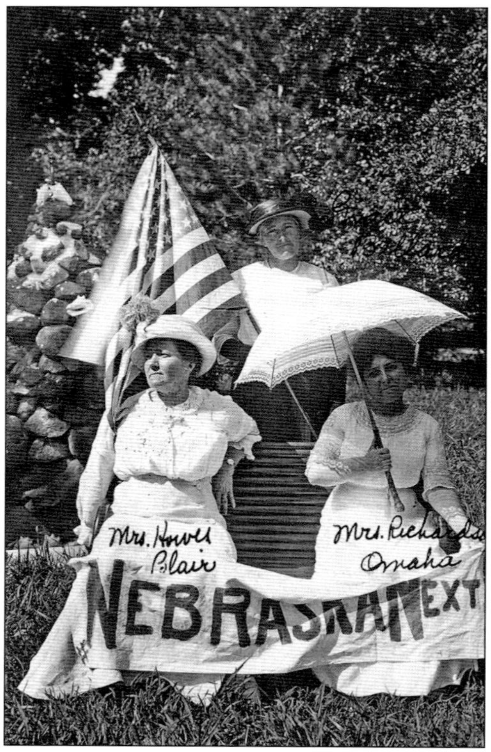

Grace Ballard (center) and two fellow suffragettes are pictured around 1916 campaigning for women's right to vote. Born in 1877, Ballard was an advocate for women's suffrage. She graduated from the University of Nebraska law school in 1914, practiced law in Blair, and became the first female Washington County attorney and was the first to fulfill that role in Nebraska, serving three terms. (Courtesy the Nebraska State Historical Society.)

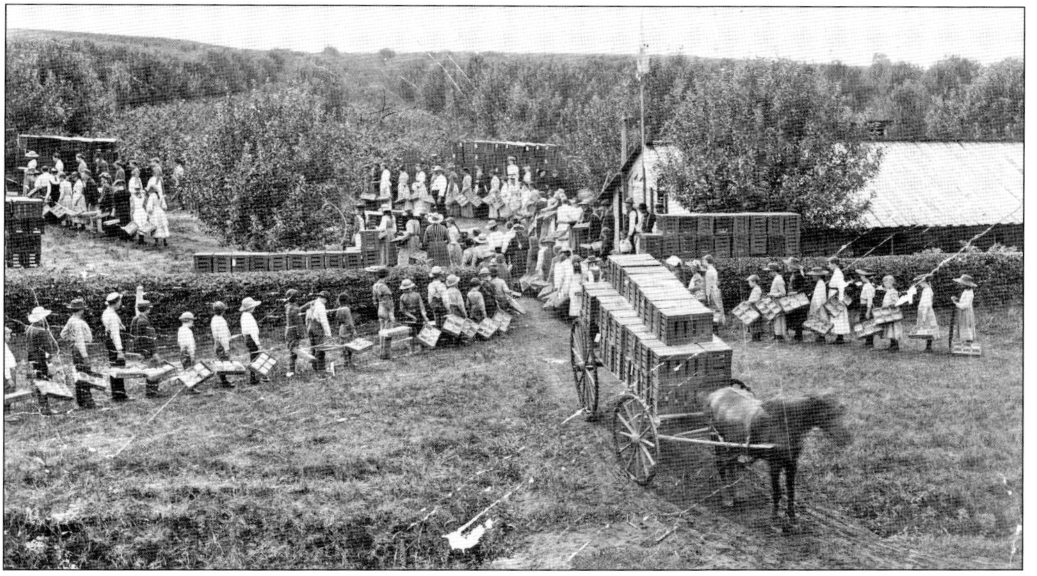

The Mount Hope Fruit Farm was started by William McCormick, who planted an orchard south of Blair. The fruit business grew, shipping fruit by rail around the state or canned at the Blair canning factory. In peak season, the farm employed as many as 200 people. The Armistice Day Freeze of 1940 destroyed the orchard. A decision not to reinvest in seedlings resulted in the closing of the business.

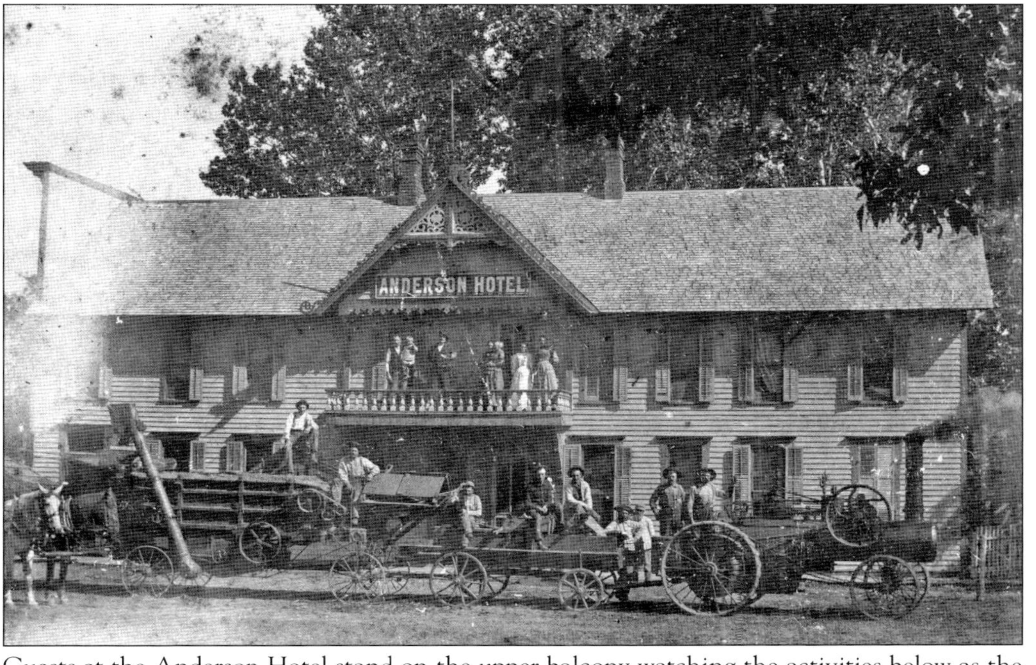

Guests at the Anderson Hotel stand on the upper balcony watching the activities below as the threshing outfit owned by Bill Schmidt passes by. Built before the turn of the 20th century on the old post road and having many owners, the old hotel still serves the public as the Longhorn Bar and Grill, in Fort Calhoun. Its original character is still recognizable.

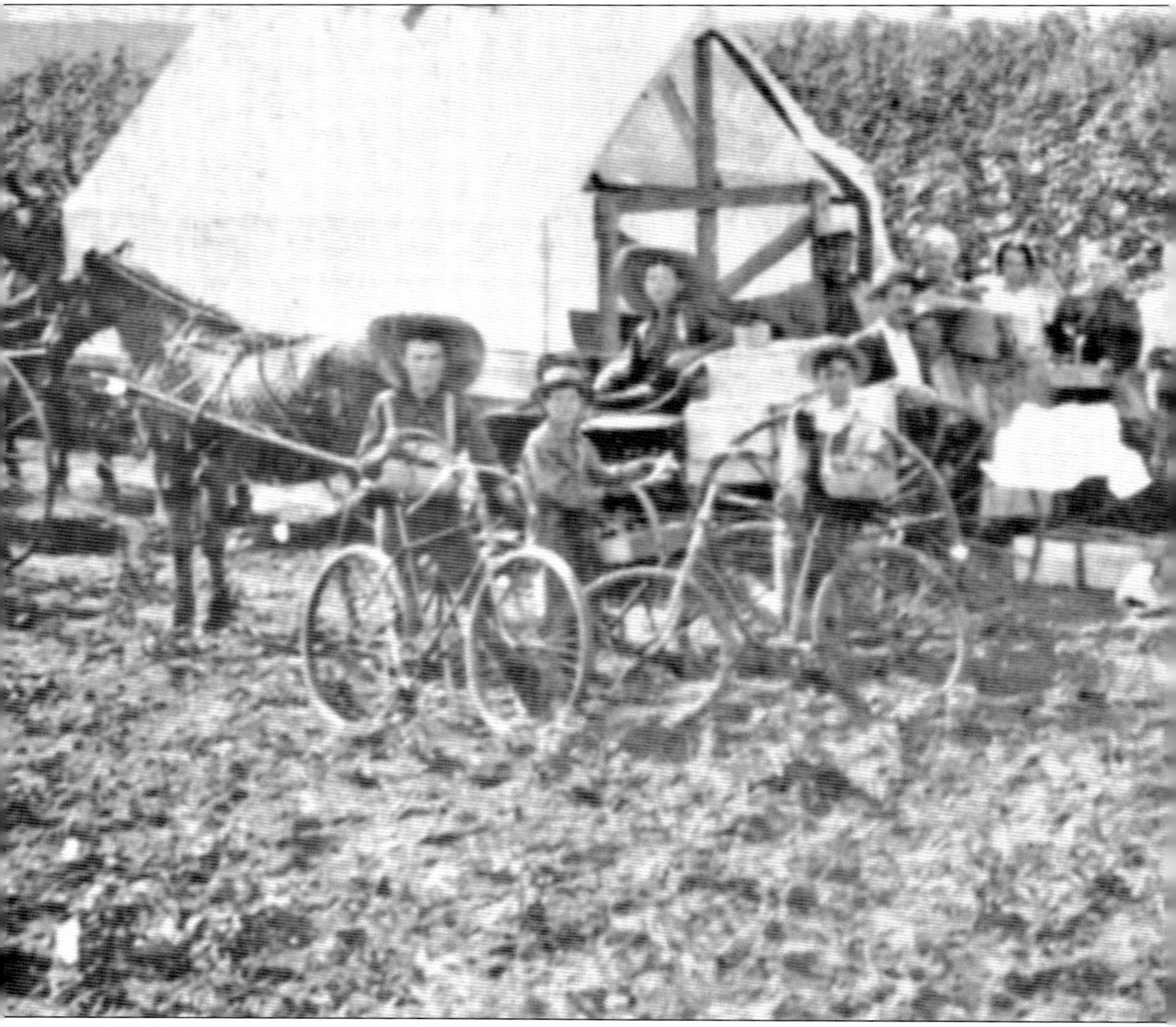

Marshall Nurseries was started in 1887 by brothers Chester Marshall and George Marshall on their family farm, two miles east of Arlington. Shade trees, Osage orange, walnut, evergreens, shrubs, berries, rosebushes, and other varieties of trees were sold and delivered by horse and buggy to customers. Business grew steadily. A showhouse was built in Arlington, and 6,500 trees were planted on 1,200 acres of land. As demand grew, they began to ship outside Washington County, their territory reaching the west central states, and employed 15 nurserymen and 50 salesmen. In

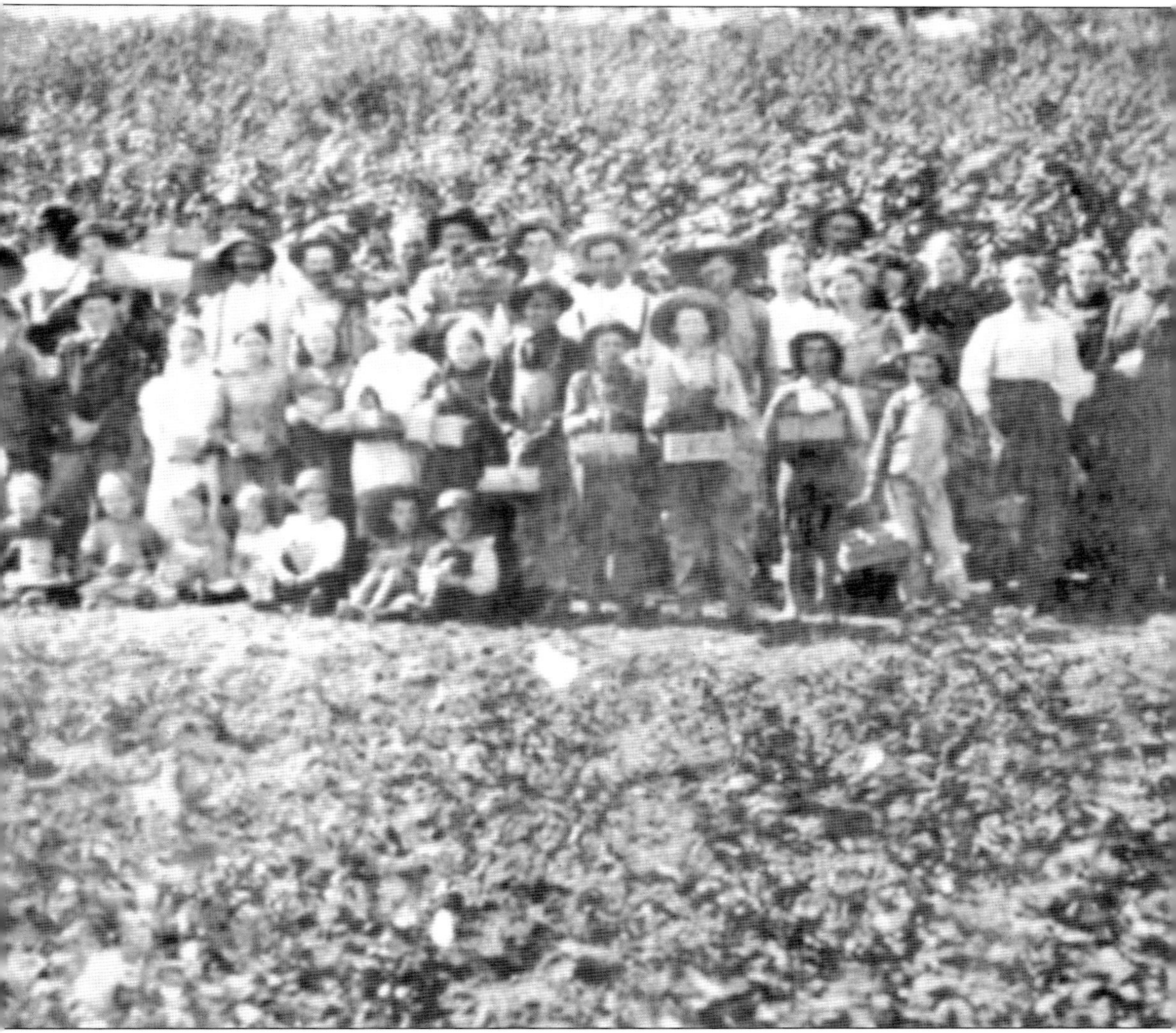

the summer, children and adults arrived early in the morning with their baskets, ready to earn money picking apples and berries on the Marshall farm. Marshall Nurseries was once the largest and oldest nursery west of Chicago. The business closed, but the beauty of Washington County communities has been greatly enriched by the trees planted throughout the landscape. The showhouse still stands in Arlington as a testimony to this once thriving business.

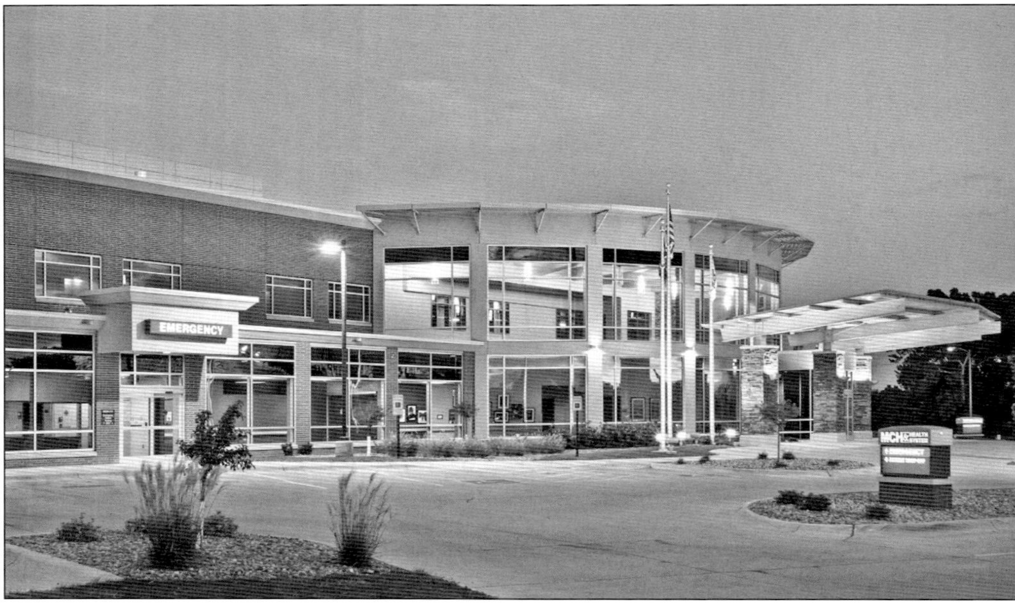

In 1956, the Blair Memorial Hospital opened. Designed as a general medical and surgical center, it serves the communities surrounding Blair and Burt County, replacing the old hospital that had previously served the town of Blair. The hospital auxiliary holds a four-day rummage sale every September on the Washington County fairgrounds; it is the largest rummage sale in the state.

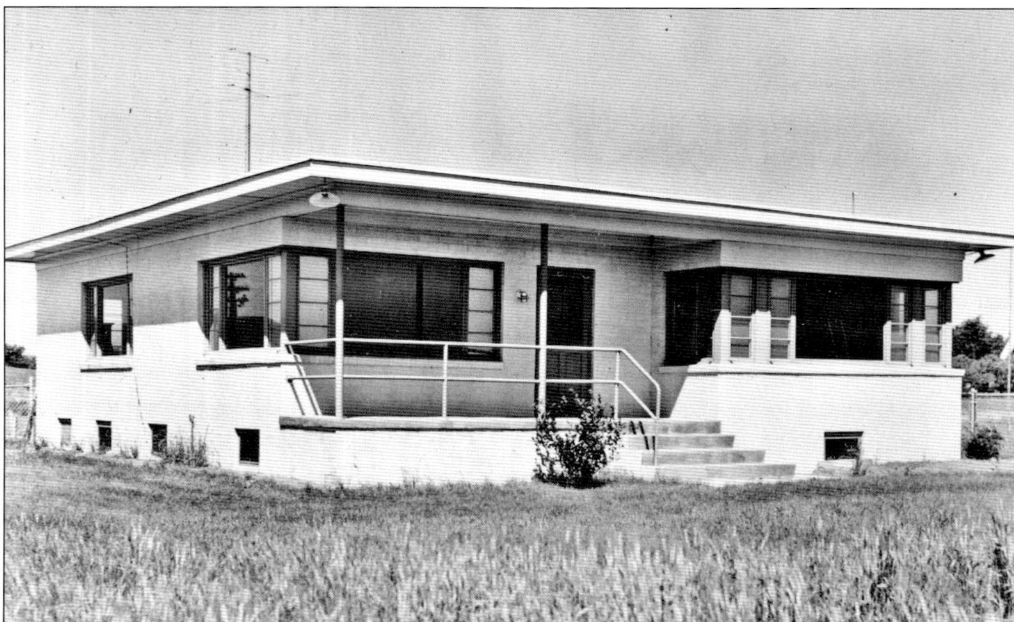

In 1944, a nine-hole golf course was built adjacent to the Blair airport, constructed around the runway. For more than a century, it was a private, members-only course. In the mid-1990s, the airport relocated seven miles south of Blair. The golf course was expanded in 1998 to an 18-hole course and remodeled. In 2001, it was opened as a public course.

Five

United We Stood

Civic Duty

Residents were pioneers and immigrants of European ancestry who migrated west and settled here in search of a better life. They were preoccupied with earning a living and providing for their families, and with possible Indian attacks and surviving their first winters in a new home, but they were equally busy building communities and cities with churches, schools, businesses, and civic offices. They discussed politics and elected city officials and territorial governors to represent them. They fought in wars and flew the American flag. They united.

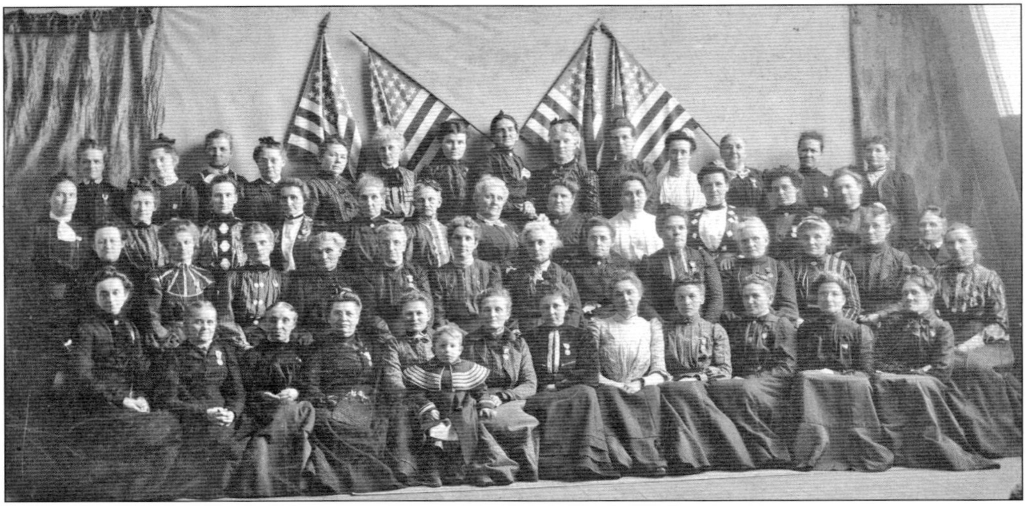

Known as the Grasshoppers Plague of 1873, grasshoppers four to six inches deep destroyed all crops and vegetation, forcing settlers to sell out or abandon their property. As a result, the Nebraska Relief Aid Society was formed in 1874. Blair's chapter took immediate action to help the farming communities, collecting money, clothing, and necessary items to be distributed to the families left destitute by the locusts.

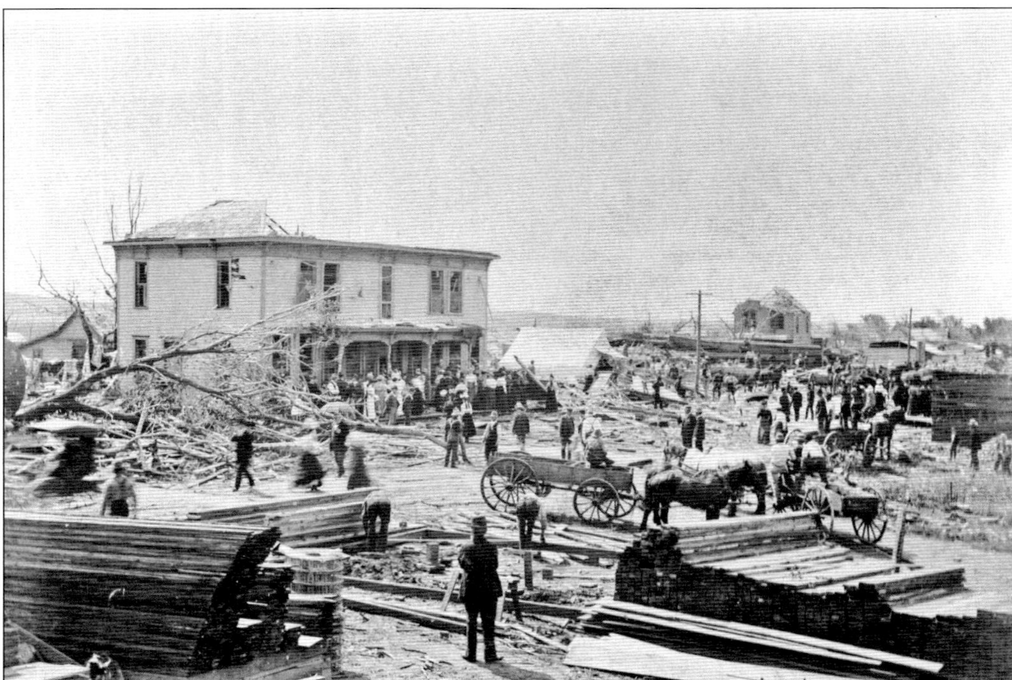

The West Hotel is a lone survivor in this part of Herman, as a tornado exhausted its fury on the town in 1899 and killed 13. The streets were a mass of debris, and hardly any building escaped damage. The town united, buried the dead, and immediately began cleaning up as lumber arrived by wagon and rail to rebuild.

The tornado of 1899, which wiped out a majority of the city of Herman, left the Methodist church standing. In the aftermath of the tornado, it served as a community hospital for the injured and dying. A relief train brought in physicians from Blair and carried back the homeless. The Methodist congregation later merged with the congregation at the First Baptist Church of Herman and Hill Creek Lutheran, forming the Herman Federated Church.

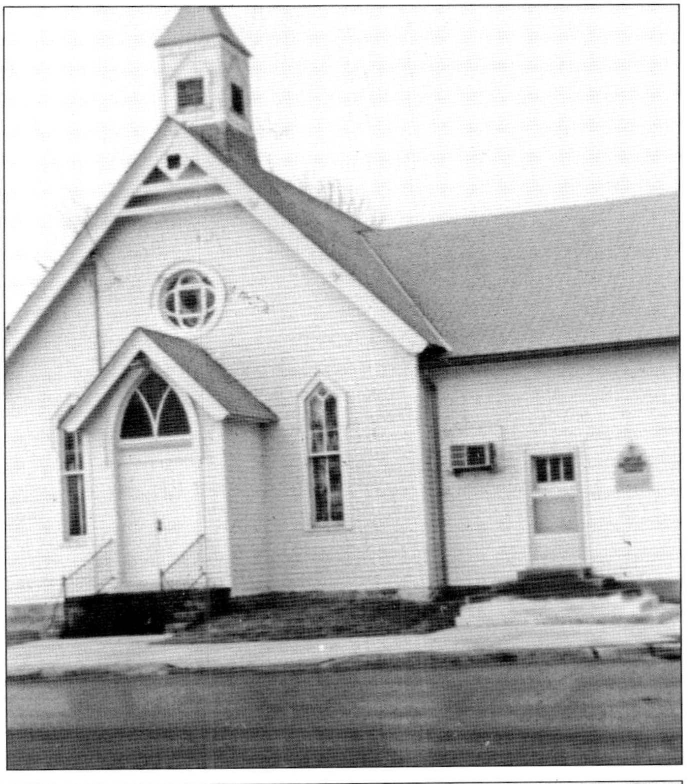

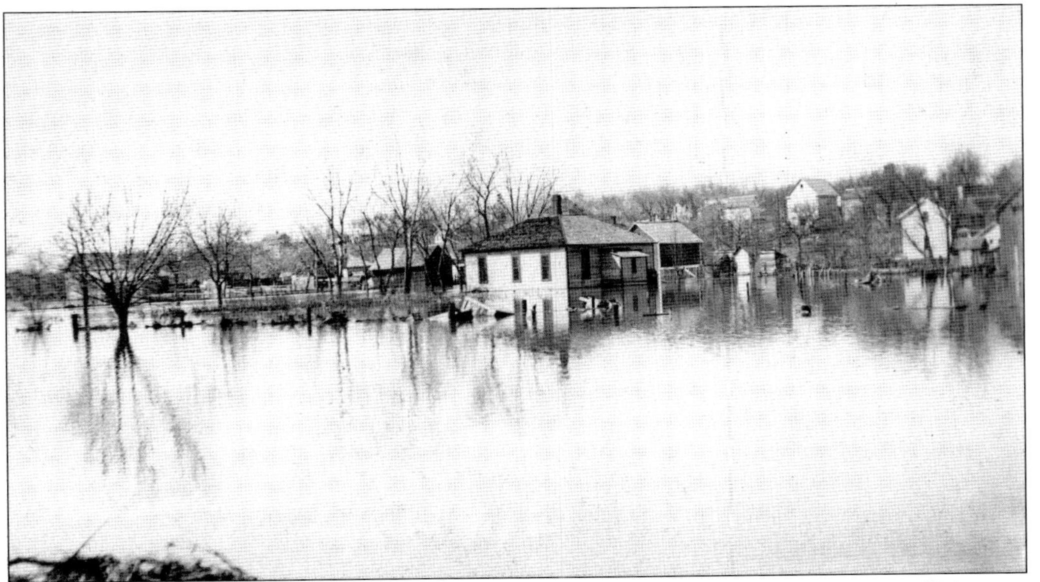

The spring rains and ice thaw threatened floods, with water rising along the Elkhorn and Missouri Rivers. The flood of 1912, in Arlington, was one of many, as residents anxiously waited for the water to subside, hoping there was not much damage. The US Army Corps of Engineers built dams and reservoirs on the Missouri to help control flooding in the bottomlands, but Mother Nature still sends occasional floods.

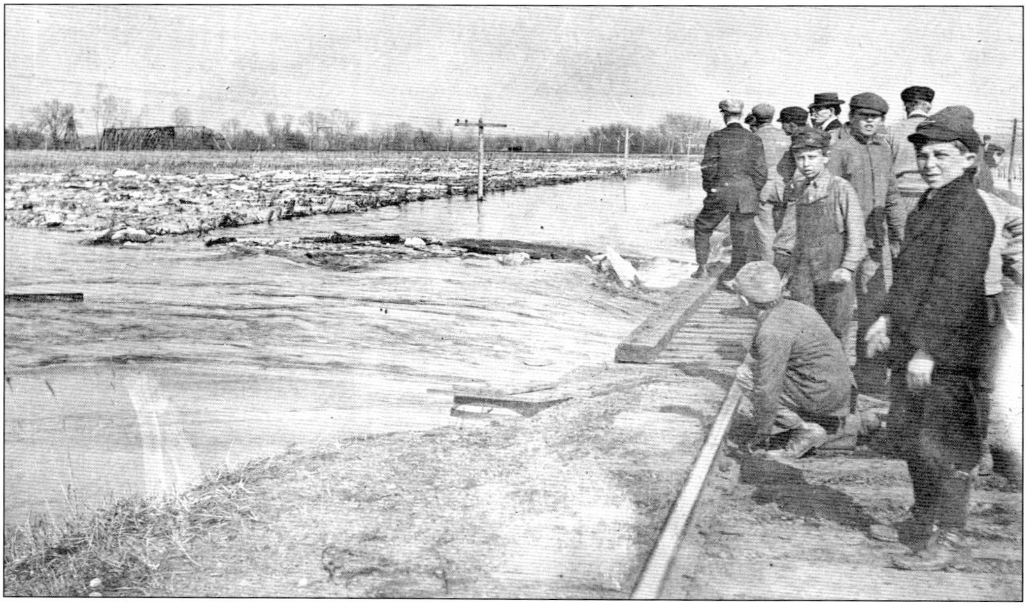

A wet, rainy spring season in 1912 raised the water levels of the Elkhorn River until the water spilled over the banks into the town, carrying mud and anything in its way. Adults and children assess the damage after floodwaters buckled rails, disrupting freight and passenger traffic along the railroad tracks in Arlington.

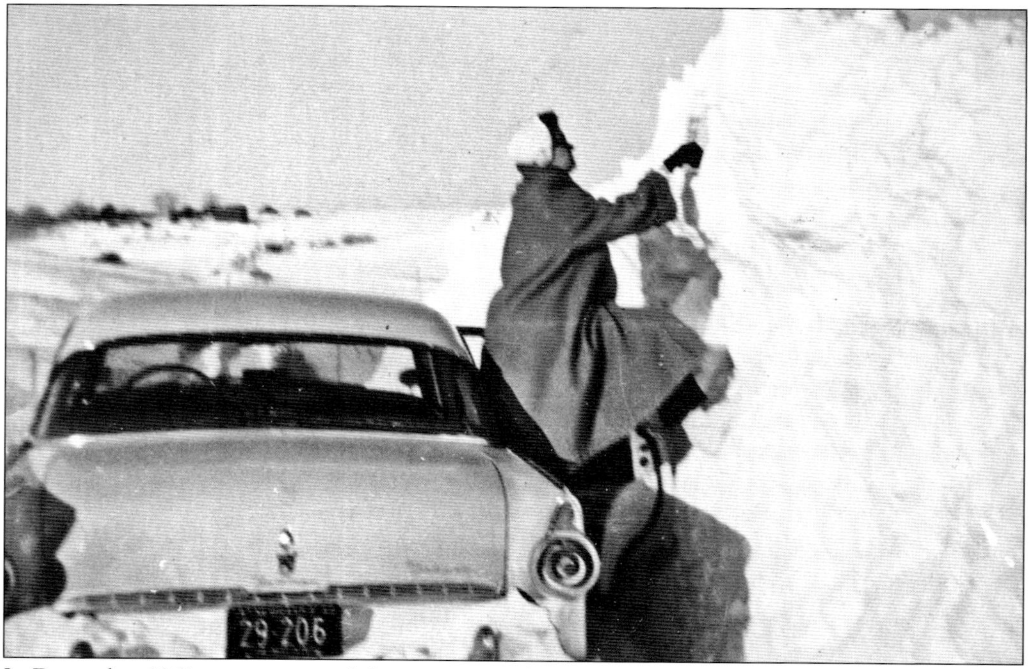

In December 1961, a snowstorm did not stop Hartha Harrison from delivering mail. The blizzards of 1856, 1888, and 1949 were also winters remembered. Note the license plate prefix of 29. In Nebraska's license plate system, Washington County had the 29th-largest number of registered vehicles when the system was introduced in 1922. All but three counties use the prefix system.

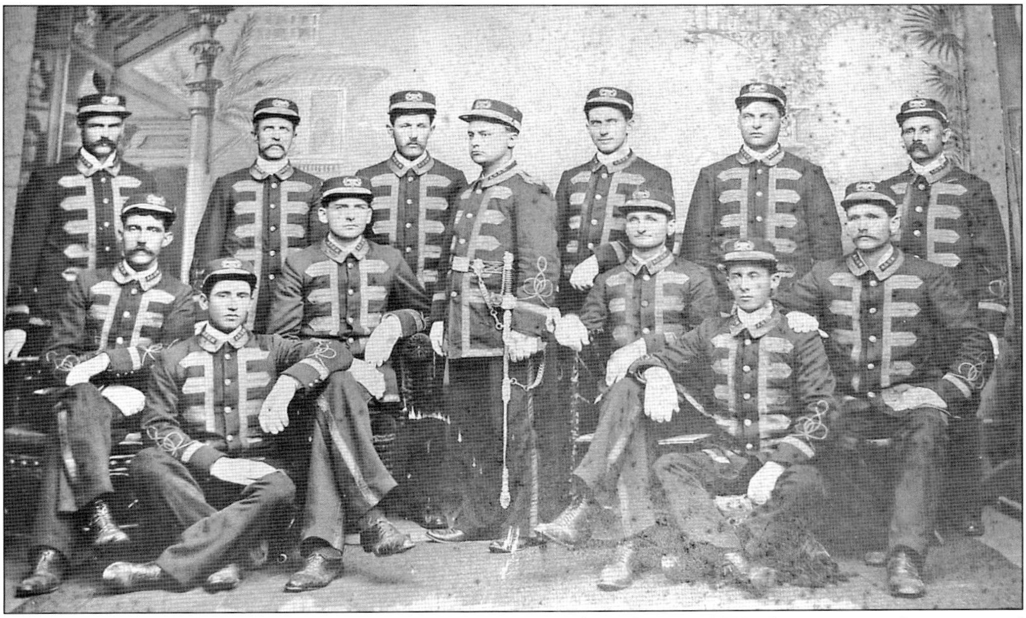

The Herman Drill Team, Lodge No. 237, Ancient Order of United Workman, was champion of the Nebraska State Fair, in Lincoln, Nebraska, on September 4, 1900. Pictured from left to right are members (first row) Charles F. Snyder and H.A. Davis; (second row) H.B. Cameron, G.R. Gray, J.B. Lowe, and Huit Lowe; (third row) G.O. Yowell, Charles Cross Jr., C.B. Baum, George M. Lydick, Captain, Capt. H.L. Hansen, John Mead, and Louis Adams.

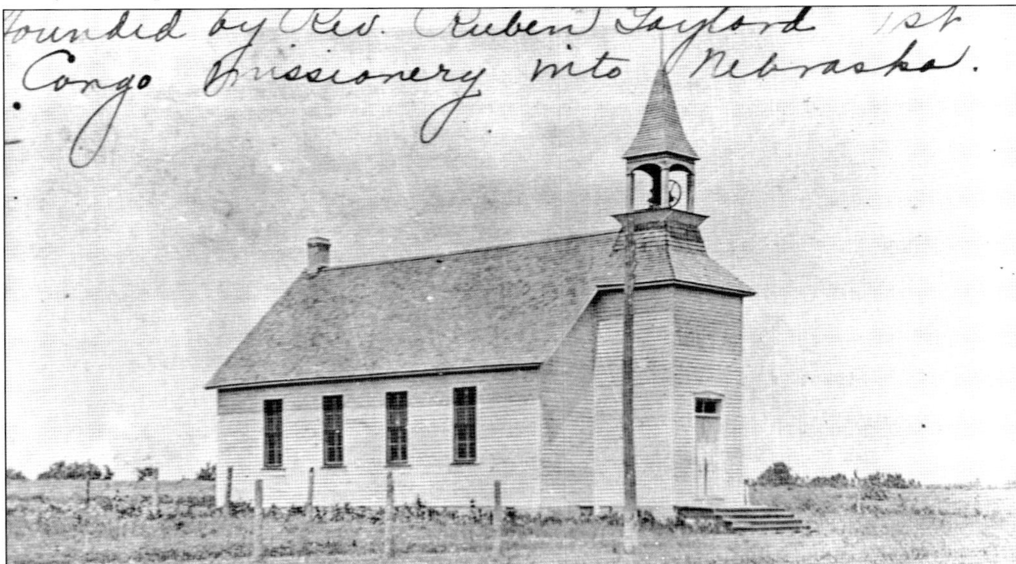

In 1856, the Congregational church located at Fontanelle. The American Sunday School Union was the oldest missionary society in America doing pioneer work. In 1916, a union Sunday school was organized at Fontanelle in the old Congregational church building by Missionary Robinson. He established a total of 13 known union schools in Washington County, organizing Sunday schools as late as 1935.

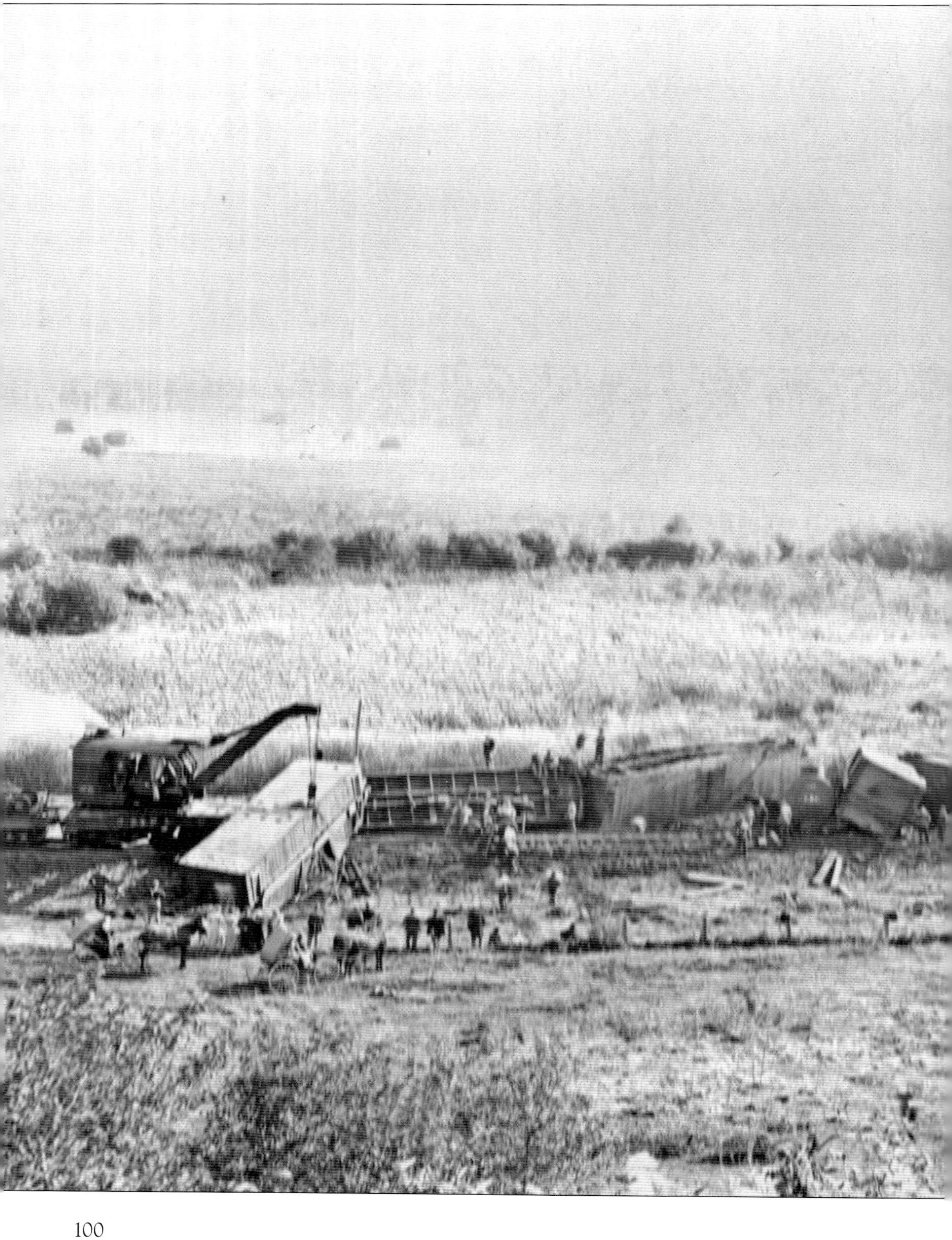

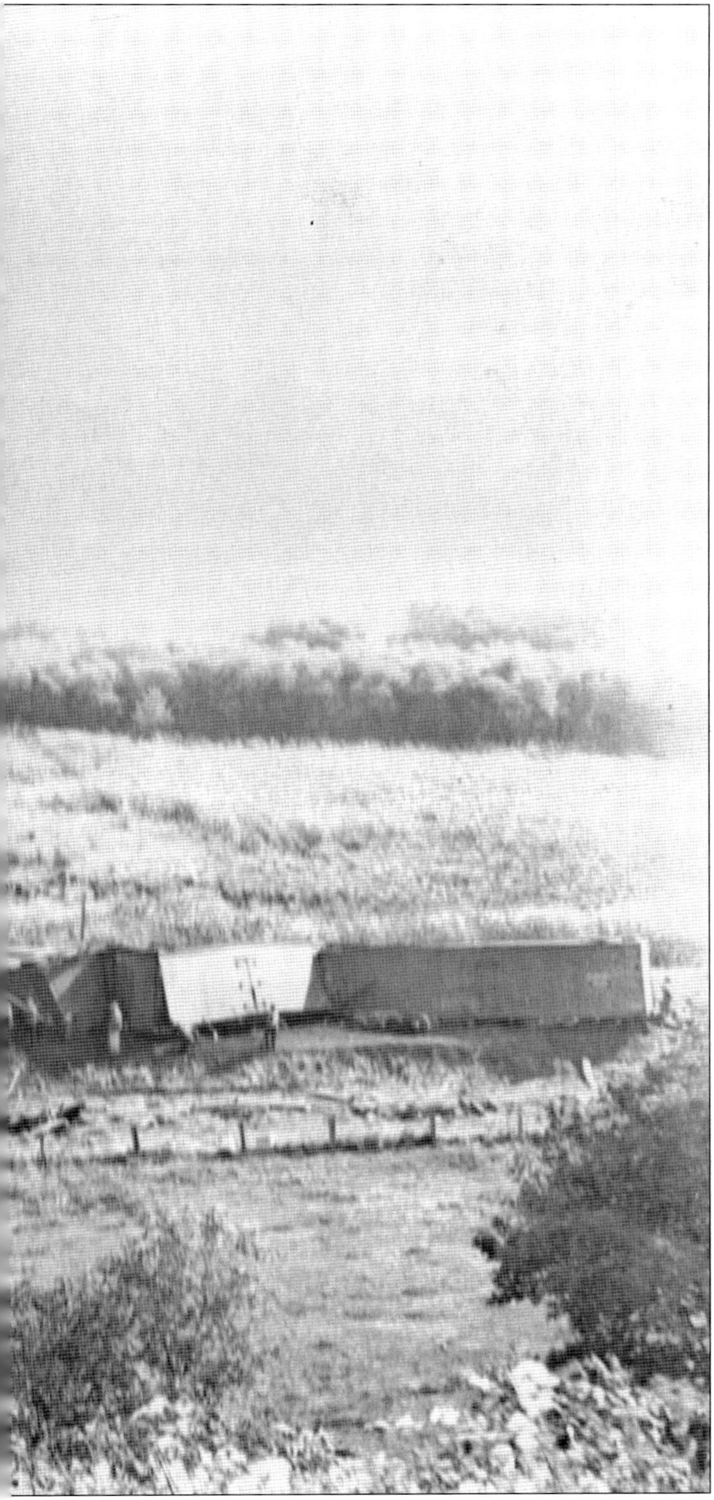

Railroads were crisscrossing the county, shipping the area's livestock, carrying its commerce, and connecting local communities, but there were hazards, as illustrated by this train derailment near Herman on October 2, 1912. The occasional train wreck on the landscape faded as train routes changed, redefining local communities. In 1903, the Sioux City and Pacific Railroad and the Fremont Elkhorn & Missouri Railway merged with the Chicago & North Western Railroad. Herman, Fort Calhoun, and Washington eventually lost rail service. In 1995, the Chicago & North Western merged with the Union Pacific Railroad. The Union Pacific continues to run on the original route established in 1869, from Blair, through Kennard and Arlington, but the elevators are gone.

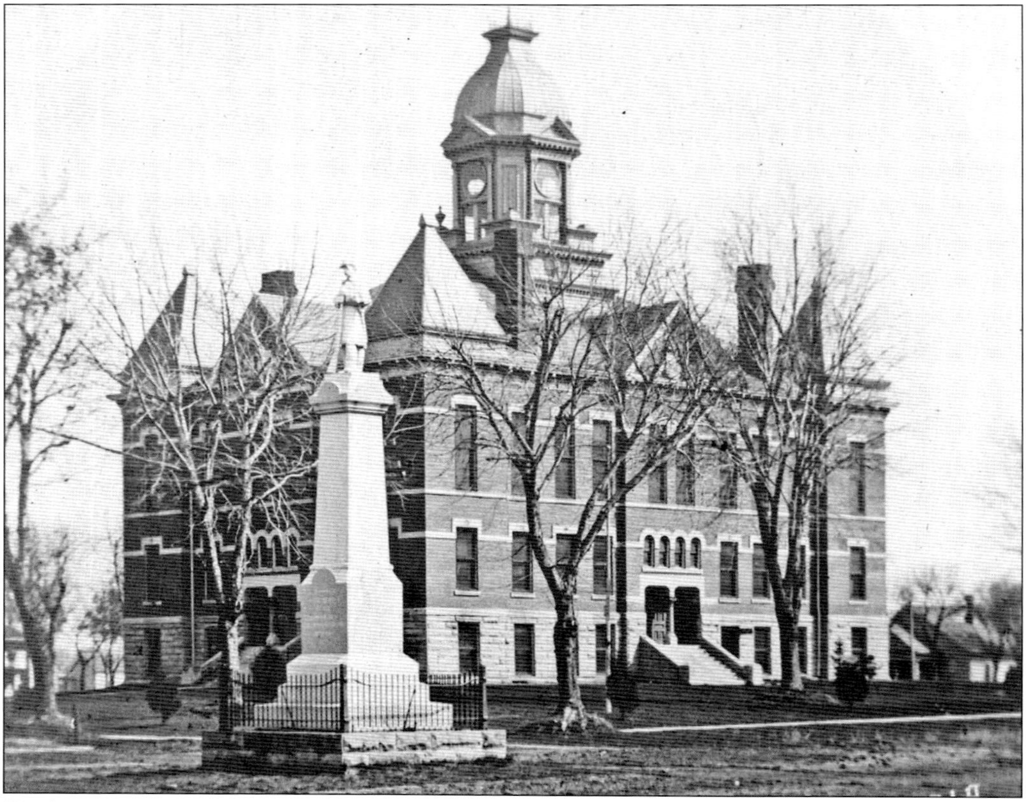

Washington County gave its sons to the Civil War. Two companies of the 2nd Nebraska Cavalry, A and B, were raised in Washington County. A memorial on the courthouse square, inscribed "1861–1865: To the memory of the Union Soldiers buried in Washington County Nebraska," pays tribute to the county's Civil War veterans. The John A. Dix Post No. 52, Nebraska G.A.R. was organized July 2, 1880, with 113 charter members.

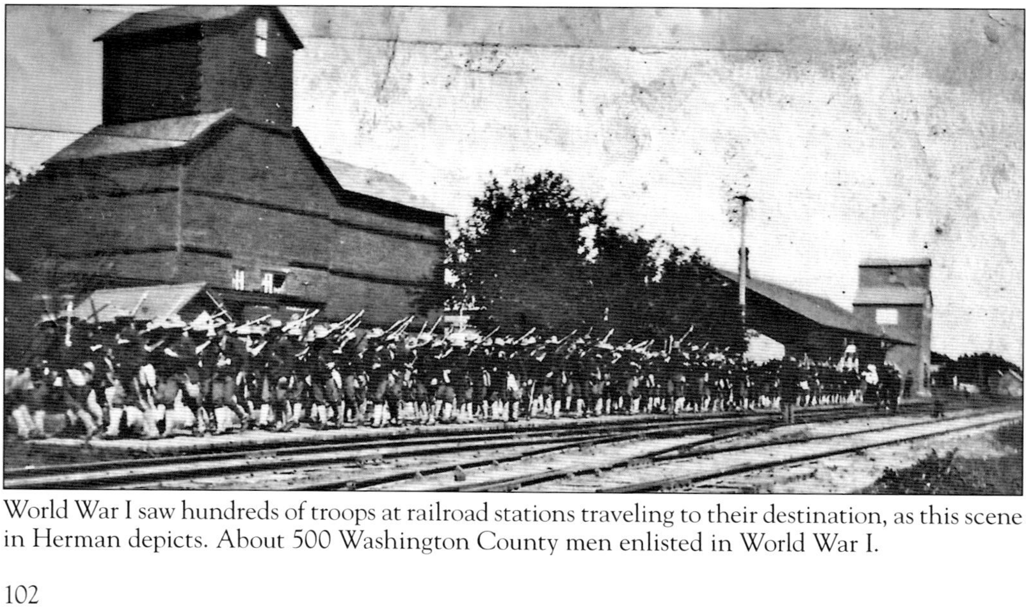

World War I saw hundreds of troops at railroad stations traveling to their destination, as this scene in Herman depicts. About 500 Washington County men enlisted in World War I.

Marshal Albert Suverkrubbe was a World War I veteran who served as Fort Calhoun's marshal and night watchman for two years. He accepted the position in 1930, when Henry Schmidt resigned. On December 5, 1932, while on patrol, he interrupted a robbery and was shot. He died 10 days later of his wound. He is the only law enforcement officer in Washington County to be killed in the line of duty.

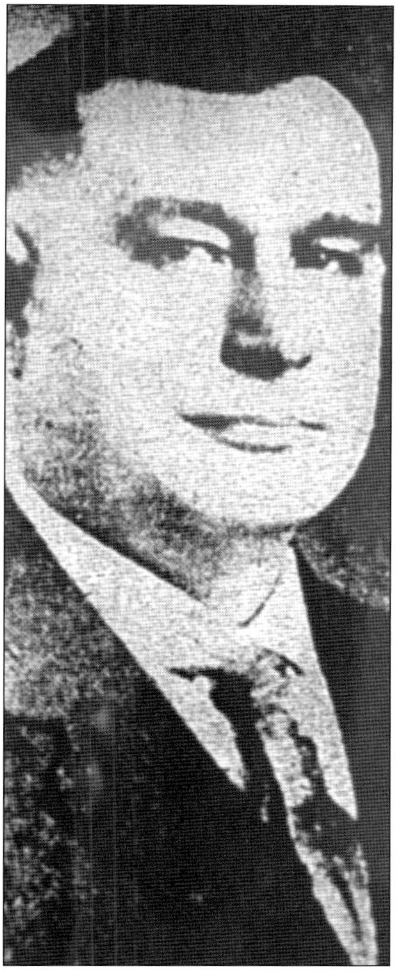

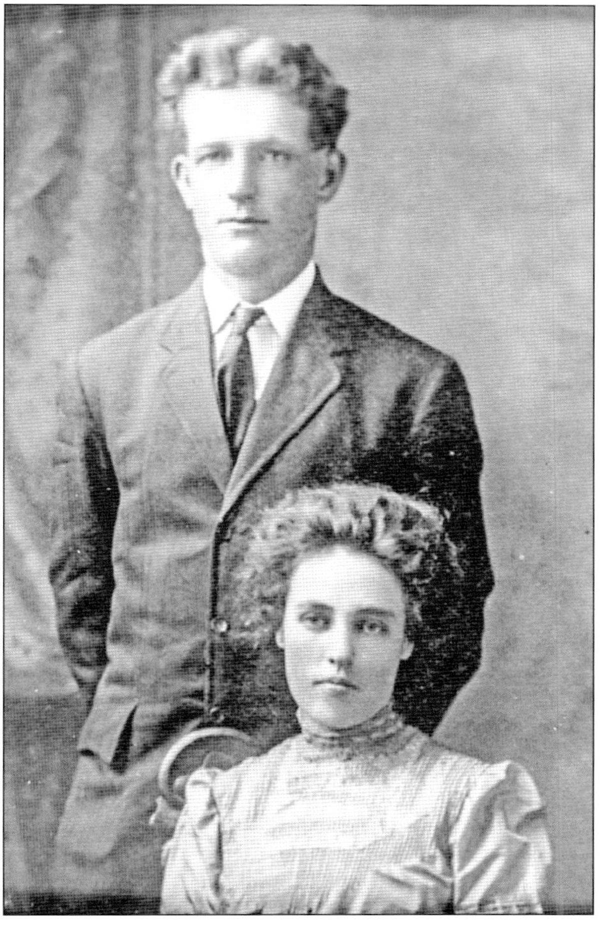

David Emory Cummings was a Herman marshal for 25 years, the cemetery caretaker, and a fan of Herman's baseball team. He published a book of poetry in 1928. David married Ruhama "Ruby" West in April 1910. They had four children and lived their married life in Herman. David was one of Herman's oldest living citizens when he died in 1979 at the age of 94. (Courtesy Bobbi Anderson.)

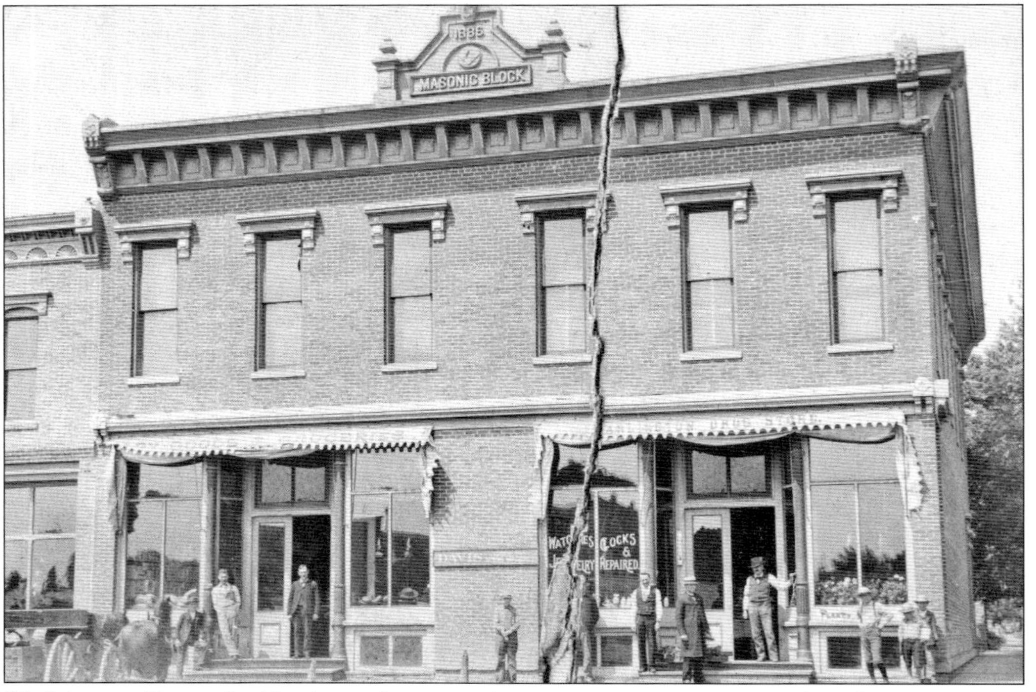

Washington County had its share of organizations—some secret, some social, and some patriotic. The oldest in the county is the Freemasons. The oldest Masonic lodge in Washington County was Solomon Lodge No. 10, organized in Fort Calhoun in 1865, with no less than 13 lodges in Washington County. Arlington's Masonic building, pictured around 1915, was representative of the lodges in the county.

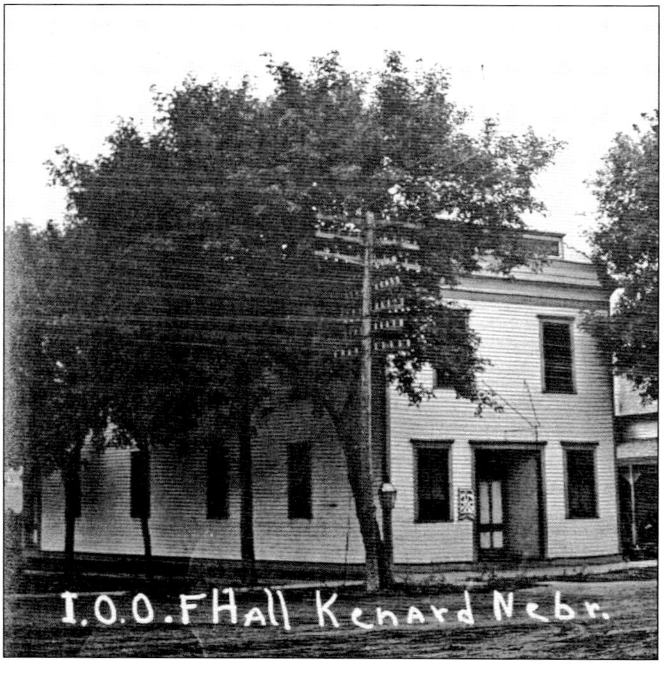

The establishing of the Independent Order of Odd Fellows dates back as early as 1869 with Blair's chapter. Kennard's lodge was organized in 1902. In 1919 and 1920, three American Legions posts were established in the area, at Blair, Arlington, and Herman. Veterans of Foreign Wars organized in Blair in November 1933 with 102 charter members, at that time the largest post in Nebraska. (Courtesy Dixie Lambert.)

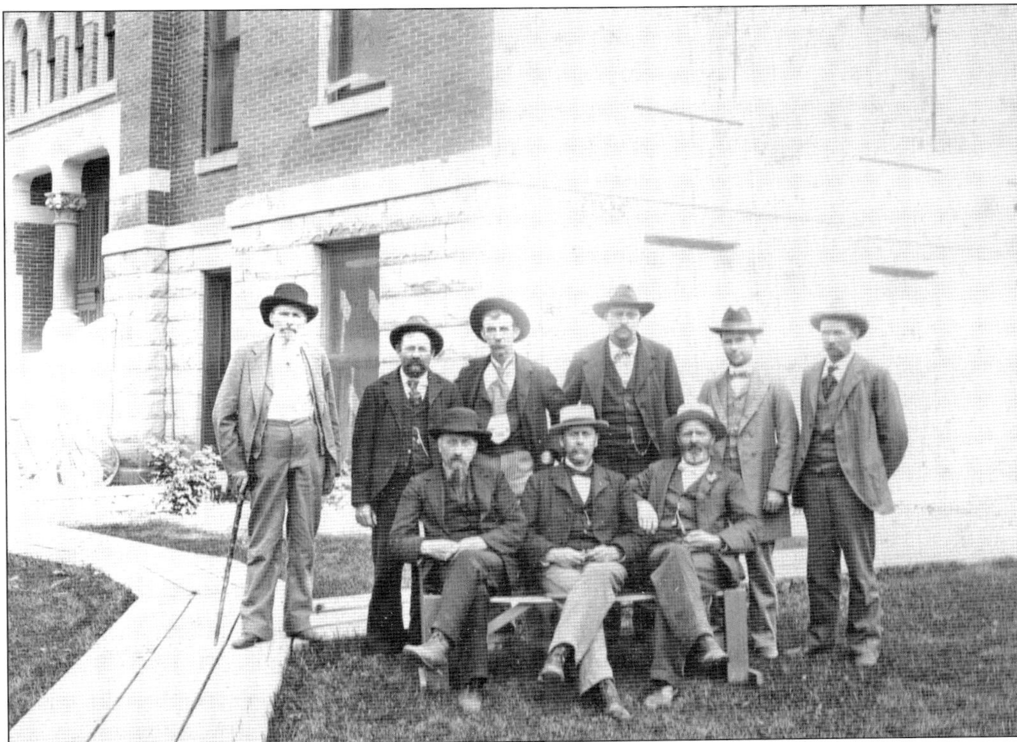

Elected by Washingtonians, Washington County legislative officials are pictured around 1895. From left to right are (standing) R. Gross, T.B. Pawling, John Akin, Magnus Johnson, Clark O'Hanlon, and Henry Rohwer; (seated) R. Broderson, William Gray, and Walt Gauldry.

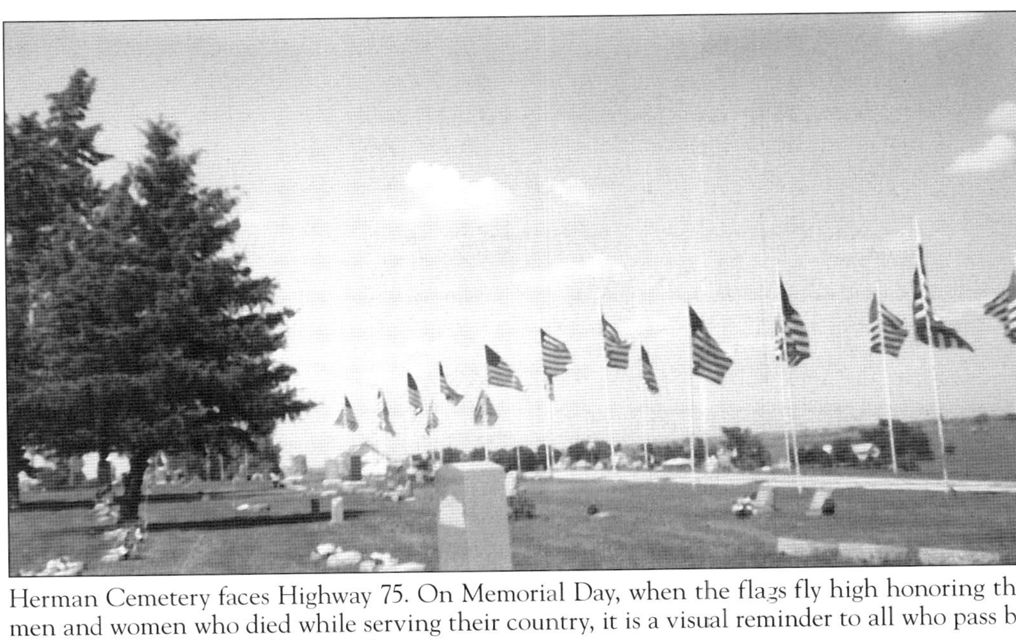

Herman Cemetery faces Highway 75. On Memorial Day, when the flags fly high honoring the men and women who died while serving their country, it is a visual reminder to all who pass by of the sacrifices these soldiers made.

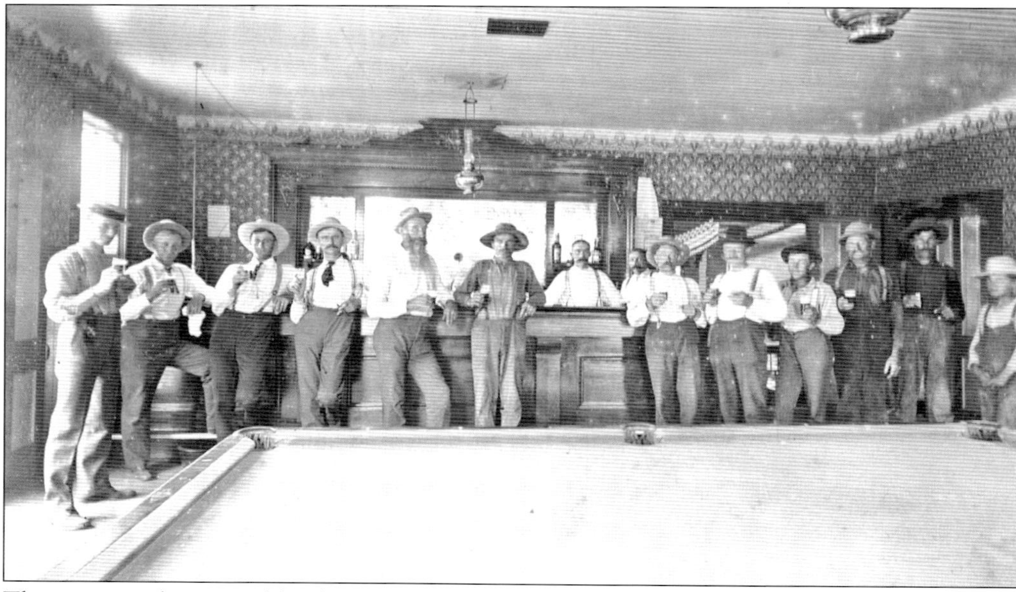

There was no shortage of drinking establishments. Before Prohibition sparked local and national agitation, Washington County's towns were banning alcohol, leading to anti-prohibition meetings in saloons and social halls. Blair went dry in 1908. Kennard did not have a saloon in 1910. Fort Calhoun entered the age of prohibition in 1917, two years before it became federal law, and stayed dry for two years after the law was repealed.

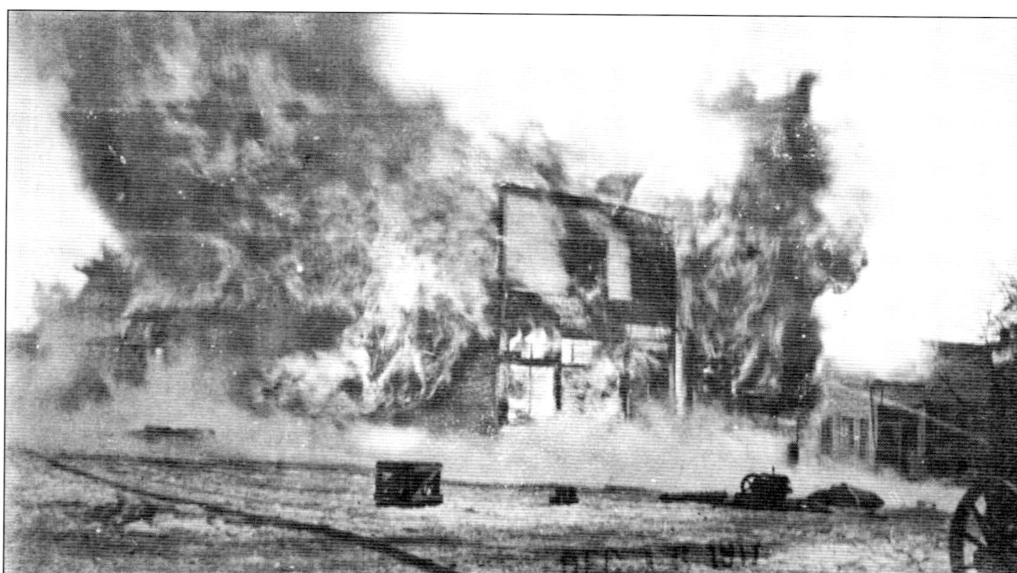

The use of a horse and cart to extinguish this blaze on Main Street Kennard was no match as flames threatened to engulf nearby buildings. One of the first municipal organizations formed in local communities was a volunteer fire department.

Six

We Danced, Sang, and Played

Community Spirit

Residents danced, sang, and played. They created a rich social life within their communities. Schoolhouses and town halls were a favorite gathering place for public entertainment, talent shows, graduations, and just giving people an excuse to get together and celebrate. They worshipped in their churches, and the congregations held ice-cream socials, potlucks, quilting bees, and fundraisers. Locals organized festivals, fairs, and civic societies. They danced, sang, played musical instruments, including the occasional piano. They picnicked, watched parades, and, of course, played baseball.

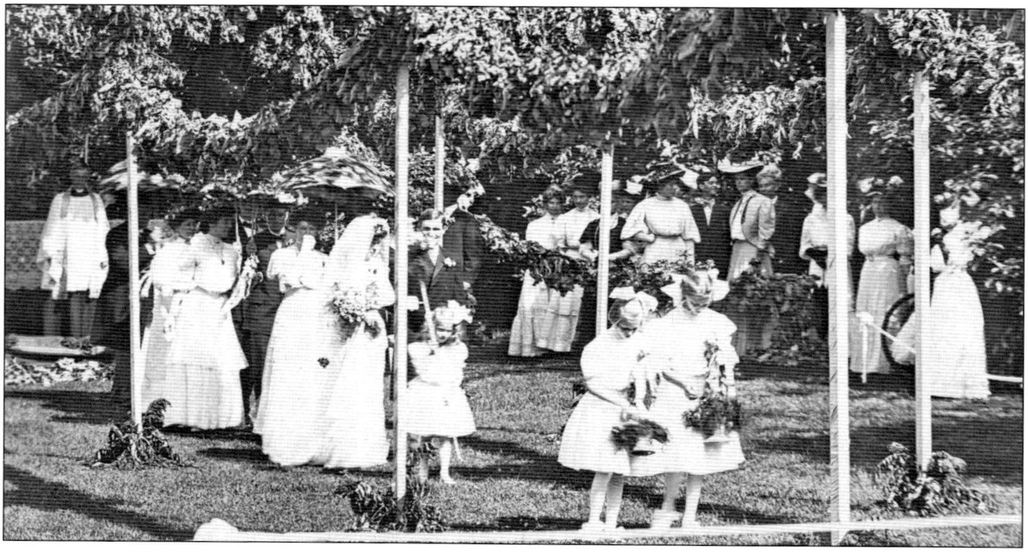

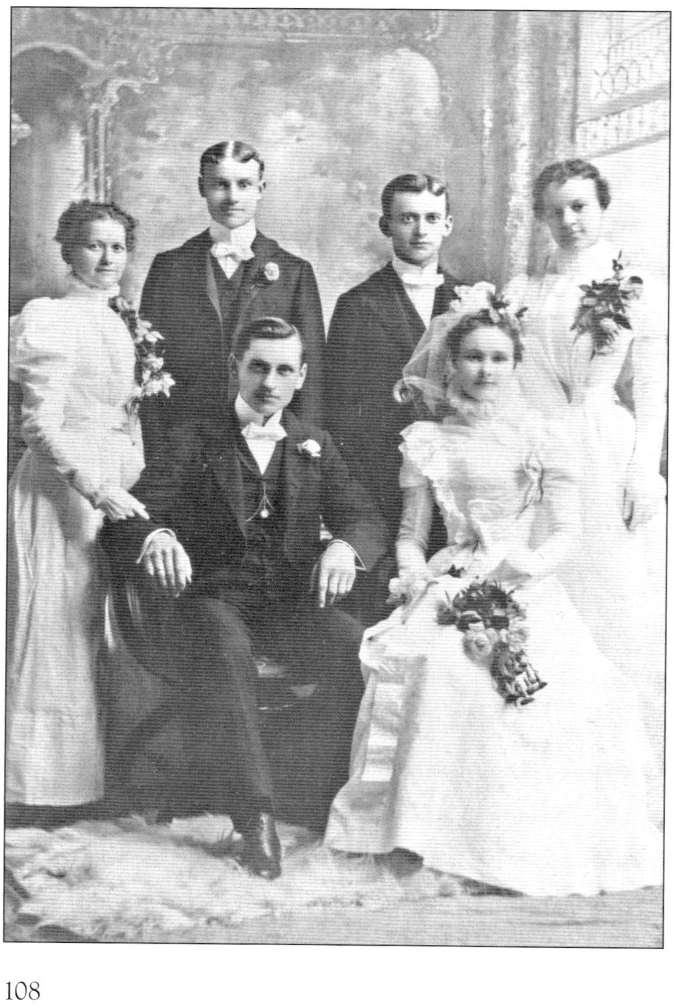

The society wedding of Helen Howe and William Haller brought two prominent Blair families together on July 29, 1907. A.P. Howes, the father of the bride, was engaged in the Crowell Lumber & Coal Co., making members of the firm wealthy during Blair's building boom. Dr. William Haller, the son of Theodore Haller of the Haller Proprietary Company, was a doctor of dentistry.

This photograph was taken at William and Lena Sierk Kruger's wedding on March 23, 1898. Standing from left to right are Dora Walker, Henry Sierk, Henry Kruger, and Anna Sierk. At first glance, it might appear that this was a triple wedding, with the wedding party all dressed in white. By the close of the 19th century, weddings were becoming more elegant, with the brides choosing silk, chiffon, white satin, and lace. White dresses were replacing darker colors.

All dressed in white, friends Mary Burgess (front), Helen Hinschman, Leona Jensen, and Adeline Haack pose for the camera in 1912. Although Kodak introduced the camera in 1900, very few families had yet to own one. Photographs were still taken in a portrait studio. Helen's aunt had a photography studio, and family and friends were often the subject of her pictures.

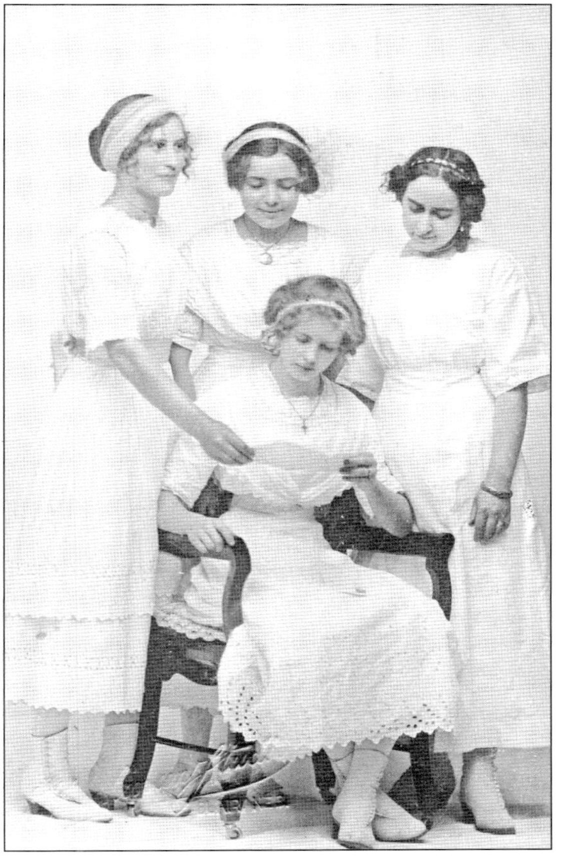

Every town had a barbershop and, later, its counterpart: a beauty shop. Ernest Schmidt, nicknamed Fiddle, is second chair as he learns the trade and watches Paul Johann Schiller, owner, shave a patron. This photograph was taken around 1918. Schmidt remained in Fort Calhoun, retiring in the barber business.

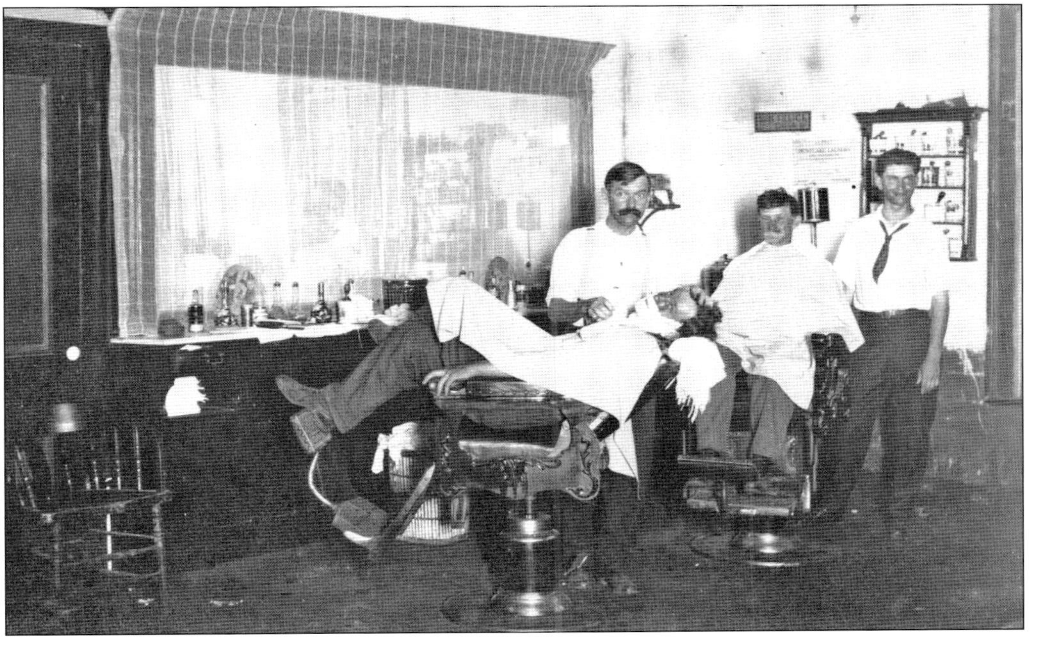

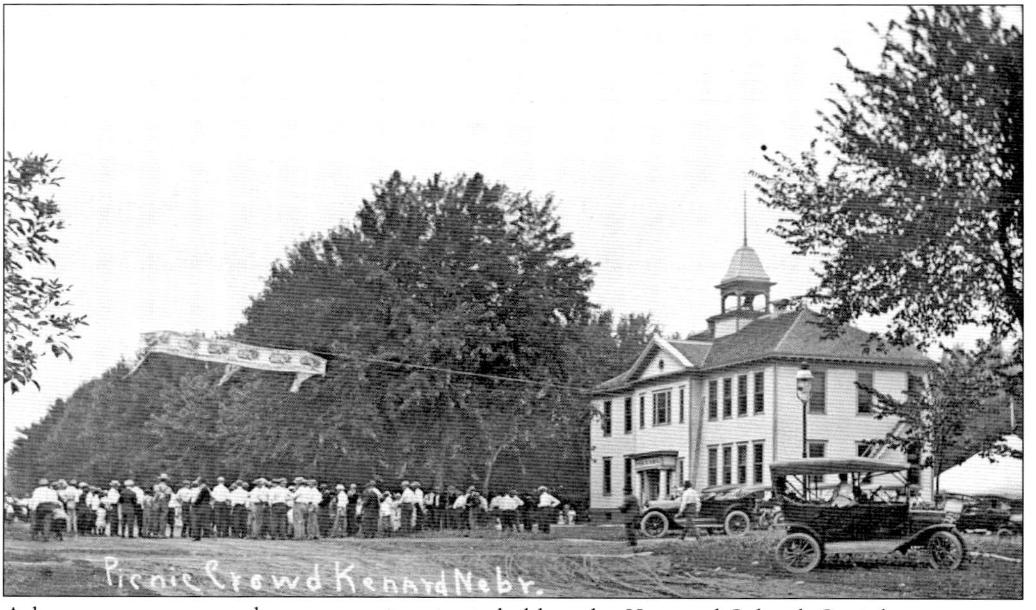

A banner announces the community picnic held at the Kennard School. Social events were anticipated by children and adults alike. Besides plenty of food, picnics usually included footraces, egg races, and sack races, and (depending on the occasion) speeches and celebrations.

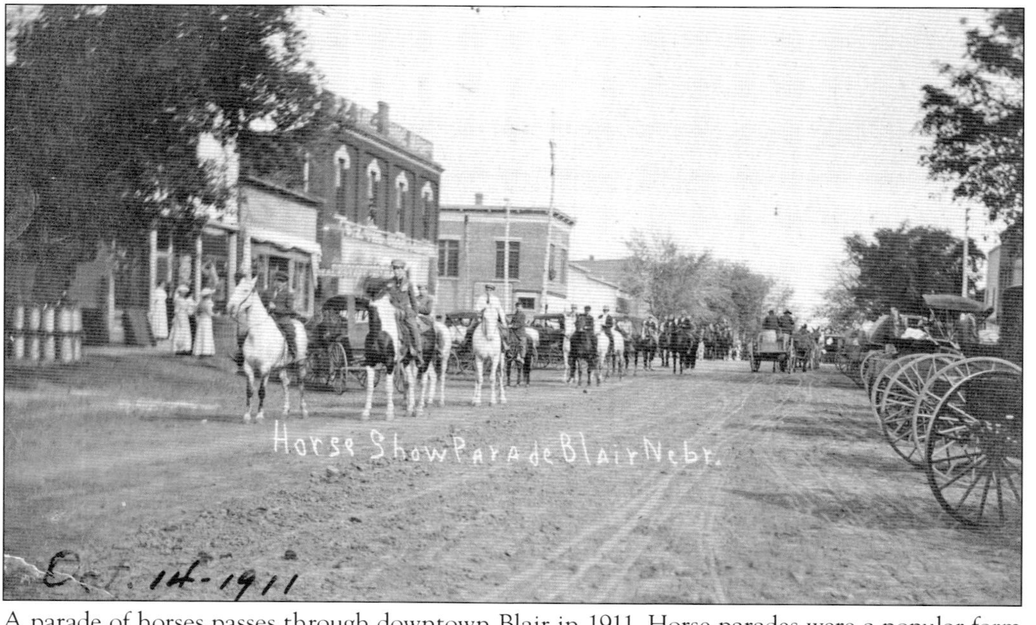

A parade of horses passes through downtown Blair in 1911. Horse parades were a popular form of entertainment and judging the horses or the floats they pulled was only part of the fun. A popular contest was the laying of potatoes on the dirt streets and watching the young men gallop to spear them. The ribbon went to the man who speared the most.

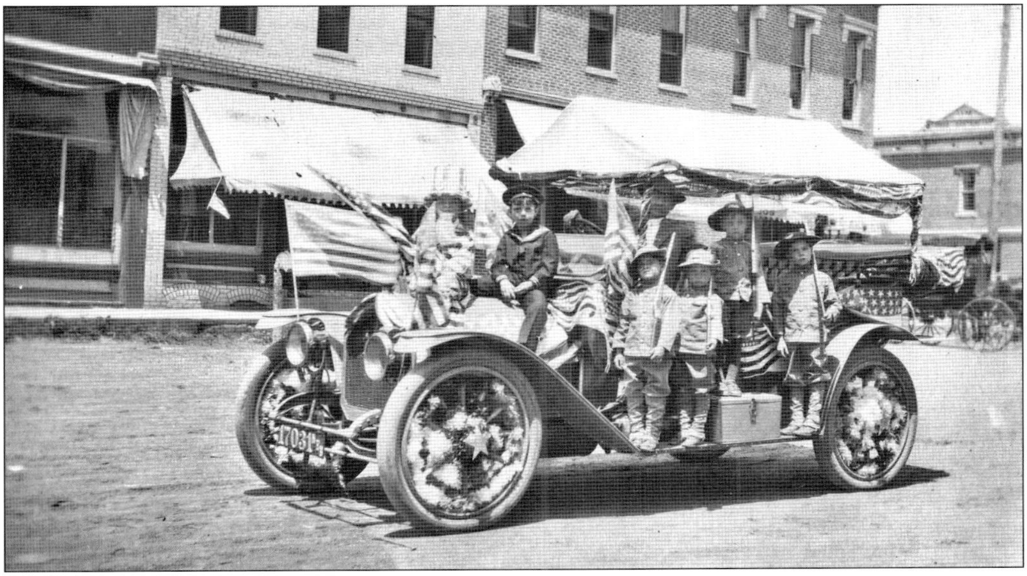

With the invention of cars, automobile parades were taking the place of horse parades and cars were being judged instead of horses. Dr. J.A. Langstaff and his wife of Fontanelle decorated their car in a patriotic theme for the Fourth of July parade. The boys riding sidecar are dressed in Army uniforms, complete with helmets and a rifle. The boy on the hood is dressed in a sailor uniform. This photograph was taken around 1914.

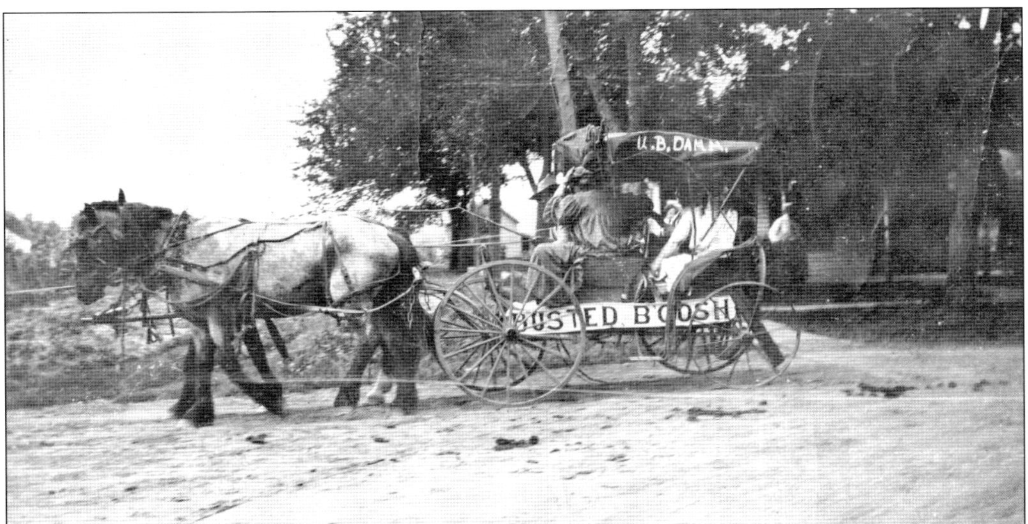

The purpose of parades and floats has changed little over time. They remain representative of the community or the individuals who participate. In this undated photograph, the banner is advertising a heartfelt sentiment, "Busted B'Gosh."

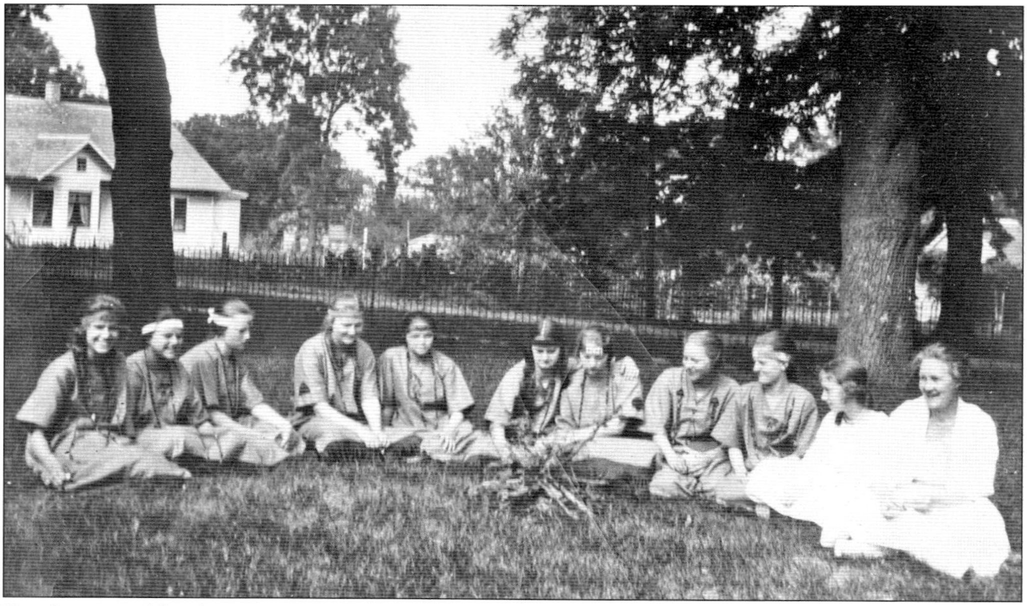

Youth groups like the Boy Scouts, Girl Scouts, and 4-H Club were forming in Washington County with adults as leaders and mentors. Organized in 1915 in Blair, the Camp Fire Girls were active in civic affairs. Fort Calhoun Camp Fire Girls pictured at Fort Calhoun Park are, from left to right, Margaret Jipp, Esther Finch, Alma Sierk, Celia Rohwer, Gladys Bivens, Josephine Retchmerk, Helen Sierk, Gertrude Frahm, Dorothy Siever, Myrtle Christensen, Eda Sierk, and Elsie Cook.

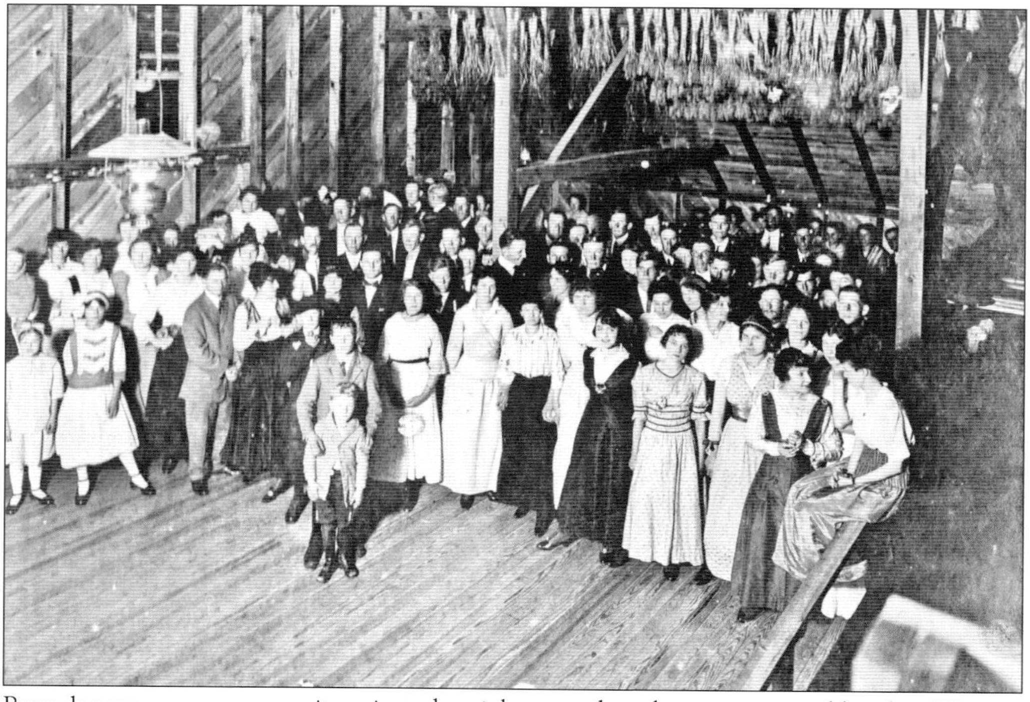

Barn dances were a community-oriented social event where large groups could gather. The top floor of the barn would become a convenient dance floor on the Slader farm.

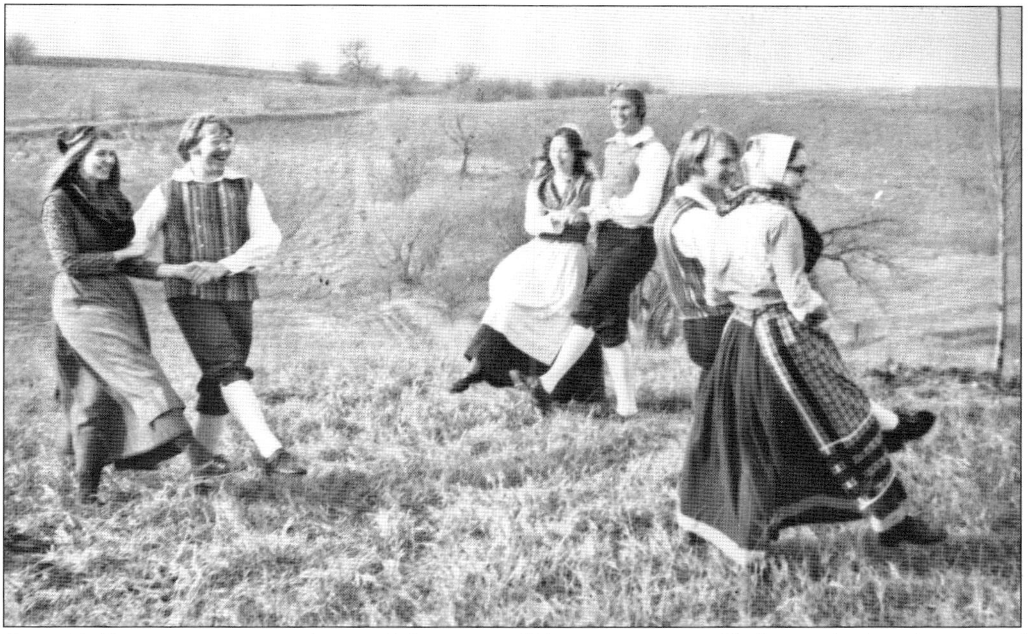

Dana College was an integral part of the town of Blair since its establishment before the turn of the century as a religious and educational institution. A dance club was organized in the 1950s, and traditional Danish dancing was taught. Partners dressed in traditional Danish outfits dance to the steps of Danish music on the grounds of the campus.

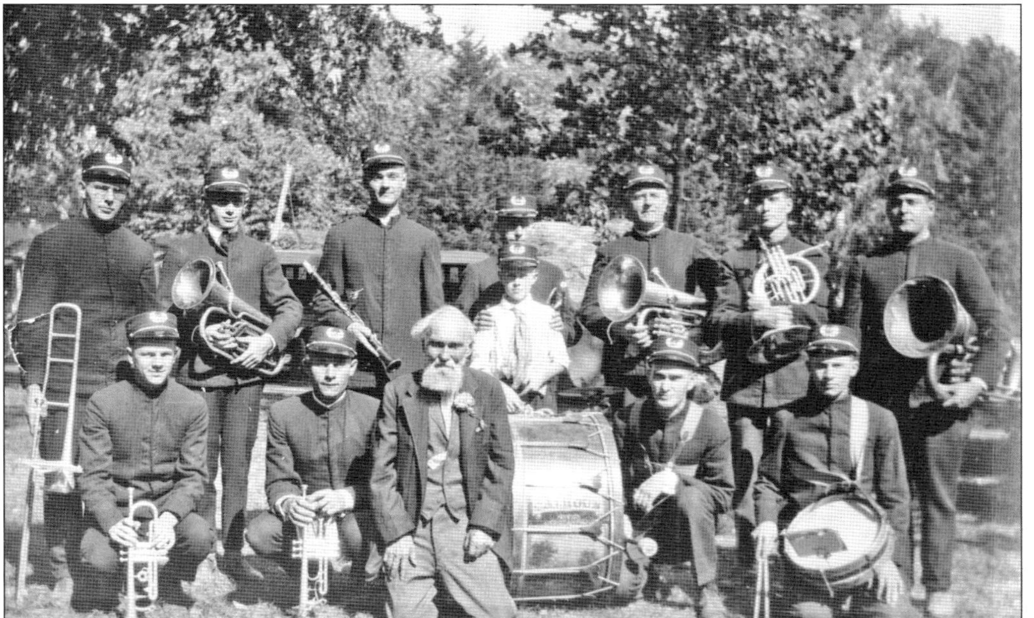

In 1921, William Henry Woods was honored during Fort Atkinson's centennial and by the Fort Calhoun Band on his 83rd birthday in 1923. Pictured from left to right are (first row) Walter Sievers, Carl Jipp, W.H. Woods, Ernest Schmidt, and Lewis Cook; (second row) Milton Cady, Paul Jipp, Richard Sievers, Henry Jipp, Earl Cook, William Sievers, Opal Brown, and Walter Gall.

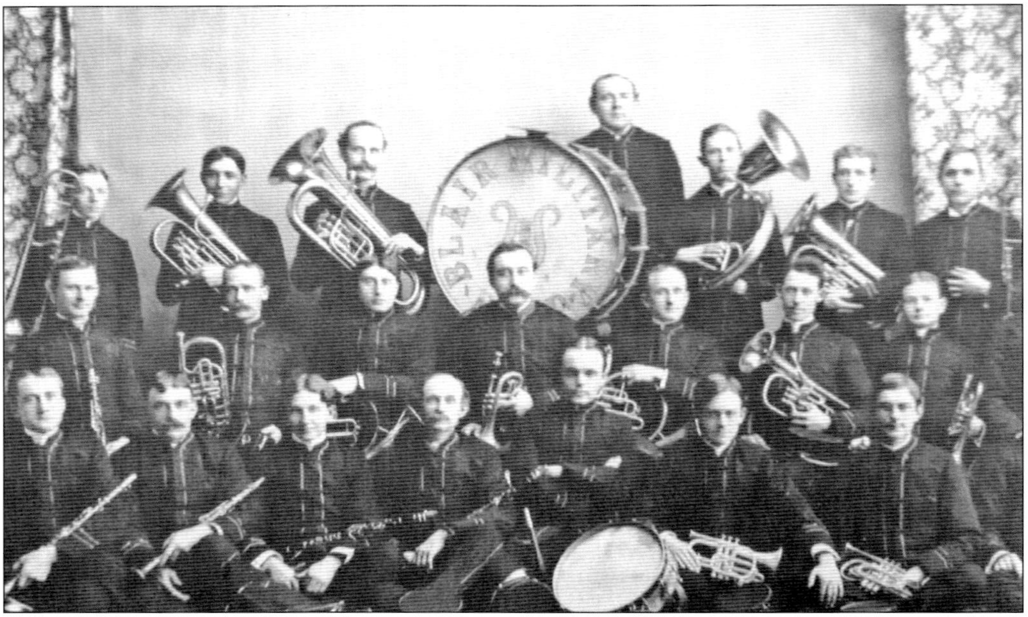

The Blair military band performed as a marching band playing for military functions, national holidays, parades, and town concerts.

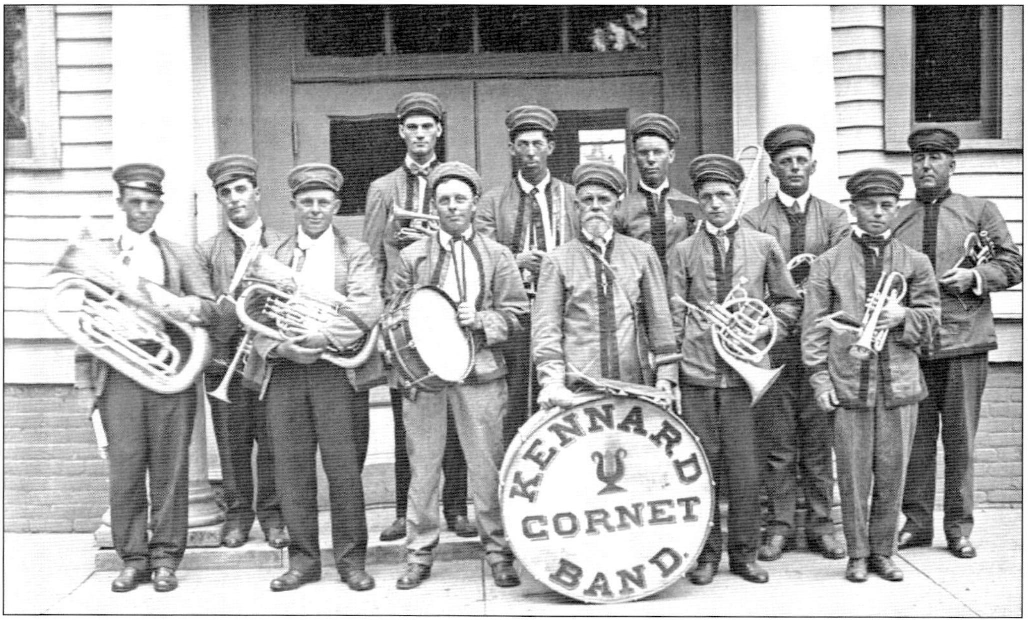

Kennard established a band when the town was in its infancy. By the turn of the century, Kennard had a cornet band of over 20 pieces and its services were in demand in several parts of the county and requested in Omaha.

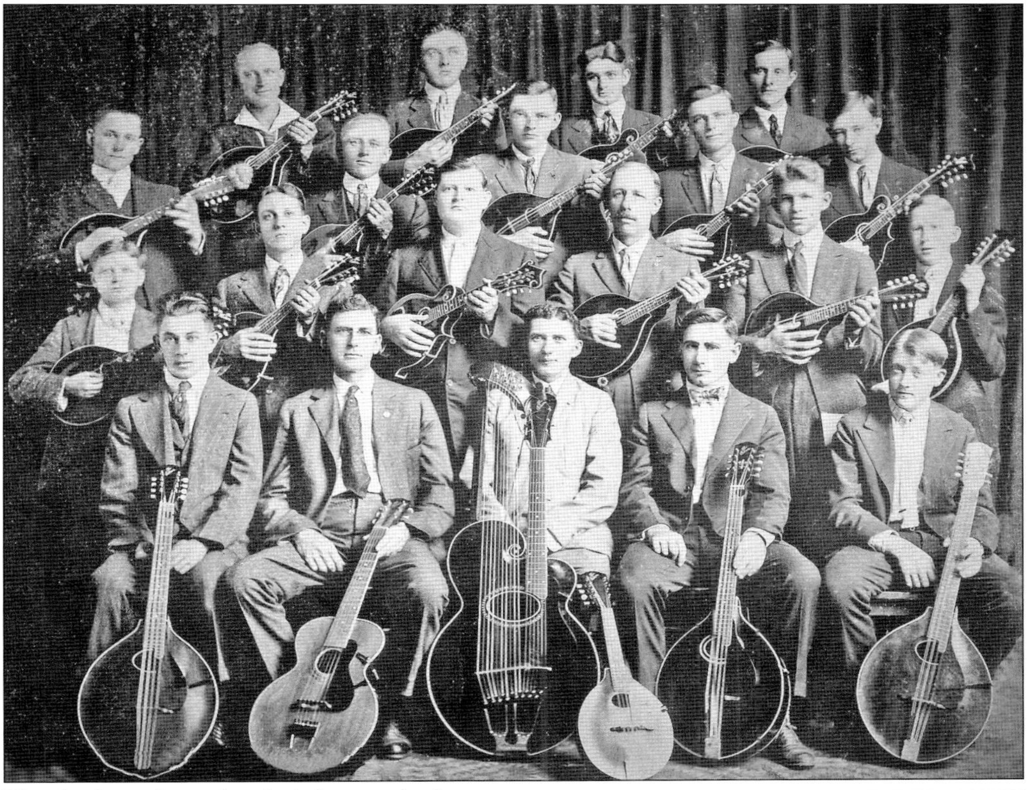

Blair had a military band, Arlington had a cornet band, and Herman had a stringed band. Pictured from left to right are Herman's musicians: (first row) Miles West, Charles Gray, William Gitke, Jessie West, and Forest Brewster; (second row) Harold Brewster, Will Barge, J.M. Brewster, Charles Blanchard, Byron Bunn, and Ted Swanson; (third row) Carl Jespersen, Charles Miller, Thomas McDonald, and Kelly VanDale; (fourth row) Ernest Kuble, Earl French, Fred Gaylord, and Carl Frandsen.

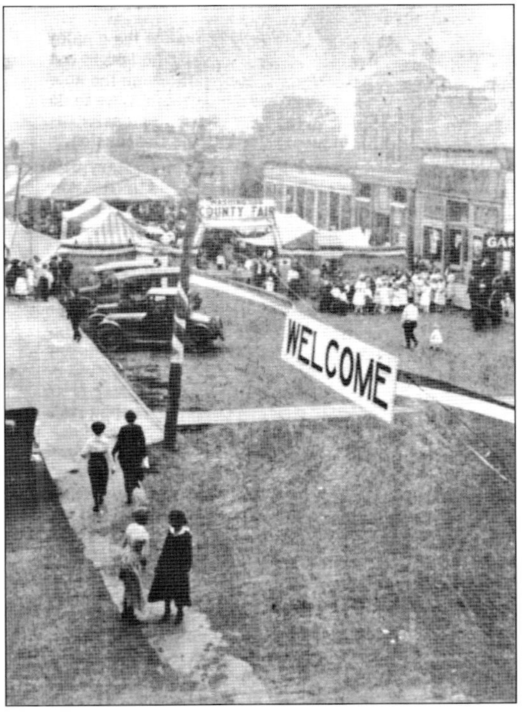

In 1918, a group of Arlington citizens organized the Washington County Agriculture Society to create interest in the agricultural opportunities in the county. In 1919, the first annual fair was held on Second Street in Arlington. Eventually, the fairground would have a permanent home where the old brickyard was located, west of town near the Elkhorn River. The fairgrounds are still located in Arlington.

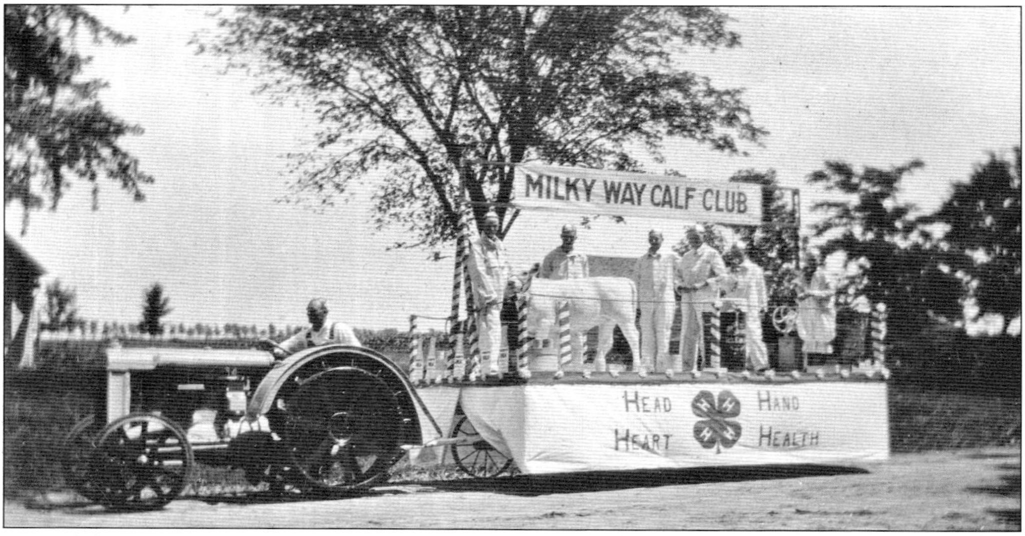

4-H Clubs began showing at the Washington County Fair in 1925, with exhibitions of rope, poultry, dairy, bees, swine, cooking, canning, and clothing. In 1935, there were 41 4-H Clubs in Washington County, and they were entering their exhibits in fairs and building floats for parades. The Milky Way Calf Club entered its float in the 1925 parade.

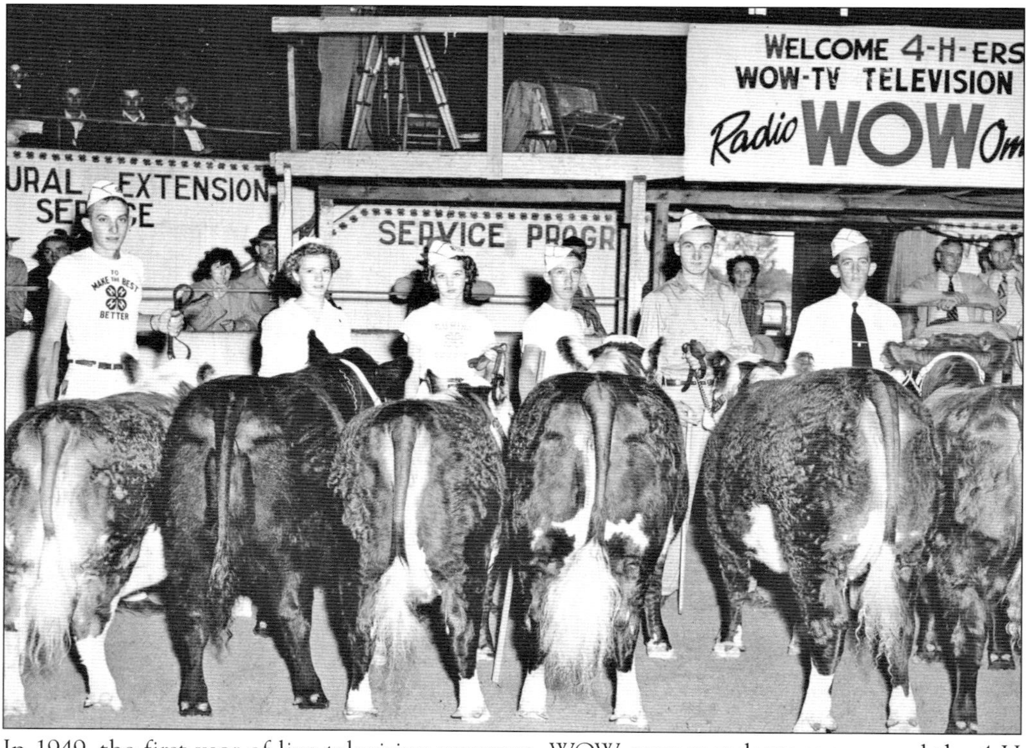

In 1949, the first year of live television coverage, WOW correspondents announced the 4-H winners. David Rasmussen of Arlington, second from right, showed a purple ribbon heifer at the 1949 state fair. The kids that show their exhibits often enter their livestock in local and state fairs and are evaluated according to breed standard, muscling, structure, and showmanship.

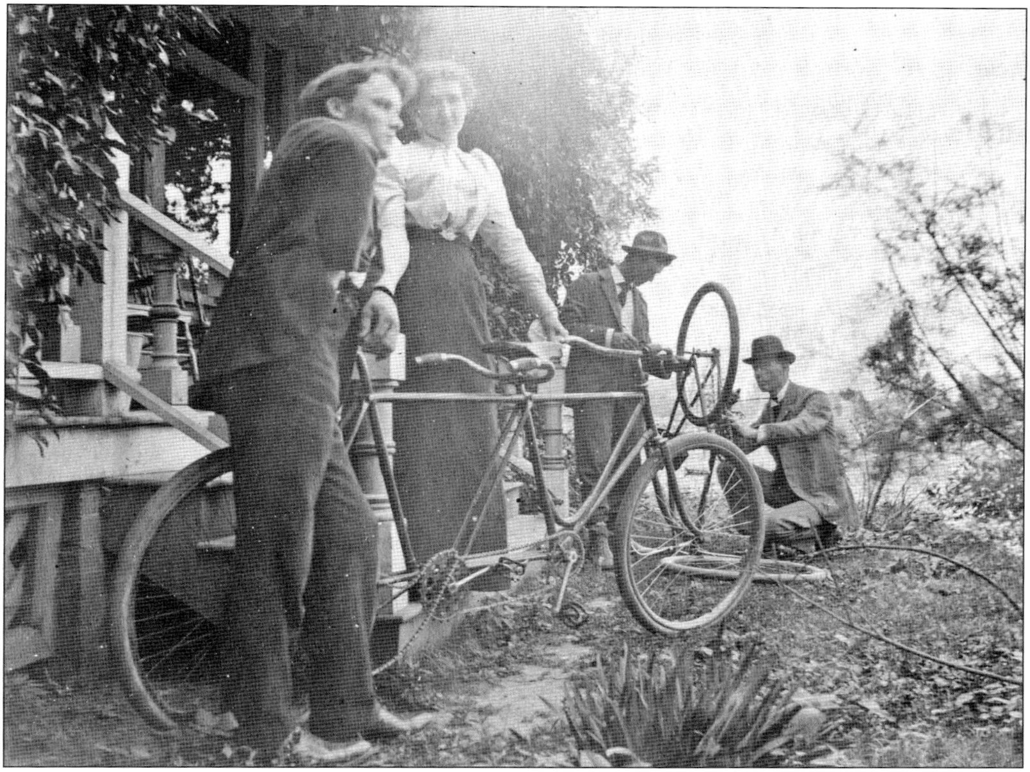

In the 1890s, local towns saw quite a bicycle craze and many businesses and residents had some form of cycle. Many bicycle clubs sprang up, and leisurely afternoon outings of riding were becoming a more common sight. Here, an unidentified man appears to be fixing his bike tire as the couple in the foreground is waiting.

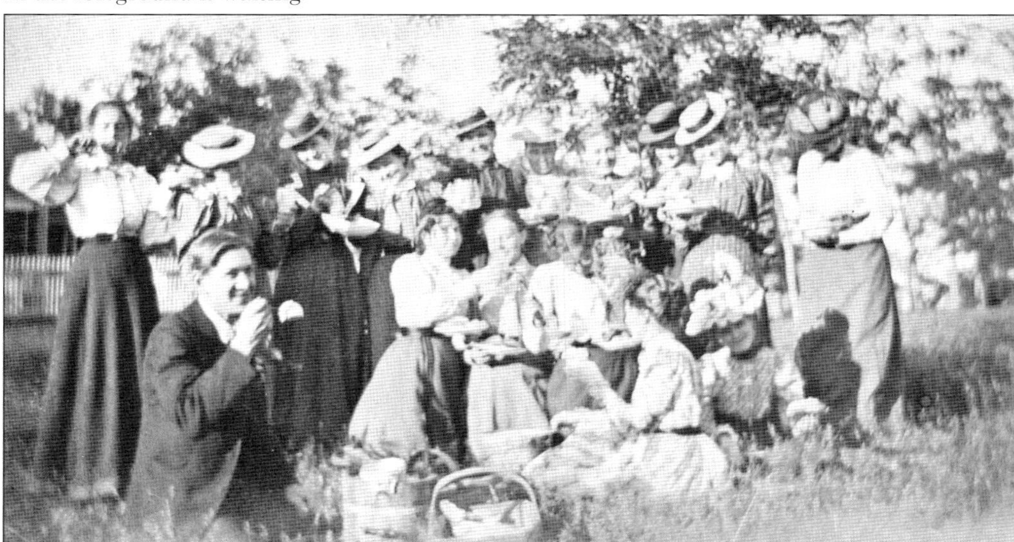

Picnickers are pictured at Stillwater Lake, near Fort Calhoun in 1898, during the Gay Nineties. Stillwater Lake no longer exists.

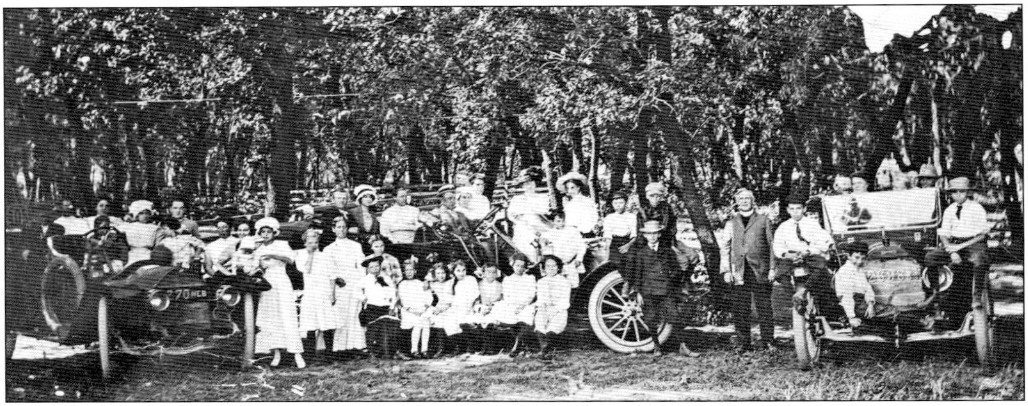

Baptisms, confirmations, and weddings were not the only time religious congregations gathered. Members of St. Mary Episcopal Church in Blair gather after services for their annual picnic in 1911. Church picnics usually included lots of food, strawberry or ice-cream desserts, and entertainment for the children and adults.

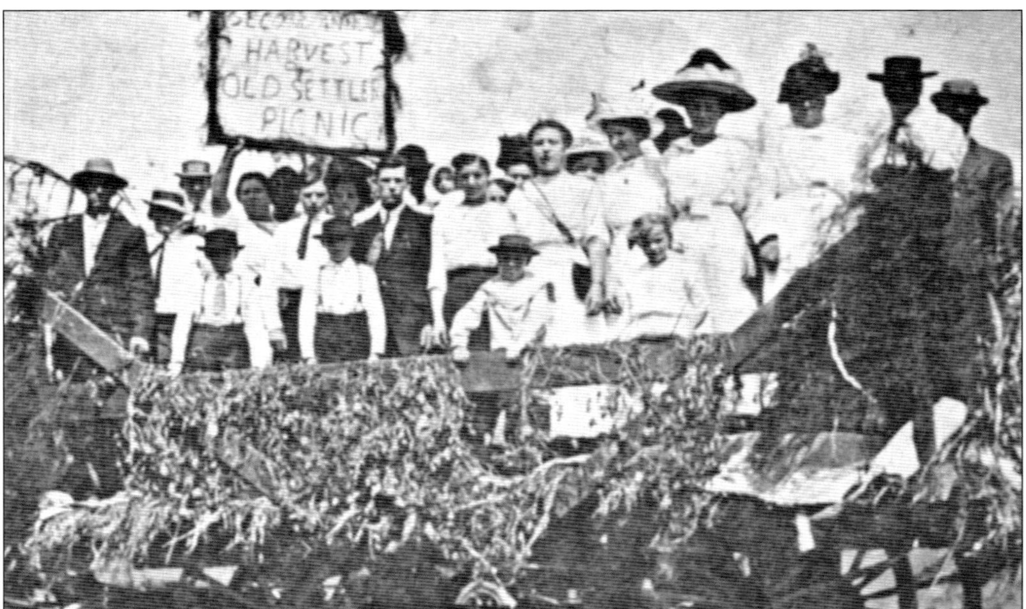

Harvest picnics and festivals were a time to be thankful but also gave the community a reason to gather in a social setting. The city of Washington's Harvest Festival included a parade with decorated wagons, footraces, horse races, baseball games, a band concert, and an evening dance. In this 1911 photograph, residents of Washington look over their float.

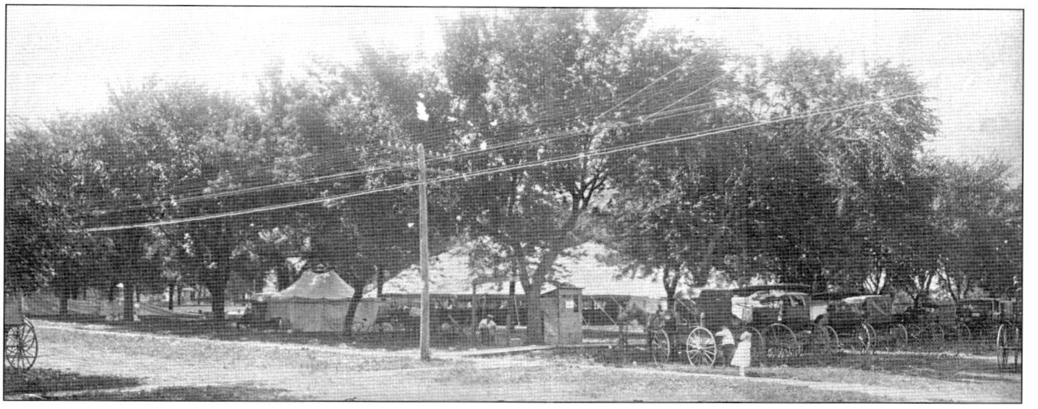

A Redpath Chautauqua is pictured. Chautauquas, designed to entertain and educate and popular in the early 1900s, reached the county in the early days of the automobile's appearance. Blair sponsored such performers as the orator William Jennings Bryan and concert musicians. Newton Gaines from Arlington entertained audiences and lectured on the Chautauqua circuit, giving speeches and delivering addresses to high school graduates, until he retired in 1918.

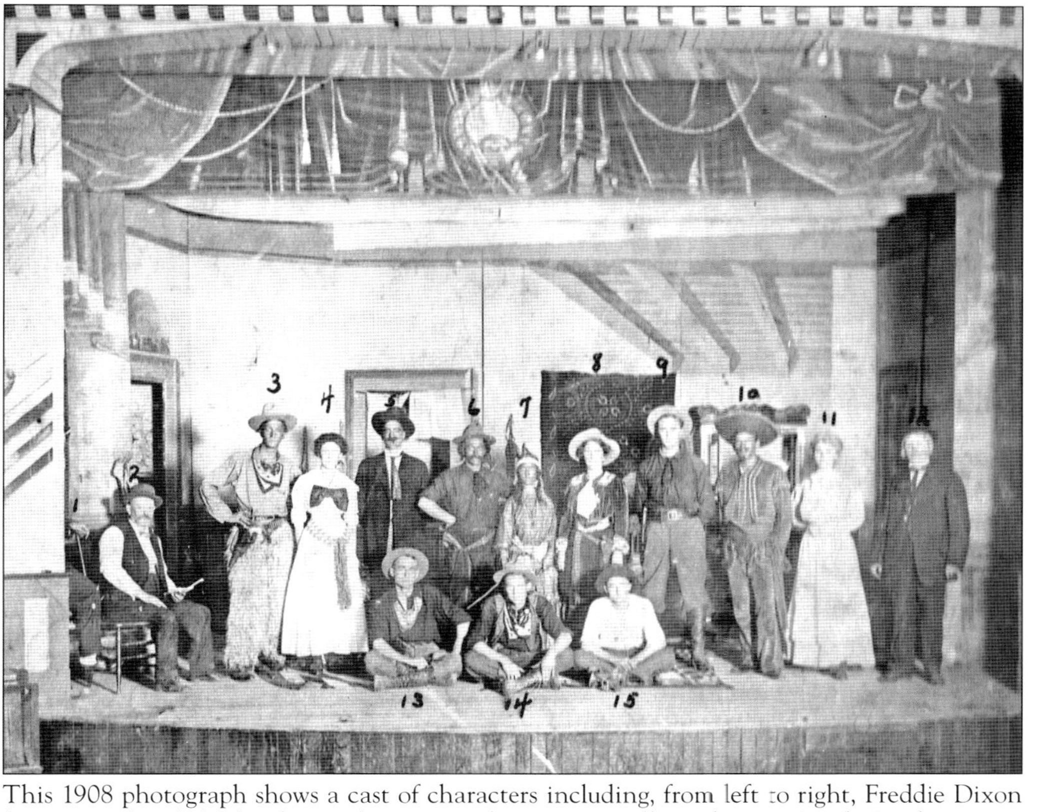

This 1908 photograph shows a cast of characters including, from left to right, Freddie Dixon (pianist, with only his leg showing), Henry Taylor, George Willsey, Florence Smith, Bertha Harris, Dick Bradley, Ben Haller, Herman Struve, Gladys Kemp, Mae Koopman, Chris Winters, Will Koopman, E.V. Capps, Maude Dixon, and Tom Osterman. They were cast members in the play *Daughter of the Desert* at the Germania Hall in Blair.

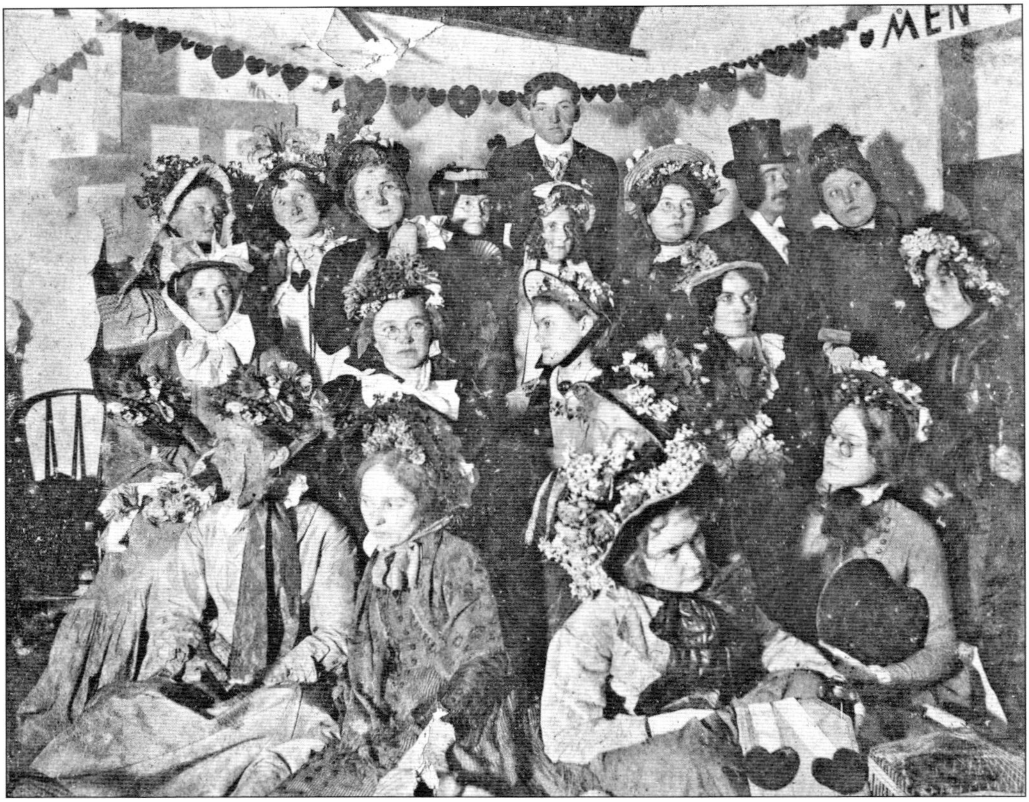

This cast performs a one-act comedy titled *The Old Maid's Convention* in Fort Calhoun in December 1901. The prices of admission were 15¢ and 25¢. The comedy play, popular at the turn of the century, raised money for churches, charitable organizations, and civic groups. The proceeds for this evening's performance were $42.50.

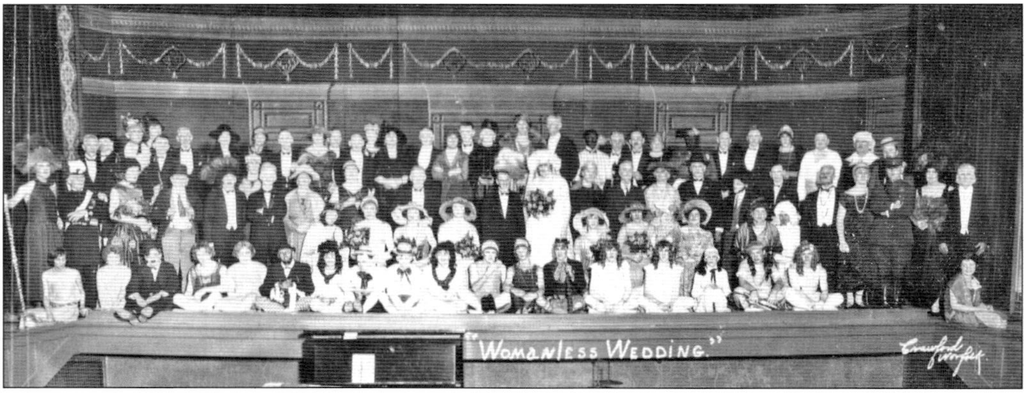

Some of the most prominent men in town entertained to a full house in the comedy *Womanless Wedding*. This cast performed in Arlington to a full audience as the town turned out to see its male neighbors dressing and playing the female roles of a traditional wedding party.

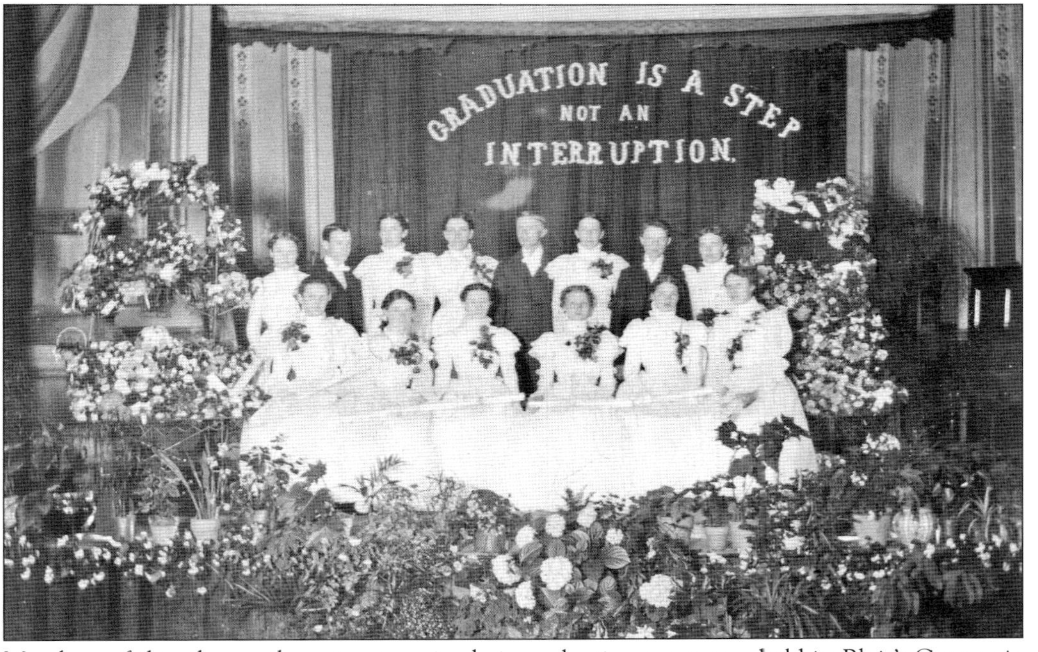

Members of this class took center stage in their graduating ceremony, held in Blair's Germania Hall. The Germania Hall and similar halls were built in German communities throughout the county to serve as their social and cultural centers. The halls were large enough to hold graduations, wedding dances, talent shows, fundraisers, boxing matches, men's club gatherings, and political meetings and were a community center for events.

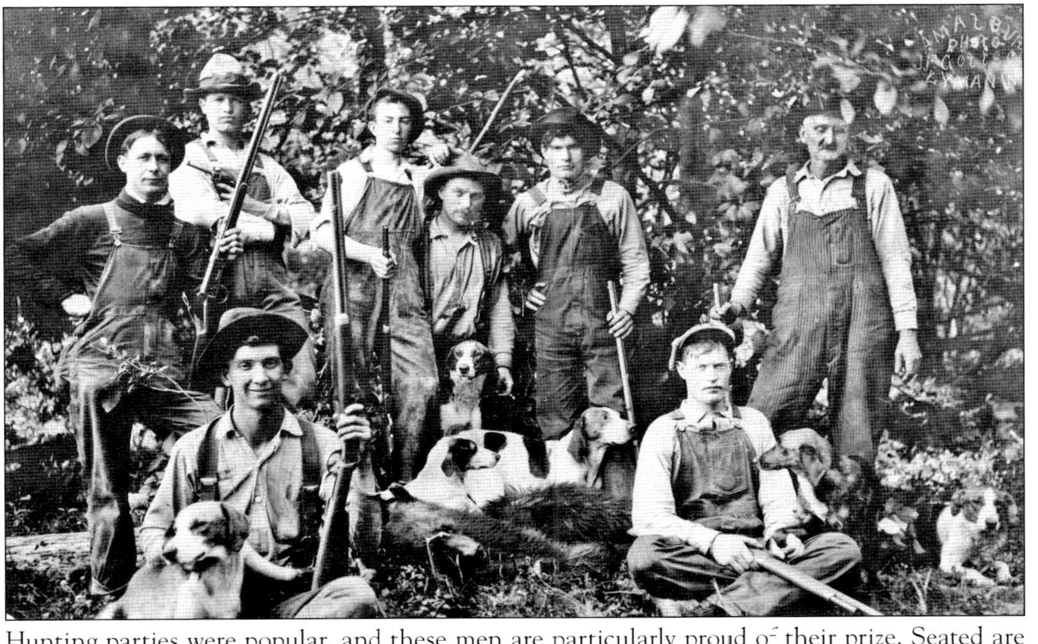

Hunting parties were popular, and these men are particularly proud of their prize. Seated are Webster McFall and Jessie West. Behind them, A.B. McFall, John West, Pat, a Mr. West, Jeff West, and Lester King pose with the bear they shot.

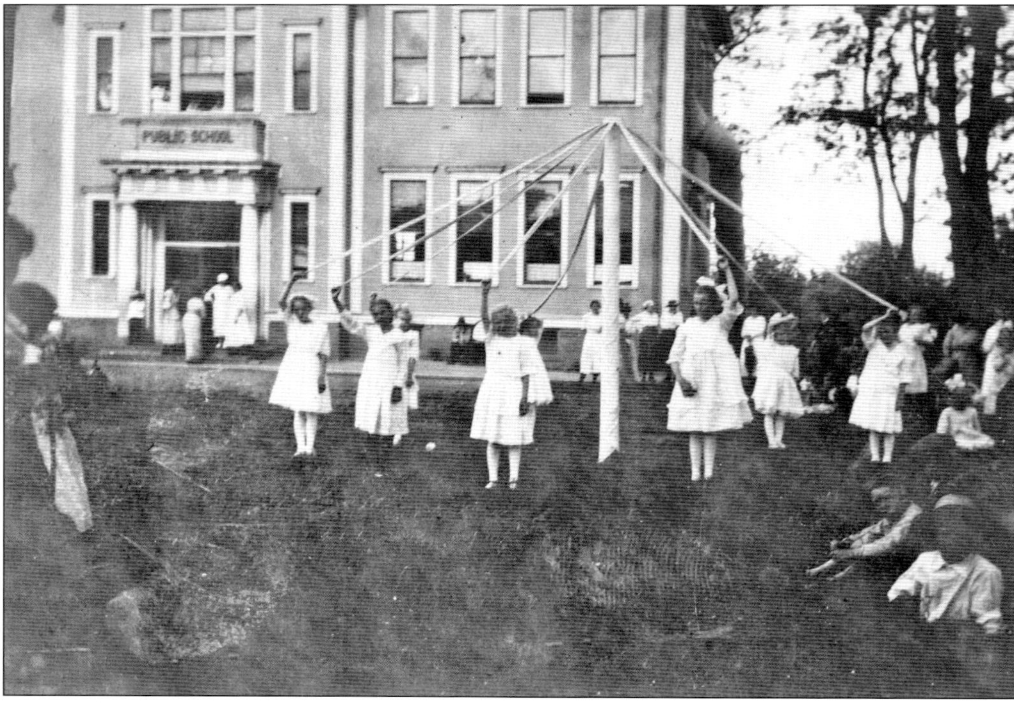

Fort Calhoun School girls celebrate spring with a maypole dance in 1913. Dorothy Sievers was May Day queen.

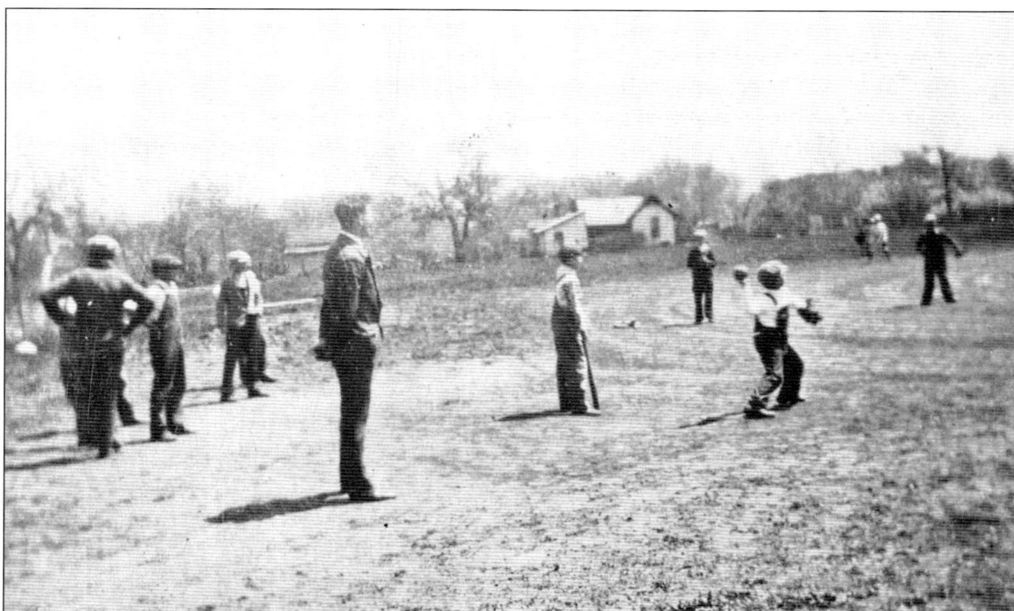

This photograph was taken around 1910. Baseball was long an enjoyable sport played on pastures, dirt lots, and city squares. Once in a while, a youngster fulfills his dream of playing ball in the big leagues. In 1947, Paul Menking came up from Junior League Baseball to play with the Chicago Cubs organization. In 1956, he retired to his hometown of Arlington and coached summer baseball.

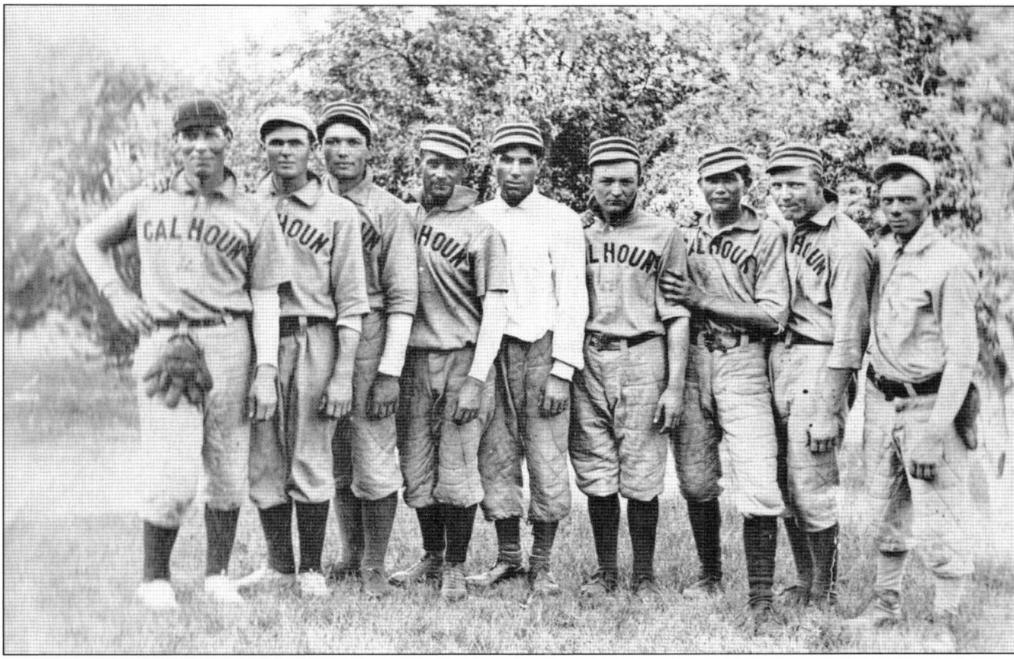

After the world war, ball leagues were sponsored by churches, the American Legion, and businesses; and for the first time players were wearing uniforms that identified the name of their team on their jerseys. The games were usually played on Sunday afternoons, and skinned diamonds were replacing the sandlots and farm fields.

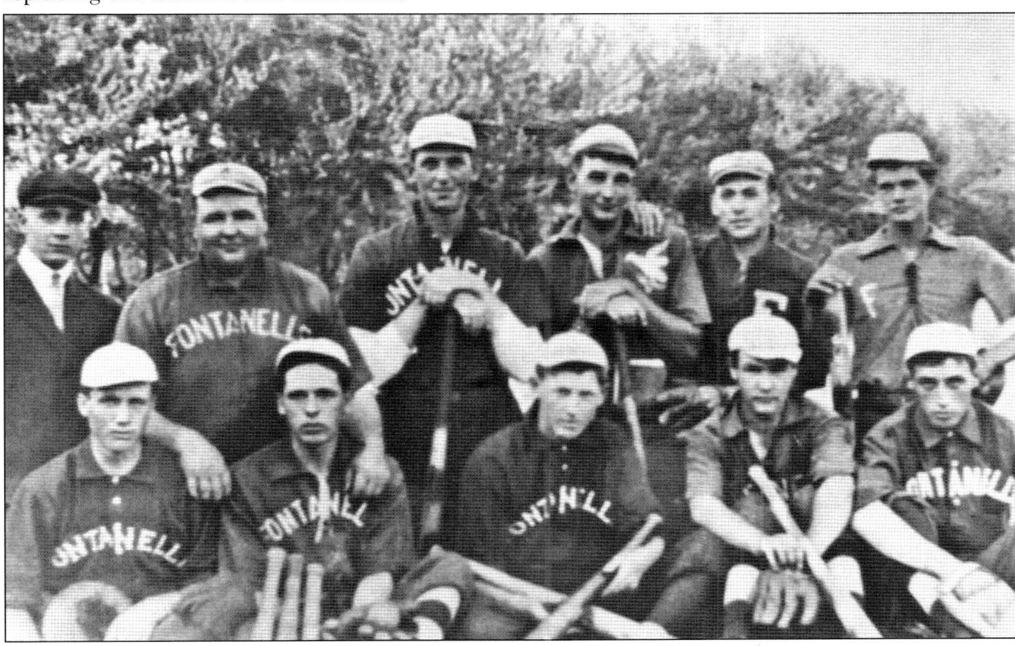

This is an early team photograph of Fontanelle ball players. Fontanelle joined the Elkhorn Baseball League when it formed in 1920, consisting of teams in western Washington and northern Dodge Counties.

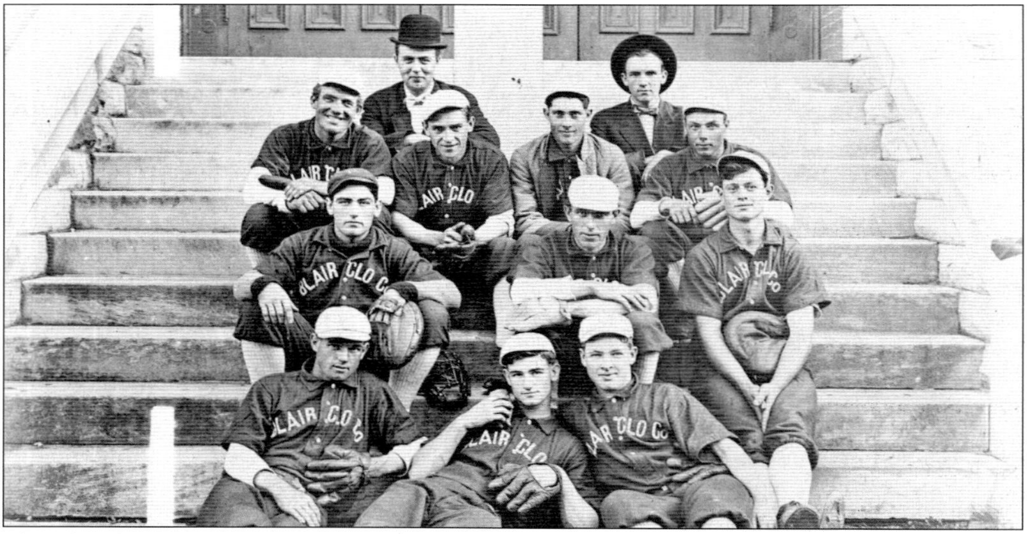

The Blair baseball team poses for a photograph on the courthouse steps. From left to right are (first row) Mengo McMurtie, Dutch Wulf, and Duck Krouse; (second row) Evert West, Dan Dixon, and unidentified; (third row) John Baston, Fred Tamms, unidentified, and Shorty Chapin; (fourth row) George Noble (with the plug hat) and Grant Mack.

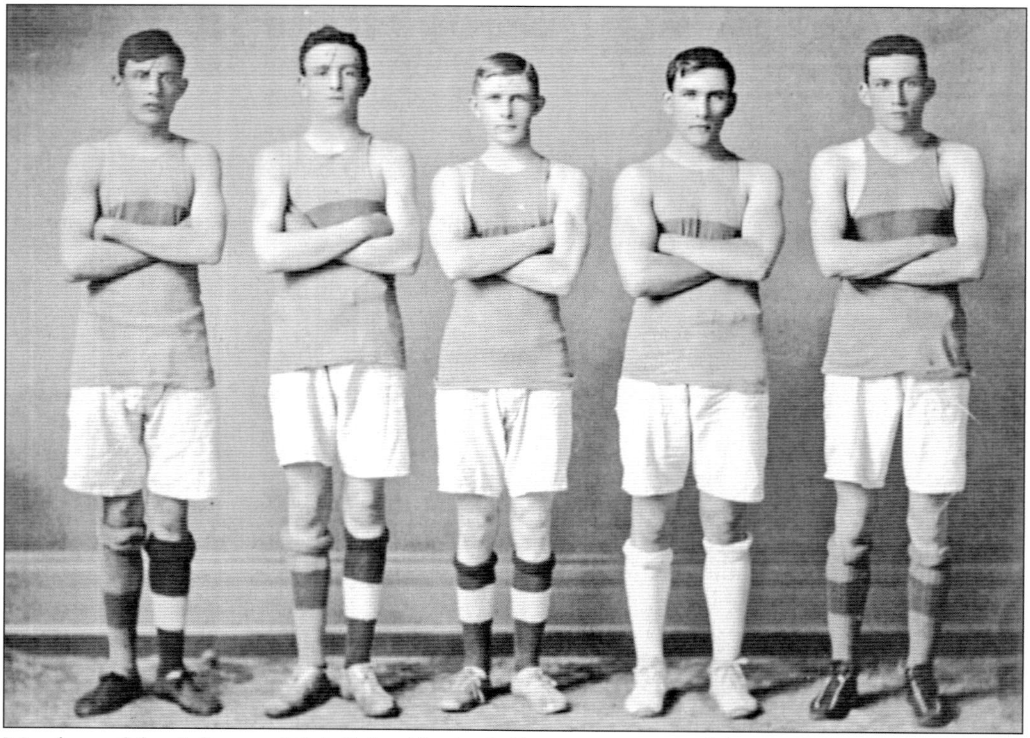

Members of the Arlington High School basketball team are pictured during the 1913–1914 season. Posing in their uniforms are, from left to right, Reed Fasset, Glen Ludwig, Walter Echtenkamp, Roscoe Rhea, and Grant Gilfry. Teams may have been small, but they were serious about their game.

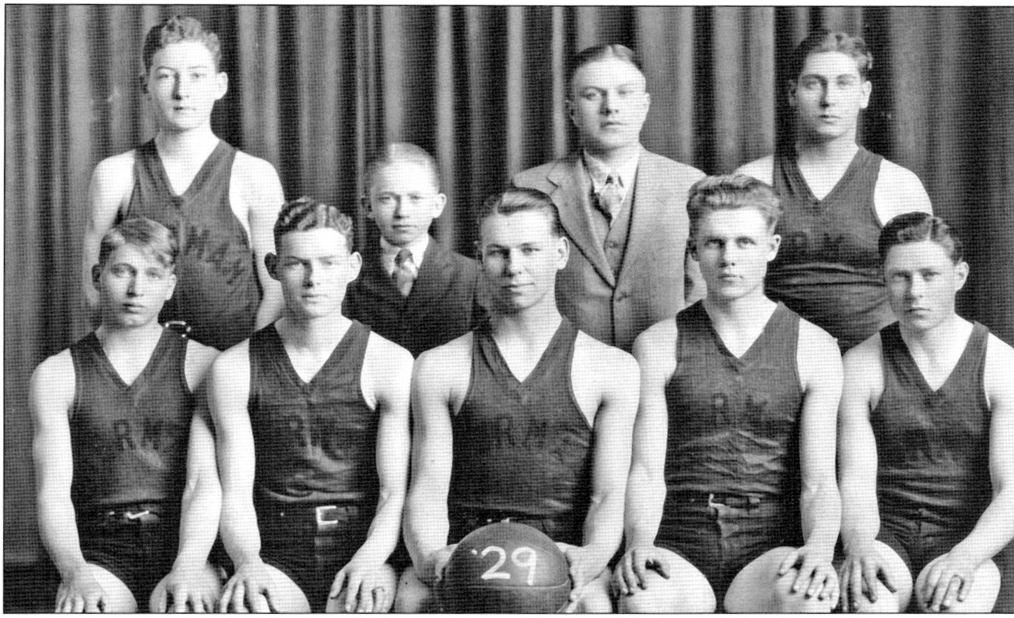

Pictured is the Herman High School state championship team of 1929. From left to right are (first row) Gordon Anderson, Harold Hancock, Elmer Jespersen, Cornell Robertson, and Aubrey Gaines; (second row) Lee Hancock, Clarence Hansen, coach Marcus Kroger, and LeRoy Spiker. Kroger, a former basketball star at Wayne State College, took the Herman boys' basketball team to state in 1929. Kroger contributed to Herman's winning basketball programs through the years. (Courtesy Jonnie Andrew.)

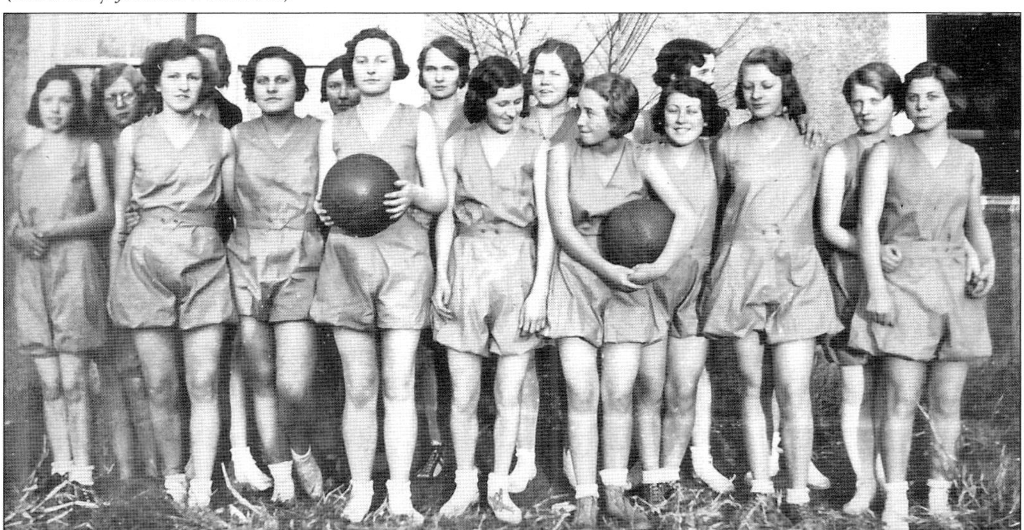

By 1932, Marcus Kroger was teaching the girls to play the game of basketball, although the girls team did not compete. The Herman bloomer players in 1932 are, from left to right, (first row) Mildred Peppmiller, Florence Kubie, Lucille Hancock, Vena Horn, Dorothy Sheets, Betsy West, Mona West, and Mardell Stokes; (second row) Alma Case, Fern Entrekin, Liberty Eriksen, Gretchen Gammel, Cora Cushman, Mildred Davis, Elaine Miller, and Mildred Sheets. (Courtesy Jonnie Andrew.)

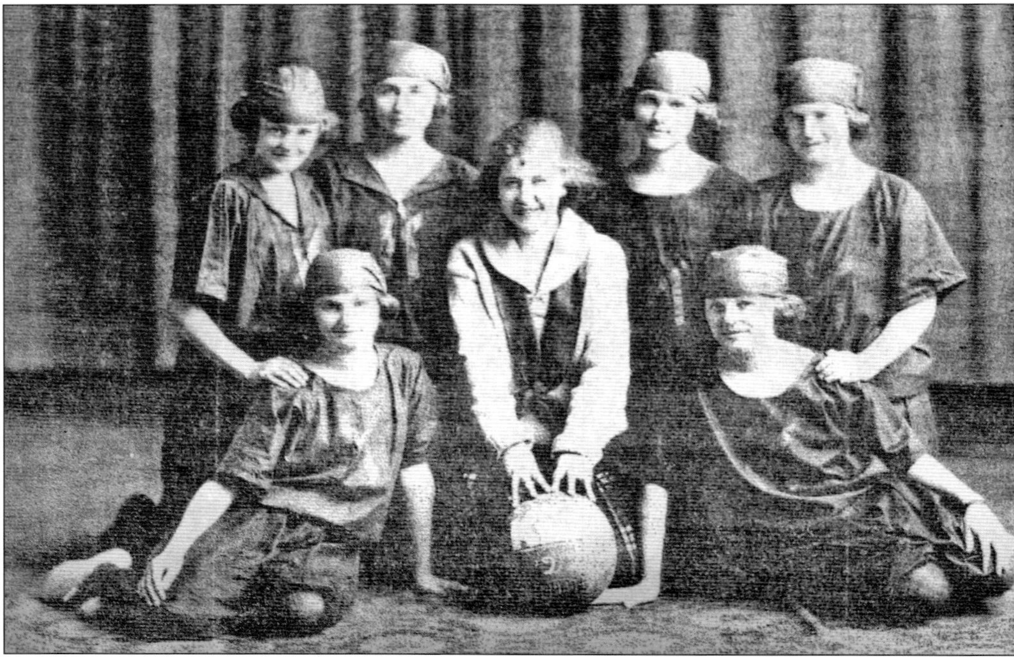

The Kennard girls' basketball team in 1922 played for the fun of the game. From left to right are (first row) Faye Stricklett, Bodwin Owen, and coach Naomi Meadows; (second row) Dorothy Widener, Helen Hall, Opal Wright, and Merle Stricklett. (Courtesy Dixie Lambert.)

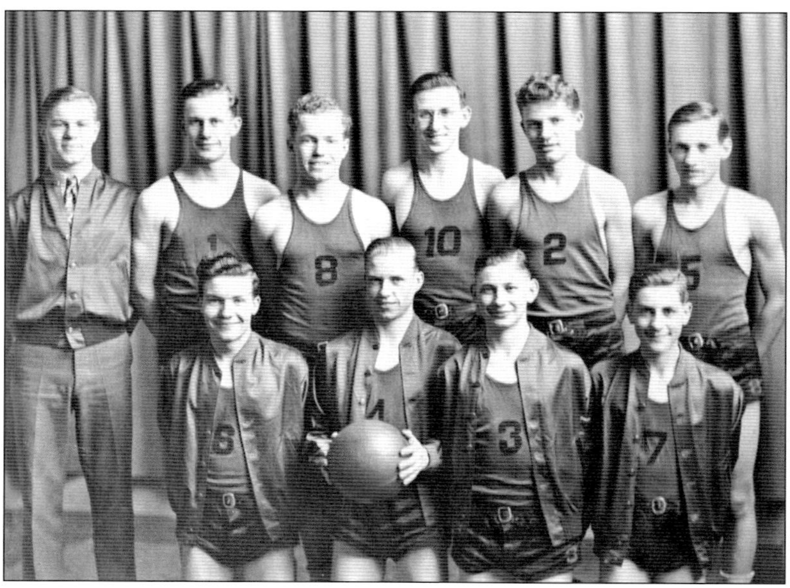

Pictured here are members of the Fort Calhoun 1943–1944 basketball team. They are, from left to right, (first row) Robert McNew, Glen Lund, Robert Wiese, and Richard Burmeister; (second row) John Rathjen, Hans Mommsen, Al Rasmussen, Charles Chaft, Merle Johnson, and Donald Deifenbaugh.

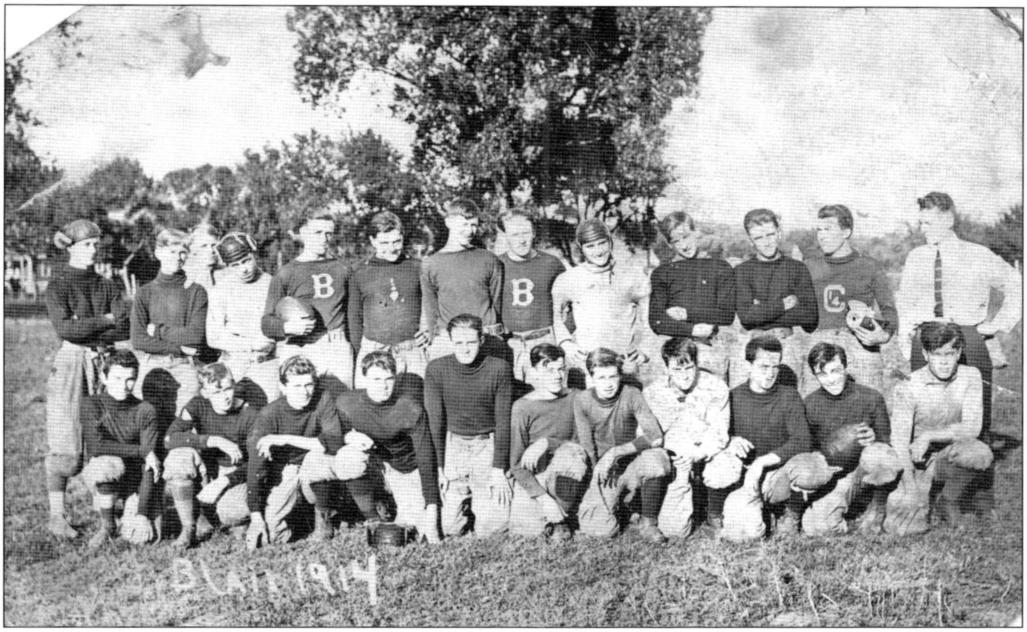

Members of the Blair football team are pictured in 1914. The team ranked no. 1 in Class B in 1932, 1973, and 1988. This photograph continues to circulate with an interest in attempting to identify the players.

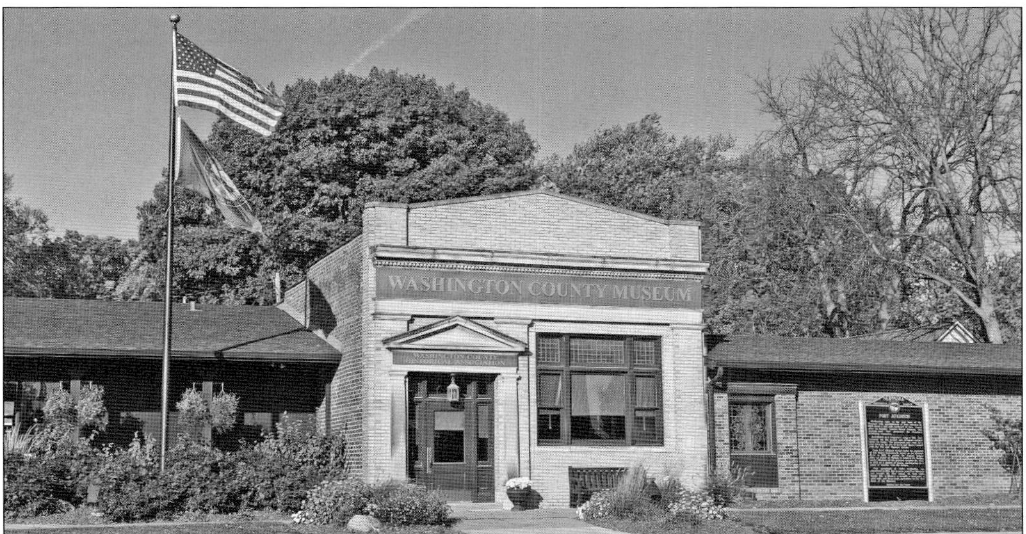

The Washington County Historical Association was organized in 1919. In 1926, the Fort Calhoun State Bank was purchased to house the museum's collection. The Washington County Historical Association Museum, the oldest county museum in Nebraska, houses Native American and prehistoric artifacts and relics from nearby Fort Atkinson and Washington County pioneers and exhibits on how the early settlers lived. The Washington County Genealogical Society was formed in 1975.